Daughters of London

Later Medieval Europe

VOLUME 8

Daughters of London

Inheriting Opportunity in the Late Middle Ages

By

Kate Kelsey Staples

BRILL

LEIDEN • BOSTON
2011

Cover illustration: Detail from *Civitas Londinum*, c. 1560, including places and streets like Chepesyde, Maidenhed lane, Distaf lane, S. Pancrees lane, and Bowe church. From the John R. Borchert Map Library, University of Minnesota, Minneapolis, Minnesota.

This book is printed on acid-free paper.

Library of Congress Cataloging-in-Publication Data

Staples, Kate Kelsey.
Daughters of London : inheriting opportunity in the late Middle Ages / by Kate Kelsey Staples.
p. cm. — (Later medieval Europe ; 8)
Includes bibliographical references and index.
ISBN 978-90-04-20311-2 (hardback : alk. paper)
1. Women—England—London—History—To 1500. 2. Women—England—London—Legal status, laws, etc. 3. Marital property—England—London. 4. Inheritance and succession—England—London. 5. England--Social conditions—1066-1485. I. Title.

HQ1147.G7S73 2011
305.409421'20902—dc22

2011001409

ISSN 1872-7875
ISBN 978 90 04 20311 2

For mom and dad

CONTENTS

ACKNOWLEDGMENTS

At the heart of this book is my doctoral dissertation. Since 2006, when I submitted the dissertation to the University of Minnesota and to UMI, I have made substantial revisions and additions to transform it into the current book. With this project, my scholarly interests converge: women's history, family history, old London, and my love for the complexities of people in the past. The opportunity to explore the ways that parents provided for their daughters and sons and to think about the world around them has been rewarding in both my research and in my teaching. It is a pleasure to take the space here to say thank you to a number of individuals and institutions who have helped throughout the course of this project. Foremost, I am indebted to my dissertation advisor, Ruth Karras, who inspired, encouraged, and guided me throughout my research and writing. Ruth Karras, Kathryn Reyerson, Michael Lower, Lianna Farber, and Steven Ruggles all read earlier versions of this work, and I thank them for their helpful advice on ways to transform the thesis into this book.

At conference meetings, I have been grateful for the chance to share my ideas and have benefited from thoughtful comments and words of encouragement. I thank Sandy Bardsley, Caroline Barron, Judith Bennett, Katherine French, Amy Froide, Jeremy Goldberg, Vanessa Harding, Jean Howard, Martha Howell, Shennan Hutton, Maryanne Kowaleski, Janet Loengard, Susan Mosher Stuard, and Shona Kelly Wray. I am also deeply appreciative of my colleagues at the University of Minnesota and at West Virginia University who continually provide that important sounding board for my ideas and who motivate me with their own brilliant work. Ellen Arnold, Katherine Aaslestad, Tovah Bender, Nikki Berg, Tyler Boulware, Liz and Ken Fones-Wolf, Don Leech, Brian Luskey, Christine Makens, Troy Osborne, Mike Ryan, Mike Sizer, Jamie Stephenson, and Matt Vester have given helpful encouragement and have generously shared suggestions. I give them many thanks. I am grateful to the anonymous readers of this manuscript for the suggestions they provided, and the tireless work of my copy editor Rachel Rosolina and my indexer Kate Mertes. All errors, of course, remain my own.

Many thanks also to the diverse audiences who heard me present my ideas at various stages of this process: the Institute of Historical Research in London, the Berkshire Conference of Women Historians, Fordham University's Center for Medieval Studies Conference, the University of Minnesota's Women's History Workshop, the International Congress on Medieval Studies at Kalamazoo, the International Medieval Congress at the University of Leeds, and the North American British Studies Conference.

Diverse funding sources helped me pull my research together including the West Virginia Humanities Council Fellowship, the Senate Grant from WVU, Faculty Travel and Development Grants from WVU, the Book Preparation Stipend Program from the Eberly College of Arts and Sciences at WVU, and the History Department Summer Research Grant at WVU. Generous grants from groups at the University of Minnesota, Twin Cities, also helped in the compilation of my research—including the Doctoral Dissertation Research Grant from the Graduate School at the University of Minnesota, the Union Pacific Microfilm Grant, and the Union Pacific Research Travel Grant from the Center for Early Modern History—as well as a research trip to London. Finally, thanks to the Medieval Academy and Richard III Society, American Branch, for the Schallek Award. I am also appreciative for access to manuscripts provided by the helpful staff at the Corporation of London Records Office.

Finally, thanks to my family, who firmly ground me. My parents, Ken and Sally, modeled for me a love of learning in their own lives and taught me the self-assurance to reach after my aspirations; Kira, Bill, and Craig provided a crucial support network with backyard get-togethers and late night (or early morning!) conversations. Thanks too, to my in-laws for their support. My greatest gratitude goes to my husband and children. Chris's sense of humor and resolute encouragement made this book possible, and the contagious laughter of William, Lillian, and Henry made it gratifying and rewarding.

LIST OF FIGURES AND TABLES

List of Figures

List of Tables

LIST OF ABBREVIATIONS

CLRO	Corporation of London Records Office
HR	Husting Roll
PRO	Public Record Office
Sharpe	Sharpe, Reginald R., ed. *Calendar of Wills Proved and Enrolled in the Court of Husting, London, A.D. 1258–A.D.1688*. 2 vols. (London: Corporation of the City of London, 1889–90)
TNA	The National Archives of the United Kingdom

CHAPTER ONE

URBAN DAUGHTERS, THEIR OPPORTUNITIES, AND LONDON WILLS

Women in the Middle Ages, as women do today, formed their identities in myriad ways. They defined who they were by the place they lived, as Londoners, Parisians, or Castilians, by their occupation or vocation, as spinners, brewsters, or nuns, by their marital status, as wives or widows, by their economic status, as nobility, gentry, or peasants, and by their religion, as Christians, Jews, or Muslims. Yet, while many scholars have written about medieval women and these various identities, little has been written about them as daughters. Locational, occupational, marital, class, and religious identification could change; women could move, marry, divorce, climb or fall socially, change jobs, and alter religious beliefs. In addition, many of these identifiers were lifecycle stages; wives would become widows and apprentices would learn the craft. Daughterhood, however, was different. Women were always daughters, and they never stopped being daughters. By considering women as daughters, we are in line with a society that frequently identified women by their relational status rather than by their occupation. By focusing on women as daughters, we can refocus the lens through which we see and understand women's lives in the medieval past.

A woman's experience, more so than a man's, was circumscribed by her family role, either as daughter, wife, mother, or widow. Men in the Middle Ages, could hold public office, attend university, and establish themselves as master craftsmen. Men, in short, could have more identities outside of the family than women were allowed. Men too were sons, husbands, fathers, and widowers, but they were less tied to the family than women because of their other identities. Women's identities were often tied to more than one family. As John Carmi Parsons explains: "a man's place in the medieval world was defined by his membership in a single patrilineal family, a woman's place by multiple family allegiances ... Women's passages from one family to another, from one stage of family life to another—daughter, wife, mother, widow—distinguished their lives from men's."[1]

Historians have studied medieval women's lives in a variety of ways for the past few decades, yet seldom as daughters. The historical study of women began in the 1920s[2] and developed as a respected subfield by the 1970s, at which time it was propelled by the women's movement and an increasing interest in social history.[3] As a result, female actors of the past have served as the focus of innumerable studies, which have considered their political, social, and economic situations in regions all over the world.[4] Some scholars have focused on the elite women of the Middle Ages and the agency they often were able to exercise through their land holdings and in their widowhood.[5] Others have considered the peasant woman, trying to

[1] John Carmi Parsons, "Mothers, Daughters, Marriage, Power: Some Plantagenet Evidence, 1150–1500," in *Medieval Queenship*, ed. John Carmi Parsons (New York: St. Martin's Press, 1993), 77.

[2] Virginia Woolf made an appeal for women's history in 1929 with *A Room of One's Own* (New York: Harcourt, Brace and Company, 1929). Eileen Power published her dissertation on medieval English nunneries in 1922, and M. M. Postan published her lectures and speeches on medieval women posthumously in 1975. See Power, *Medieval English Nunneries c. 1275 to 1535* (Cambridge: Cambridge University Press, 1922) and *Medieval Women* (New York: Cambridge University Press, 1975). See also Barbara Hanawalt's article in which she discusses the historiography of medieval English women, tracing trends from the nineteenth century to the present. Hanawalt, "Golden Ages for the History of Medieval English Women," in *Women in Medieval History and Historiography*, ed. Susan Mosher Stuard (Philadelphia: Pennsylvania Press, 1987), 1–24.

[3] Hanawalt, "Golden Ages," 12, 18. For a discussion of the development of the subfield of medieval women's legal history, see Janet Senderowitz Loengard, "'Legal History and the Medieval Englishwoman' Revisited: Some New Directions," in *Medieval Women and the Sources of Medieval History*, ed. Joel T. Rosenthal (London: University of Georgia Press, 1990), 210–36. In this article, Loengard emphasizes the role social history has played among medieval historians of women and makes a plea to legal historians to consider legal documents for what they can reflect about women's experiences in the Middle Ages.

[4] See Joan Wallach Scott, *Gender and the Politics of History* (New York: Columbia University Press, 1999), 15–27, for a good discussion on the development of women's history, specifically how scholars have approached the subfield by either adding women to the traditional historical narrative or by rewriting history with different questions in mind.

[5] For examples of scholarship on elite women, see Thomas Evergates, ed., *Aristocratic Women in Medieval France* (Philadelphia: University of Pennsylvania Press, 1999); Barbara J. Harris, *English Aristocratic Women, 1450–1550: Marriage and Family, Property and Careers* (New York: Oxford University Press, 2002); J. C. Ward, *English Noblewomen in the Later Middle Ages* (New York: Longman, 1992); and John Carmi Parsons, ed., *Medieval Queenship* (New York: St. Martin's Press, 1993). For examples of scholarship on widows, see Sandra Cavallo and Lyndan Warner, eds., *Widowhood in*

access her life through her appearance in manor documents, like court records.[6] In these studies and others, medieval women, and the economic opportunities afforded them, are often considered in their rural locale and often as widows. This is with reason, as women who appear in the primary sources as actors most frequently are widows. Widows often appear as free agents, liberated from the controlling men in their lives. This is a view we hungrily seek in a world teaming with literature that speaks to ideas of women's innate inferiority and their economic disadvantages. Furthermore, many elite women, both widows and wives, appear in the sources because they frequently exercised power through their rural estates.

This book offers a different, two-fold approach: urban daughters. Through the particular avenue of inheritance, a consideration of daughterhood in London will afford a wider landscape in which to view the opportunities presented to some women in the late Middle Ages. Instead of considering women as widows and wives, considering women as daughters—as well as the property they inherited in an urban space in particular—will permit a more nuanced view of medieval women.

Most daughters in medieval England did marry and become wives. Marriage was expected for most women and men, although perhaps as much as 15 percent of the population never married in northern Europe.[7] However, women's experiences as wives in medieval England can be difficult to decipher, as they fell legally under their husband's control when they married. Upon marrying, a woman became a *femme couverte* (literally a covered woman), or as Wil-

---

Medieval and Early Modern Europe, (New York: Pearson Education Inc., 1999); Louise Mirrer, ed., *Upon My Husband's Death: Widows in the Literature and Histories of Medieval Europe* (Ann Arbor: University of Michigan Press, 1992); Ann Morton Crabb, *The Strozzi of Florence: Widowhood and Family Solidarity in the Renaissance* (Ann Arbor: University of Michigan Press, 2000); Caroline Barron and Anne F. Sutton, eds., *Medieval London Widows 1300–1500* (London: Hambledon Press, 1994); C. E. King, *Renaissance Women Patrons: Wives and Widows in Italy c. 1300–1550* (Manchester: Manchester University Press, 1998); Mavis Mate, *Daughters, Wives and Widows after the Black Death: Women in Sussex 1350–1535* (Woodbridge, Sussex: Boydell Press, 1998); Sue Sheridan Walker, ed., *Wife and Widow in Medieval England*, (Ann Arbor: University of Michigan Press, 1993).

[6] For example, Judith Bennett, *Women in the Medieval English Countryside: Gender and Household in Brigstock Before the Plague* (New York: Oxford University Press, 1987) and Barbara Hanawalt, *The Ties That Bound: Peasant Families in Medieval England* (New York: Oxford University Press, 1986).

[7] Ruth Mazo Karras, *Sexuality in Medieval Europe: Doing Unto Others* (New York: Routledge, 2005), 59.

liam Blackstone, an eighteenth-century lawyer, explained coverture, "By marriage, the husband and wife are one person in law: that is, the very being or legal existence of the woman is suspended during the marriage, or at least is incorporated and consolidated into that of the husband."[8] A wife's property in England was controlled by her husband; he in fact owned her property while married, unlike on the Continent,[9] and she could not make a will, nor contract a debt, without her husband's consent. The historical phenomenon of coverture has not halted scholars' efforts to illuminate the lives of medieval wives; indeed, considerable research has been conducted on wives, and they are approached most commonly through the topics of marriage and family,[10] property exchange,[11] and marital dispute.[12]

When individuals married depended, in part, on geography and the economy. It has been argued that marriage rates were lower in towns than in the countryside.[13] Despite the possibilities of more

[8] William Blackstone, *Commentaries on the Laws of England, 1765–1769,* book I, chapter 15, part III, accessed September 1, 2005, www.lonang.com/exlibris/blackstone/bla-115.htm.

[9] Amy Louise Erickson, "Coverture and Capitalism," *History Workshop Journal* 59 (2005): 3. Erickson further explains that common law coverture is the reason for the practice of women taking their husbands' surnames. It was a practice specific to England until 1800, when it spread more broadly to the Continent. The practice of coverture did not end until the nineteenth century. See also Amy Louise Erickson, "Common Law Versus Common Practice: The Use of Marriage Settlements in Early Modern England," *Economic History Review* XLIII (1990): I.

[10] For example, Pauline Stafford, *Queens, Concubines and Dowagers: The King's Wife in the Early Middle Ages* (Athens, GA: University of Georgia Press, 1998); George Duby, *The Knight, the Lady, and the Priest: The Making of Modern Marriage in Medieval France* (New York: Pantheon Books, 1983); Isabel Davis, Miriam Müller, and Sarah Rees Jones, eds., *Love, Marriage, and Family Ties in the Later Middle Ages* (Brepols: International Medieval Research 11, 2003); Linda E. Mitchell, *Portraits of Medieval Women: Family, Marriage and Social Relationships in Thirteenth Century England* (New York: Palgrave McMillan, 2003); and Suzanne Wemple, *Women in Frankish Society: Marriage and the Cloister, 500–900* (Philadelphia: University of Pennsylvania Press, 1987).

[11] Martha Howell, *The Marriage Exchange: Property, Social Place, and Gender in Cities of the Low Countries, 1300–1550* (Chicago: University of Chicago Press, 1998); Barbara Harris, *English Aristocratic Women*; Maria Ågren and Amy Louise Erickson, eds., *The Marital Economy in Scandinavia and Britain, 1400–1900* (Burlington, VT: Ashgate, 2005).

[12] Shannon McSheffrey, "Place, Space, and Situation: Public and Private in the Making of Marriage in Late-Medieval London," *Speculum* 79, no. 4 (2004): 960–90; Frederik Pederson, *Marriage Disputes in Medieval England* (London: Hambledon, 2000).

[13] Maryanne Kowaleski, "Singlewomen in Medieval and Early Modern Europe: The Demographic Perspective," in *Singlewomen in the European Past, 1250–1800,* ed.

daughters as single women in medieval towns, coverture is often the point of departure for scholars working with women in medieval England. If we instead consider the types of property that women inherited as daughters, whether married or not, we can perhaps gain a keener insight into their parents' intentions for them and the possibilities available to them as owners, managers, and renters of that property.

Some exciting recent studies have focused on the lifecycle category of the single woman, for example, the collections edited by Judith Bennett and Amy Froide, and Katherine Lewis, Noël Menuge, and Kim Phillips, as well as Cordelia Beattie's new book *Medieval Single Women*. In the latter, Beattie explores the use of the category of single woman in a variety of texts from across late medieval England.[14] "Single women," as a category, can be difficult to pin down, as it is in some cases a lifecycle status that could fluctuate with a woman's circumstances.[15] Yet, while difficult, it is a worthwhile effort, since a single status reflected the reality of so many women (and men). As Judith Bennett and Amy Froide point out, "Marriage might have been normative, but many people never married, and many others lived single for many years."[16] Kim Phillips's book on young unmarried women is likewise inspiring for the avenues of discussion she initiates with her idea of the "active docility" that society suggested for young, unmarried, and hence single women.[17] In contrast to their focus on the category of single women (whether lifelong or temporary) and maidenhood respectively, this study is more inclusive and is not limited by age of the daughters or by marriage. Since all women were daughters, we are allowed to imagine women's oppor-

Judith Bennett and Amy Froide (Philadelphia: University of Pennsylvania Press, 1999), 49, 64.

[14] Judith Bennett and Amy Froide, eds., *Singlewomen in the European Past, 1250–1800* (Philadelphia: University of Pennsylvania Press, 1999); Katherine J. Lewis, Noël James Menuge, and Kim M. Phillips, eds. *Young Medieval Women* (New York: St. Martin's Press, 1999); Cordelia Beattie, *Medieval Single Women: The Politics of Social Classification in Late Medieval England* (Oxford: Oxford University Press, 2007).

[15] For a terrific exposition of the difficulty in locating and counting single women in the past, see Maryanne Kowaleski's article, "Singlewomen in Medieval and Early Modern Europe: The Demographic Perspective," in *Singlewomen in the European Past 1250–1800,* ed. Judith Bennett and Amy Froide (Philadelphia: University of Pennsylvania Press, 1999), 38–81.

[16] Bennett and Froide, *Singlewomen in the European Past 1250–1800*, 1.

[17] Kim M. Phillips, *Medieval Maidens: Young Women and Gender in England, 1270–1540* (Manchester: Manchester University Press, 2003), 13.

tunities on a greater scale, not inhibited by marital status, which did not apply to all women.

By considering inheritance, we gain a different vantage point. All medieval women were hemmed in by the patriarchal structures of their society, yet taking inheritance into account permits us to see the chances they had to maneuver, confound, and support those structures. Through the last wills and testaments of their parents,[18] enrolled in London Husting Court in the late Middle Ages, it is the aim of this study to shed light on women's social and economic positions as property owners. By considering how much and what types of property daughters inherited, in comparison to what their brothers inherited, it is possible to acquire a better sense of their lived experiences. Finally, although the situation of daughters may have varied from city to city, I propose that daughters in urban settings in the late medieval England may have had opportunities different from their sisters in the countryside.

In over three thousand wills enrolled in the Husting Court, 1,529 daughters and 1,854 sons received some amount of property. Scholars have long assumed that if daughters in the Middle Ages inherited any property from their parents, it was in the form of movable wealth rather than real property. The Husting wills instead indicate that daughters often inherited real estate such as houses, shops, and land along with their brothers, and were not limited to legacies of movable property. From these wills it becomes clear that their fathers and mothers viewed these women as viable heirs to real estate and gave them many opportunities to own, rent, and manage property. In addition, many of these parents equipped their daughters with the tools to conduct business and to pursue a livelihood, and through a

[18] Originally a will and testament were separate documents. A will preserved intentions for the devolution of real estate, and a testament preserved intentions for the devolution of movable goods and chattels, otherwise known as *personalty*. See Barron and Sutton, *Medieval London Widows*, xvi, and Karen Grannum and Nigel Taylor, *Wills and Other Probate Records* (Kew: The National Archives, 2004), 5. See also Reginald Sharpe, *Calendar of Wills Proved and Enrolled in the Court of Husting, London, A.D. 1258–1688* (London: John C. Francis, 1889), I:xxxi; and Peter Walne, *English Wills: Probate Records in England and Wales with a Brief Note on Scottish and Irish Wills* (Richmond: Virginia State Library, 1964), 15. In the Husting wills, testators appear to have used the terms as synonyms. While separate wills and testaments do appear in the rolls on occasion, usually intentions for all types of property are included in one will. Sharpe, *Calendar of Wills*, I:xxv. Further mention of *will* in this study includes both real estate and movable property.

consideration of bequests of money and goods in the Husting wills, it becomes evident that movable wealth was valuable to daughters and sons alike, indicating flexible domestic spaces that were gendered both feminine and masculine.

Women, Family, and Inheritance

Many scholars have agreed that women—widows, wives, and daughters—lost relative power and influence by the late Middle Ages due to changes in family structure and inheritance patterns, as families shifted to a patrilineal family arrangement and to placing emphasis on the first male heir. Both George Duby and David Herlihy argued for the shift in family structure from cognatic and kindred oriented to patrilineal and lineage based in the central Middle Ages, although they disagreed on why this change occurred—whether political and social (Duby) or religious and cultural (Herlihy)—and exactly when it took place (eleventh and twelfth centuries versus twelfth and thirteenth centuries).[19] Jo Ann McNamara argues that after the year 1000, women lost power that they previously held as wives in the conjugal unit. In the second millennium, change was afoot in the gender system due to a myriad of reasons including the development of primogeniture, as well as "more centralized states, a more hierarchical church, and an urban society based on the money economy."[20] Following this theory, the couple became less powerful—men were able to exercise power in other spheres, and women were barred from the particularly manly avenues of power they had access to in the first millennium; in MacNamara's words, "their masculinity gave way to a heightened concept of femininity."[21] Women became more or less pawns in the marriage game, transferring property and building family wealth. Italy, and southern Europe more generally, is often

[19] George Duby, *Medieval Marriage: Two Models from Twelfth-Century France*, trans. Elbourg Forster (Baltimore: Johns Hopkins University Press, 1978), 8–11. David Herlihy, "The Making of the Medieval Family," in *Women, Family and Society in Medieval Europe: Historical Essays 1978–1991* (Providence: Berghahn Books, 1995), 146.

[20] Jo Ann McNamara, "Women and Power through the Family Revisited," in *Gendering the Master Narrative*, ed. Mary C. Erler and Maryanne Kowaleski (Ithaca: Cornell University Press, 2003), 17–30, quotation at 22. Also see her original work with Suzanne Wemple, "The Power of Women through the Family," *Feminist Studies* 1(1973): 126–41.

[21] McNamara, "Women and Power," 25.

singled out as the case that proves this rule. By the late Middle Ages women were increasingly blocked from inheritance with their dowries if they had brothers, as families sought to keep the patrimony together. There have been few exceptions to this general argument.[22]

In northern Europe, too, scholars have put forth the argument that with a shift in family structure and inheritance laws went a decrease in economic opportunities for women. For example, in England around the twelfth and thirteenth centuries there was a concrete shift toward enforcing primogeniture to the detriment of daughters' inheritances. In her study of charters from rural England, Claire de Trafford argues that with the development of the statute of *De donis* in the thirteenth century, families became more restrictive in terms of inheritance. Prior to the statute of *De donis*, which prevented the alienation of any of the heir's inheritance, a widow could divide the lands in her *maritagium* (marriage portion or dowry) as she wished, which gave widows significant influence and provided financial resources for children in the family besides the heir. In her words, "Given that many women in turn passed their *maritagia* on to their sons and daughters, it is probable that the family in this period was more inclusive in terms of how it shared its land than in the later Middle Ages.... Over time, however, this generosity seems to have eroded, resulting in the legislation enacted in *De donis*."[23] De Trafford's argument coincides with those noted above: as people began to emphasize lineage, daughters (and younger sons) lost out. In a review of relevant scholarship, Mary Charles Murray argues that for England, the dissolution of corporate kin groups through the development of private property, a class society, and primogeniture saw the loss of power for many women, as they became more dependent on men and had less control over property. Many scholars point to

[22] One notable exception was elucidated by Amy Livingstone's work. In northern Europe among the nobility, Livingstone has documented women inheriting and controlling property in the charters of the eleventh- and twelfth-century Blois-Chartres region controlling land, fiefs, serfs, customs, tithes, pasture land, houses, and so on. Amy Livingstone, "Noblewomen's Control of Property in Early Twelfth-Century Blois-Chartres," *Medieval Prosopography* 18 (1997): 55–72. Contributors to the volume *Aristocratic Women in Medieval France* also have argued for women playing active roles in public life more generally. Theodore Evergates, ed., *Aristocratic Women in Medieval France* (Philadelphia: University of Pennsylvania Press, 1999).

[23] Claire de Trafford, "Share and Share Alike? The Marriage Portion, Inheritance and Family Politics," in *Studies on Medieval and Early Modern Women: Pawns or Players?*, ed. Christine Meek and Catherine Lawless (Dublin: Four Courts Press, 2003), quotation at 48.

patriarchy to explain a lessening of women's power; however, Murray points out that the change to primogeniture was not patriarchal in intent as many men also lost economic power.[24]

It has been well established for rural medieval Europe that primogeniture stamped on daughters' opportunities to inherit. However, urban sites, which often followed partible inheritance schemes, have not been excluded from the theory. Martha Howell, in her study of wills and other records from late medieval Douai, finds that Douaisiens formed a new marital property regime in the late Middle Ages, moving from a preference for the conjugal unit and the household to kinship and lineage, thus favoring children rather than wives as inheritors of property.[25] They solidified this shift with a parallel move from custom to contract, and with this move, these city-dwellers became interested in preserving their wealth rather than accumulating it. Although this shift affected women differently depending on their personal situations, as Howell is keen to point out, the result she explains is that women began to be seen less as active economic agents. Society began to view them as "carriers of property" rather than as "creators of property."[26] Under custom, then, the daughter entering a marriage had more freedoms in her partnership with her husband, and under contract she could be assured a certain marriage portion if her husband was irresponsible in business. Both systems *could* benefit daughters; however, overall this change in marital property regime brought about a new gender construct in which women were viewed as weaker and less productive as economic actors. Indeed, Howell argues, the emphasis shifted away from the woman as a potential producer and partner to a more emotional and maternal being. Interestingly, companionate marriage came about in Douai as husband and wife shifted from positions of economic partners to occupying two distinctly different halves of a whole, each with their own role to play in the union.[27]

The shift to an emphasis on primogeniture in inheritance certainly negatively affected women's opportunities to exercise influence in many situations. However, medieval London does not follow the same pattern that these scholars outline for other rural and urban

---

[24] Mary Charles Murray, "Property and 'Patriarchy' in English History," *Journal of Historical Sociology* 2 (1989): 309–316.

[25] Martha Howell, *The Marriage Exchange: Property, Social Place, and Gender in Cities of the Low Countries, 1300–1550* (Chicago: University of Chicago Press, 1998).

[26] Howell, *The Marriage Exchange*, 233.

[27] Howell, *The Marriage Exchange*, 236–37.

sites in medieval Europe. I argue here that the Husting wills reveal a different situation. The practice of burgage tenure in London, and in other English towns, is an important caveat in the larger argument of women's loss of power by the late Middle Ages.

Daughters and Burgage Tenure in Late Medieval Towns

Daughters in towns had a better chance than their counterparts in the countryside of acquiring real estate whether as a part of, or in addition to, their dowries. Inheritance customs were different in towns like the capital because, as Caroline Barron explains, Londoners "held their lands directly of the king in free burgage (or socage) tenure: these lands were free of the obligation of military service and so could be freely devised, just as if they were chattels."[28] In rural areas, the division or non division of land was crucial because of the services due to the lord from whom the tenant held land. The tenant had to obtain permission from the lord before selling or dividing the land.[29] Since burgesses did not have similar obligations, they could divide their land as they wished. This meant that in towns, daughters, along with their brothers, could receive real estate from their fathers and mothers. A married daughter could also inherit property, whereas her rural counterpart would likely have been excluded from inheritance with the acquisition of her dowry. In addition, testators also included sisters, nieces, female servants, and friends as beneficiaries of their property in their wills.[30]

[28] Caroline M. Barron, "The 'Golden Age' of Women in Medieval London," in *Medieval Women in Southern England*, ed. Keith Bate, Anne Curry, Christopher Hardman, and Peter Noble (Reading, England: Graduate Centre for Medieval Studies, University of Reading, 1989), 35–58. Indeed, Albert Kiralfy explains that in towns, "houses, flats, shops, workshops were regarded as personal property rather than as real property." Kiralfy, "Wills of Personality (Movables) in England from 1066–1500 A.D.," in *Actes à cause de mort, Deuxième partie*, Société Jean Bodin pour l'Histoire Comparative des Institutions (Bruxelles: De Boeck Université, 1993), 42. See also Frederick Pollock and Frederick Maitland, *History of English Law before the Time of Edward I* (Cambridge: Cambridge University Press, 1924), 2:330–31; and Michael M. Sheehan, *The Will in Medieval England: From the Conversion of the Anglo-Saxons to the End of the Thirteenth Century*, vol. 6 (Toronto: Pontifical Institution of Mediaeval Studies, 1963), 274–78.

[29] Morley de Wolf Hemmeon, *Burgage Tenure in Mediaeval England* (Cambridge: Harvard University Press, 1914), 4–5, 49.

[30] In her study of Sussex boroughs, Mate includes a number of examples in which females inherited property in addition to, or instead of, males. See Mate, *Daughters, Wives and Widows*, 80.

Despite this concession of more options to daughters in towns where partible inheritance was common, historians have not pursued very far the opportunities and economic influence that partible inheritance may have provided for these urban women.[31] Some historians have generalized that, despite the partible inheritance custom of burgage tenure, men in towns predominantly inherited real property, while women inherited movable goods, as was common among the non elite in the countryside. For example, through her research on Sussex towns, Mavis Mate asserts that even though a father had the option in medieval English towns to divide his property as he wished and to give tenements or businesses to his daughters, he "preferred to give them cash marriage portions."[32] In Sussex, Mate found that "most burgesses gave their daughters cash marriage portions, with amounts varying from five to one hundred marks, rather than an urban tenement."[33] She accepts that burgage tenure may have given these adult unmarried women opportunities to live on their own and start a business for themselves. However, she argues that this was probably unlikely since no mention of such women exists in the records, the medieval ideological structure did not tolerate single female entrepreneurs, and a single woman who controlled an urban tenement would have been seized quickly off the marriage market.[34] In contrast, the wills enrolled with the Husting Court of London indicate intentions of fathers for their daughters to own and control domestic and commercial real estate, either on their own or with their husbands.

Women from medieval London have been a popular subject of study, in part because of the wealth of sources that survive from this

---

[31] For example, Maryanne Kowaleski suggests that the ability for daughters to inherit in towns may have influenced familial relationships. Kowaleski, "The History of Urban Families in Medieval England," *Journal of Medieval History* 14 (1988), 49. Derek Keene also proposes that in towns during the later Middle Ages daughters provided continuity in the descent of property and businesses within families, but that it is difficult to trace them and their family connections in the sources. Derek Keene, *Survey of Medieval Winchester* (Oxford: Clarendon Press, 1985), 1:235.

[32] Mavis Mate, *Women in Medieval English Society* (Cambridge: Cambridge University Press, 1999), 91.

[33] Mate, *Daughters, Wives and Widows*, 80. One mark equaled about 2/3 of £1. See Alan M. Stahl, "Coins and Coinage," in *Medieval England: An Encyclopedia*, ed. Paul E. Szarmach, M. Teresa Tavormina, and Joel T. Rosenthal (New York: Garland, 1998), 202.

[34] Mate, *Daughters, Wives and Widows*, 80.

borough.[35] Following the general trend in medieval women's historiography, wives and widows have also been the focus of study of women's experience in London. Shannon McSheffrey, the leading scholar on marriage in medieval London, has examined women's roles within marriage dispute cases.[36] Numerous scholars have examined widowhood as experienced by London widows, the details of whose lives are recorded in wills, court documents, deeds, church records, chronicles, and letters. Derek Keene conducted a group biography of tanners' widows in London, while Jennifer Ward studied Elizabeth de Burgh, a widow whose connections reached well beyond London but who was active and had interests in the capital.[37] As with many urban studies, medieval women in this locale have also been considered as workers, exploring various trades in which women participated, such as silkwomen, brewsters, and prostitutes.[38] Despite the

[35] Derek Keene and Vanessa Harding, *A Survey of Documentary Sources for Property Holding in London before the Great Fire,* vol. 22 (London: London Record Society, 1985). For principal works on medieval London itself, see Gwyn A. Williams, *Medieval London: From Commune to Capital* (London: Athlone Press, 1962); Caroline Barron, *London in the Later Middle Ages: Government and People, 1200–1500* (Oxford: Oxford University Press, 2004); Caroline M. Barron, "London 1300–1540," in *The Cambridge Urban History of Britain*, ed. by D.M. Palliser (Cambridge: Cambridge University Press, 2000) , I:395–440.

[36] McSheffrey, "Place, Space, and Situation."

[37] Derek Keene, "Tanners' Widows, 1300–1350," in *Medieval London Widows*, 1–28; Jennifer C. Ward, "Elizabeth de Burgh, Lady of Clare (d. 1360)," in *Medieval London Widows,* 29–46. Other scholars contributed to this volume of London widows, examining widows who ranged from paupers to ladies to bell-founders. See Caroline M. Barron and Anne F. Sutton, ed., *Medieval London Widows*. For other biographies, see Hanes Kleineke, "Alice Martyn, Widow of London: An Episode from Richard's Youth," *The Ricardian: Journal of the Richard III Society* 14 (2004): 32–36; Margaret Connolly, "Another Medieval London Widow: The Story of Beatrice Cornburgh," *The Ricardian: Journal of the Richard III Society* 13 (2003): 148–58; and Claire A. Martin, "Dame Margery Astry," *The Ricardian: Journal of the Richard III Society* 14 (2004): 1–31. See also Barbara Hanawalt's discussion of widowhood in London. Hanawalt, "The Widow's Mite: Provisions for Medieval London Widows," in *Upon My Husband's Death: Widows in the Literature and Histories of Medieval Europe*, ed. Louise Mirrer (Ann Arbor: University of Michigan Press, 1992), 21–45.

[38] Kay Lacey, "Women and Work in Fourteenth and Fifteenth Century London," in *Women and Work in Pre-Industrial England*, ed. Lindsey Charles and Lorna Duffin (Dover, NH: Croom Helm, 1985), 24–82; Caroline Barron and Matthew Davies, "Ellen Langwith: Silkwoman of London (died 1481)," *The Ricardian: Journal of the Richard III Society* 13 (2003): 39–47. Stephanie Trigg, "'Ye louely ladyes with youre longe fyngres': The Silkwomen of Medieval London," *Studia anglica Posnaniensia* 38 (2002): 469–84. Judith Bennett, "Women and Men in the Brewers' Gild of London, ca. 1420," in *The Salt of Common Life: Individuality and Choice in the Medieval Town, Countryside and Church: Essays Presented to J. Ambrose Raftis*, ed.Edwin Brezette DeWindt (Kalamazoo:

wealth of studies of women in medieval London, their experiences as daughters remain relatively unexplored.[39] Burgage tenure afforded opportunities to daughters in London, perhaps a broader category of women than those above, which were not available elsewhere in rural England or on the Continent. In addition, daughters who inherited property in late medieval London, as well as in other towns in England, could go on to exercise influence through that property, even if it was through the family rather than as an individual. Laws and customs may partially obscure such women's influence in the sources, but it remains an avenue worth pursuing, and it is an idea I will return to at the end of the book.

Wills and Social History

Scholars have used wills for some time as entry points to understanding women's lives and the lives of many others.[40] Linda Guzzetti, Barbara Harris, Katherine Lewis, Patricia Skinner, Shona Kelly Wray, and others have examined wills from all over Europe to consider women's statuses and personal interests in medieval Europe, most

---

Medieval Institute Publications, 1995), 181–232. Some works that address prostitution in the capital include, Ruth Mazo Karras, *Common Women: Prostitution and Sexuality in Medieval England* (Oxford: Oxford University Press, 1996); Cordelia Beattie, "Governing Bodies: Law Courts, Male Householders, and Single Women in Late Medieval England," in *The Medieval Household in Christian Europe c. 850–c. 1550: Managing Power, Wealth, and the Body,* ed. Cordelia Beattie, Anna Maslakovic, and Sarah Rees Jones (Turnhout: Brepols, 2003), 199–220; Henry Ansgar Kelly, "Bishop, Prioress, and Bawd in the Stews of Southwark," *Speculum* 75, no. 2 (2000): 342–88.

Another vocation medieval women could choose was that of nun, and many scholars have written about religious women. For examples, see JoAnn McNamara, *Sisters in Arms: Catholic Nuns through Two Millennia* (Cambridge: Harvard University Press, 1996); Bruce Vernarde, *Women's Monasticism and Medieval Society: Nunneries in France and England, 800–1215* (Ithaca: Cornell University Press, 1997); John A. Nichols and Lillian Thomas Shank, ed., *Medieval Religious Women* (Kalamazoo, MI: Cistercian Publications, 1984–1995).

[39] Shannon McSheffrey's work on women's voices in marriage cases is an exception. See McSheffrey, "'I will never have none ayenst my faders will': Consent and the Making of Marriage in the Late Medieval Diocese of London," in *Women, Marriage, and Family in Medieval Christendom: Essays in Memory of Michael M. Sheehan, C.S.B.,* ed. Constance M. Rousseau and Joel T. Rosenthal (Kalamazoo: Medieval Institute Publications, 1998), 153–74.

[40] See Michael Zell's article for an early assessment of the various avenues of social and church history for which wills permit an exploration. Zell, "Fifteenth- and Sixteenth-Century Wills," 67–74.

often as widows.[41] Joel Rosenthal and Clive Burgess have considered wills for what they reveal about medieval spiritualities and lay piety.[42] In three volumes, W. K. Jordan has studied wills for the light they shed on charitable giving.[43] Stephen Epstein, who uses the will predominantly to study the family, published one of the first monographs to use wills as the primary source base.[44] His work was followed by that of Daniel Lord Smail on family networks in medieval

[41] Linda Guzzetti, "Women's Inheritance and Testamentary Practices in Late Fourteenth- and Early Fifteenth-Century Venice and Ghent," in *The Texture of Society: Medieval Women in the Southern Low Countries*, ed. Ellen E. Kittell and Mary A Suydam (New York: Palgrave MacMillan, 2004), 79–108; Barbara Harris, *English Aristocratic Women*; Katherine J. Lewis, "Women, Testamentary Discourse and Life-Writing in Later Medieval England," in *Medieval Women and the Law*, ed. Noël James Menuge (Woodbridge, Suffolk: Boydell Press, 2000): 57–75; Skinner, "Women, Wills, and Wealth"; Shona Kelly Wray, "Women, Family, and Inheritance in Bologna during the Black Death," in *Love, Marriage, and Family Ties in the Later Middle Ages*, ed. Isabel Davis, Miriam Müller, and Sarah Rees Jones (Turnhout: Brepols, 2001), 205–16; Ann J. Kettle, "'My Wife Shall Have It': Marriage and Property in the Wills and Testaments of Later Mediaeval England," in *Marriage and Property*, ed. Elizabeth M. Craik (Aberdeen: Aberdeen University Press, 1984), 89–103.

[42] Joel T. Rosenthal, *The Purchase of Paradise: Gift Giving and the Aristocracy, 1307–1485* (London: Routledge, 1972); Clive Burgess, "Late Medieval Wills and Pious Convention: Testamentary Evidence Reconsidered," in *Profit, Piety, and the Profession in Later Medieval England*, ed. Michael Hicks (Gloucester: Alan Sutton, 1990), 14–33. Also see Lisane Lavanchy, *Écrire sa mort, decrier sa vie: Testaments de laics lausannois (1400–1450)* (Lausanne: Université de Lausanne, 2003); and Peter Heath considers lay piety from 1400 to 1529 in Hull, "Urban Piety in the Later Middle Ages: The Evidence of Hull Wills," in *The Church, Politics and Patronage in the Fifteenth Century*, ed. Barrie Dobson (New York: St. Martins Press, 1984), 209–34. There has been a lengthy discussion among scholars of early modern England about using wills to discuss lay piety, specifically by examining religious preambles and how they changed from pre- to post-Reformation. See, for example, A. G. Dickens, *Lollards and Protestants in the Diocese of York, 1509–1558* (London: Oxford University Press, 1959), 28–29, 32. Margaret Spufford was one of the first to point out the dangers of using preambles as indicators of piety as scribes, rather than testators, were often the authors of preambles. Spufford, "Religious Preambles and the Scribes of Villagers' Wills in Cambridgeshire, 1570–1700," revised and reprinted in Spufford, *Contrasting Communities: English Villagers in the Sixteenth and Seventeenth Centuries* (Cambridge: Cambridge University Press, 1974), 320–34. See also Michael Zell, "The Use of Religious Preambles as a Measure of Religious Belief in the Sixteenth Century," *Bulletin of the Institute of Historical Research* 50, no. 122 (1977), 246–49.

[43] W. K. Jordan, *Philanthropy in England, 1480–1660: A Study of the Changing Pattern of English Social Aspirations* (New York: Russel Sage Foundation, 1959), *The Charities of London, 1480–1660* (New York: Russel Sage Foundation, 1960), and *The Charities of Rural England, 1480–1660* (London: G. Allen & Unwin, 1961). See also Barbara Hanawalt's article that focuses on charity in London. Hanawalt, "Reading the Lives of the Illiterate: London's Poor," *Speculum* 80 (October 2005): 1067–86.

[44] Epstein, *Wills and Wealth in Medieval Genoa.*

Marseille, Shona Kelly Wray on medieval Bologna, and Jacqueline Murray on sixteenth-century London.[45] Teofilo F. Ruiz has studied medieval mentalities about property as revealed in wills,[46] and Jennifer Kermode used merchants' wills to inform her about merchant society and merchant networks.[47]

At least five other scholars have used the Husting wills in particular as the focus of their studies. In her dissertation, Kristen Burkholder used a selection of the wills enrolled in the Husting Court, along with a selection from the Prerogative Court of Canterbury, to study aspects of material culture.[48] In his master's thesis, Jamieson Weetman studied the Husting wills enrolled from 1315–1359 to examine changes in piety due to the Black Death.[49] J. M. Jennings focused on the testators (rather than on recipients, as this study does primarily), their interests, and the types of real estate bequests in the wills enrolled in the Husting Court from 1400 to 1450.[50] In his study of 1,515 wills enrolled between 1271–1330, Harry Miskimin explored questions of demography,[51] as did Barbara Megson in her study examining the mortality rates of the Black Death.[52]

As with all sources of the past, wills have their limitations, and many scholars have commented on the challenges of and opportuni-

---

[45] Daniel Smail, "Mapping Networks and Knowledge in Medieval Marseille, 1337–1362: Variations on a Theme of Mobility" (PhD diss., University of Michigan, 1994); Shona Kelly Wray, "Last Wills in Bologna During the Black Death" (PhD diss., University of Colorado, 1998) and *Communities and Crisis: Bologna during the Black Death* (Leiden: Brill Academic Publishers, 2009); Murray, "Kinship and Friendship," 369–85.

[46] Teofilo F. Ruiz, *From Heaven to Earth: The Reordering of Castilian Society, 1150–1350* (Princeton: Princeton University Press, 2004). Ruiz also discusses the charitable giving and family inheritance strategies of Castilians.

[47] Jennifer Kermode, *Medieval Merchants: York, Beverley and Hull in the Later Middle Ages* (Cambridge: Cambridge University Press, 1998).

[48] Kristen Burkholder, "Material Culture and Self-Presentation in Late Medieval England" (PhD diss., University of Minnesota, 2001).

[49] Jamieson Floyd Weetman, "London Wills and the Black Death: The Pursuit of Stability in Religious Practise in the Husting Rolls Wills, 1315–1359," (master's thesis, University of Calgary, 1999).

[50] John M. Jennings, "The Distribution of Landed Wealth in the Wills of London Merchants 1400–1450," *Mediaeval Studies* 39 (1977): 261–80.

[51] Harry A. Miskimin, "The Legacies of London: 1259–1330," in *The Medieval City*, ed. Harry A. Miskimin, David Herlihy, and A. L. Udovitch (London: Yale University Press, 1977), 209–27.

[52] Barbara E. Megson, "Mortality among London Citizens in the Black Death," *Medieval Prosopography* 19 (1998): 125–33.

ties for using wills as a source of the past.[53] First, in terms of the type of source itself, as with all medieval documents, scholars deal with survivability. Only the wills that have survived the potential ravages of time remain. In addition, because wills were orally dictated to executors, and then enrolled by scribes at the Court of Husting,[54] it is possible that these individuals altered the original intentions of the testators by using formulaic phrases or terminology, rather than the words used by the testator.

Second, these wills give us only a snapshot of a section of late medieval London society. Individuals who proved and enrolled wills at the Husting Court needed to have possessions to bequeath, and these possessions are also difficult to estimate the value of without inventories attached. There are a few inventories that survive from medieval England, but it is not until the early modern period that they survive in any great amount. Church law required inventories from 1342, but only after 1529—when the requirement appears in statute—do we see an increase in them.[55] Thus, these testators represent the upper crust and middling sorts of medieval society. Wills in late medieval London are also limited by gender; they were predominantly enrolled by men, which will be discussed in depth in chapter two.

Historians also need to be wary of the scope of the last will and testament and the silences that this type of document does not address. Wills provide a modern audience with only a glimpse of a

[53] For examples, see Eric Josef Carlson, "The Historical Value of the Ely Consistory Probate Records," in *Index of the Probate Records of the Consistory Court of Ely 1449–1858 Part I: A–E*, ed. Elisabeth Leedham-Green and Rosemary Rodd (London: British Record Society, 1994), xvii–lix; and Nigel Goose and Nesta Evans, "Wills as an Historical Source," in *When Death Do Us Part: Understanding and Interpreting the Probate Records of Early Modern England*, ed. Tom Arkell, Nesta Evans, and Nigel Goose(Oxford: Leopard's Head Press, 2000), 38–71.

[54] Barron and Sutton, *Medieval London Widows*, xvi.

[55] Grannum and Taylor, *Wills and Other Probate Records*, 91. For example, John S. Moore begins his study of inventories from south Gloucestershire in 1539. The Prerogative Court of Canterbury holds no probate inventories before 1417. Moore, ed., *The Goods and Chattels of our Forefathers* (London: Phillimore, 1976), 5. In his study, Christopher Dyer uses a few late medieval (pre-1540) inventories. Dyer, *An Age of Transition? Economy and Society in England in the Later Middle Ages* (Oxford: Oxford University Press, 2005), 116–22. For studies using early modern inventories, see the collection of articles in Goose and Evans, *When Death Do Us Part*. For a discussion of the limitations of inventories as sources of the past, see Margaret Spufford, "The Limitations of the Probate Inventory," in *English Rural Society, 1500–1800: Essays in Honour of Joan Thirsk*, ed. John Chartres and David Hey (Cambridge: Cambridge University Press, 1990), 139–74.

person's intentions, values, interests, and piety as he or she faced a particular and final event in his or her life. Wills are documents that reveal a snapshot of the past, and the historian must recognize the danger of drawing too many generalizations, as often times other gifts of property and pious conditions were dealt with *inter vivos*.[56]

The Husting wills, too, are silent about the size and shape of families. While the wills delimit the heirs of the testator, they are silent about whether these heirs are the only children in the family, as well as the age and order of the children. There is no way of reconstituting family structure with any certainty.

Finally, wills reveal the wishes of the testators, but just that. By their nature, they deal with intention rather than real action. Thomas Kuehn has warned social historians against using wills to tell the whole story of inheritance by reminding them that inheritance did not stop with the wishes of the testator but went beyond the will and into the courts to be contested.[57]

As long as one recognizes the limits of the source material, as one must with all sources, wills remain valuable for understanding the past. In her study of Bolognese wills, Shona Kelly Wray, for example, concedes that the rest of the legal process behind inheritance is important, but she explains that this does not negate the importance of the testament. While wills could be contested, this did not happen frequently. Wray suggests that the scarcity of contested wills supports the idea that testators expected their intentions to be carried out.[58] Wills may not tell the entire story—they may represent

---

[56] Burgess, "Late Medieval Wills." For another discussion of the limits of using wills to shed light on personal piety, see Philippa Maddern's discussion, "Friends of the dead: Executors, Wills and Family Strategy in Fifteenth-Century Norfolk," in *Rulers and Ruled in Late Medieval England: Essays Presented to Gerald Harriss*, ed. G. L. Harriss, Rowena E Archer, and Simon Walker (London: Hambledon Press, 1995), 155–74.

[57] Thomas Kuehn, "Law, Death, and Heirs in the Renaissance: Repudiation of Inheritance in Florence," *Renaissance Quarterly* 45 (1992): 484–516. Also see his reviews of the work of Epstein, *Wills and Wealth in Medieval Genoa*, and Samuel Cohn, *Death and Property in Siena, 1205–1800: Strategies for the Afterlife* (Baltimore: Johns Hopkins, 1988), and their study of testaments. Kuehn, review of *Wills and Wealth in Medieval Genoa*, by Steven Epstein, *Speculum* 61, no.1 (1986): 143–45, and Kuehn, review of *Death and Property in Siena, 1205-1800: Strategies for the* Afterlife, by Samuel Cohn, *Journal of Modern History* 62 (1990): 624–26. Kuehn applies his critique to his study of contested inheritance cases on behalf of women in Florence in Kuehn, *Law, Family and Women: Toward a Legal Anthropology of Renaissance Italy* (Chicago: University of Chicago Press, 1991), 238–57.

[58] Wray, "Last Wills in Bologna."

only a sliver of society, or they may leave out a family member or an earlier gift—but a detailed examination of testators' wishes over an expanse of time can reveal useful information about actors in the past. Patterns in inheritance can be determined, social networks traced, opportunities for heirs elucidated, and familial relationships illuminated. While daughters' voices are absent from these sources directly, indirectly through these wills it is possible to reconstruct the world within which they lived and operated.

The Husting Wills

The Husting Court was the county court of London,[59] and the wills enrolled in the Husting Court of Deeds and Wills are the focus of this study.[60] To preserve their intentions concerning the devolution of their property (goods, chattels, money, land, and businesses), by law, London citizens—like their rural counterparts—first dictated a will and/or testament in the presence of at least two witnesses, who could be either clerks or laymen; executors were either present or named, and a scribe was usually hired for a fee to record the document.[61] The testator could name whom he liked as executor, but if he named no one, then the responsibility fell to family members.[62]

---

[59] Sharpe, *Calendar of Wills*,I:iii, x–xi.

[60] For the chief study of wills in medieval England in general, see Sheehan, *The Will in Medieval England*. Also see his other articles, Sheehan, "English Wills and the Records of the Ecclesiastical and Civil Jurisdictions," *Journal of Medieval History* 14 (1988): 3–12; Sheehan, "Wills and Testaments," in *Medieval England: An Encyclopedia*, ed. Joel T. Rosenthal, et al. (New York: Garland, 1998); Sheehan, "The Bequest of Land in England in the High Middle Ages: Testaments and the Law," in *Marriage, Property, and Succession*, ed. Lloyd Bonfield (Berlin: Duncker and Humblot, 1992), 326–38; Sheehan, "A List of Thirteenth-Century English Wills," *Genealogists' Magazine* 13 (1961): 259–65.

[61] Pollock and Maitland, *History of English Law*, II:336-7. Grannum and Taylor, *Wills and Other Probate Records*, 72–73. George Casper Homans explains that in an ideal situation the testator would dictate his will in the presence of a parish priest as well. Homans, *English Villagers of the Thirteenth Century* (Cambridge: Harvard University Press, 1941), 134. See also the twelfth-century legal treatise, Glanvill, *A Treatise on the Laws and Customs of the Kingdom of England*, ed. G. D. G. Hall (London: Thomas Nelson Ltd., 1965), 80. Sharpe explains that the executors, or any beneficiary, proved the will before the Husting Court to authenticate the testator's will. In addition, the testator had to affix his seal for it to be enrolled with the court, witnesses' testimony needed to match, and the testament had to be enrolled "within a reasonable time," I:xliii–iv.

[62] Glanvill, *A Treatise*, 80. Executors first appeared in England in the will of King Henry II, in 1182. Pollock and Maitland, *History of English Law*, II:334–35. For a com-

In practice, a testator most often named his wife first, and sometimes other family members, friends, or business associates.[63] Naming one's wife as an executor, or executrix, was a common practice among the landed elite. Among a selection of knights and noblemen in late medieval England, 77% named their wives as executors, with 35% of them named as sole executors.[64] In a selection of wills from sixteenth-century London, 77% of male testators named their wives as sole executors.[65] The practice predates early modern London and can be seen in late medieval provincial towns, like Bristol.[66] Between the thirteenth and fifteenth centuries in Bristol, as well as Lincoln, the percentage of wives as executors was nearly 82% and 80% respectively.[67] In merchants' wills from late medieval York, Beverley and Hull, over 90% named their wives as executors.

In contrast, naming wives as executors was not as common on the Continent, especially in areas of southern Europe. In wills from early medieval southern Italy (800–1100), executors were usually family members and often spouses as well. However, in those areas under Lombard law, wives could not be executors because under that legal system women were considered "legally incompetent."[68] No mat-

parison of the custom of executors on the Continent, see Steven Epstein, *Wills and Wealth in Medieval Genoa, 1150–1250* (Cambridge: Harvard University Press, 1984), 220. In Genoa, tutors or guardians appointed by the testator also served as executors. If a testator was childless, often the principal heir or a beneficiary would serve as an executor.

[63] See Caroline M. Barron, "Introduction: The Widow's World," in *Medieval London Widows 1300–1500*, ed. Caroline M. Barron and Anne F. Sutton (London: Hambledon Press, 1994), xxix–xxxii; and Michael L. Zell, "Fifteenth- and Sixteenth-Century Wills as Historical Sources," *Archives* 14, no. 62 (1979): 67. For discussion of executors in common law and in wills from rural England, see Maddern, "Friends of the Dead," and Kiralfy, "Wills of Personality," 35–45. Maddern argues that examining executors, instead of legatees, can inform us to a greater extent of the values of the testators and of family strategy. Kiralfy argues that the institution of executor is "peculiarly English, although Germanic precursors have existed," and the word *executor* indicates influence from the Continent. Kiralfy, "Wills of Personality," 38.

[64] Harris, *English Aristocratic Women*, 129, see also 152–60.

[65] Jacqueline Murray, "Kinship and Friendship: The Perception of Family by Clergy and Laity in Late Medieval London," *Albion* 20, no. 3 (1988): 376.

[66] Peter Fleming, *Women in Late Medieval Bristol* (Bristol: Bristol Branch of the Historical Association, 2001), 12–17.

[67] Ann J. Kettle, "My Wife Shall Have It," 100.

[68] Patricia Skinner, "Women, Wills and Wealth in Medieval Southern Italy," *Early Medieval Europe* 2 (1993): 136–37. See also Ellen Kittell, "Testaments of Two Cities: A Comparative Analysis of the Wills of Medieval Genoa and Douai," *European Review of History* 5 (Spring 1998): 47–83.

ter the relationship between testator and executor, executors could expect an often lengthy commitment involved in executing a will, such as recovering debts. For this reason, the choice of executors can reveal networks and friendships among individuals and families.[69]

After the testator dictated his will to his executors and witnesses, the executors had the will submitted for probate and then proved, which made the document legally valid.[70] Proving the will involved swearing an oath that the executors would carry out the wishes of the testator. Finally, the executors had the will enrolled at the Court of Husting for a certain price, ranging between 2 s. 8d. and 16 s. 8d.[71] An example of such a document appears in figure 1.1.

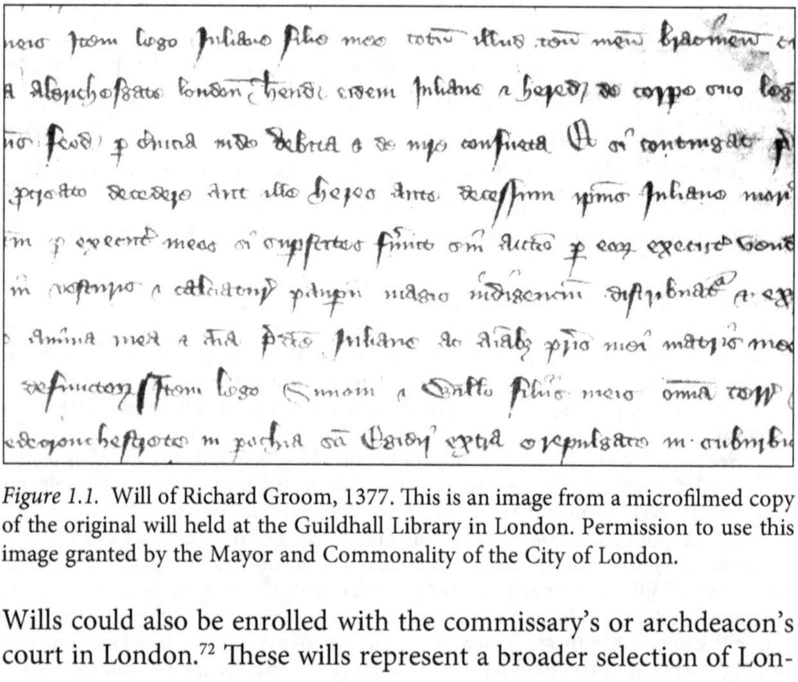

Figure 1.1. Will of Richard Groom, 1377. This is an image from a microfilmed copy of the original will held at the Guildhall Library in London. Permission to use this image granted by the Mayor and Commonality of the City of London.

Wills could also be enrolled with the commissary's or archdeacon's court in London.[72] These wills represent a broader selection of Lon-

[69] Kermode, *Medieval Merchants*, 107.

[70] Pollock and Maitland, *History of English Law*, II:343.

[71] Sharpe, *Calendar of Wills*, I:xiv. Reginald R. Sharpe, ed., *Calendar of Letter-Books Preserved among the Archives of the Corporation of the City of London at the Guildhall: Letter-Book K* (London: J. E. Francis, 1908), 181, 292. Walne, *English Wills*, 31. In medieval England, 12d. was equal to 1s. and 20s. was equal to £1. The silver penny (1d.) was the coin in use at the time. See Stahl, "Coins and Coinage," 202.

[72] Marc Fitch, ed., *Index to Testamentary Records in the Commissary Court of London* (London: British Record Society, 1969), 1:1374–488 and *Index to Testamentary Records*

doners as compared with those enrolled in the Husting Court, as anyone could enroll their will in these courts. Yet, in general, these wills were concerned with the testator's place in the afterlife. The church encouraged testators to leave a portion of their wealth in their wills for pious works.[73] In rural England, wills were often enrolled in ecclesiastical courts, unlike on the Continent. On the Continent, law followed the rule laid down by St. Cyprian, Bishop of Carthage, in 255 CE that the church was not to meddle in testamentary affairs.[74] In England, the church also encouraged women to enroll wills, and for this reason perhaps it is more common to find women's wills enrolled among the ecclesiastical courts than in the London Husting Court. For example, of all the people appearing in ecclesiastical probate courts in early modern England to prove wills and file accounts and inventories, almost three quarters were women.[75]

Marc Bloch pointed out that "a will, in the eyes of that age, was a work of piety as much as of wise provision and was intended above all to ensure the salvation of the soul by devout bequests."[76] Although the Husting wills often included details about pious bequests, a great portion of the bequests included were secular in nature. These wills, hence, can tell us about a portion of London society in terms of their plans for their property. The testators of the Husting wills were wealthy artisans and merchants primarily, since a Londoner needed to possess a substantial amount of land, tenements, or chattels of £10 or more in order to lodge one's *post obit* concerns over the division of that property with the court.[77] Furthermore, testators needed to be citizens of London. These testators were also overwhelmingly male. Since married women needed to have the permission of their husbands to make a will, and since women lost personal control over

in the Archdeaconry Court of London, British Record Society (London: British Record Society, 1979), 1:1363–649.

[73] See Hanawalt, "The Widow's Mite," 41, n. 11; Pollock and Maitland, *History of English Law*, II:314; Hanawalt, "Reading the Lives of the Illiterate," 1074–75. According to Hanawalt, the Archdeaconry Court includes 228 wills from 1393 to 1409, and the Commissary Court includes more wills from 1377 to 1480.

[74] Kiralfy, "Wills of Personality," 35, 40–42.

[75] Amy Louise Erickson, *Women and Property in Early Modern England* (New York: Routledge, 1993), 32.

[76] Marc Bloch, *Feudal Society*, trans. L. A. Manyon, vol. 1 (Chicago: University of Chicago Press, 1961), 125.

[77] Jeremy Sumner Gibson, *Probate Jurisdictions: Where to Look for Wills* (Baltimore: Genealogical Pub. Co., 1997), 7. Grannum and Taylor, *Wills and Other Probate Records*, 13.

their property upon marriage due to the law of coverture, most of the women who enrolled wills with the Husting Court were widows. Of the 3,081 wills enrolled with the court between 1300 and 1500, 2,720 (88%) were enrolled by men, and only 361 (12%) were enrolled by women. These testators are a sampling of late medieval society; around 1300, the total population of London was perhaps as high as eighty thousand, falling to half that number by 1400 and at around fifty thousand in 1500.[78] We are not, then, dealing with the majority of the population, rather only a portion. Even so, what their wills reveal can speak to their daughters' experiences and opportunities.

The recipients in the wills ranged widely from members of the immediate family to godchildren, other relatives, servants, apprentices, and business associates (figure 1.2). It is not always possible to determine the relationship of the recipient to the testator if the testator did not specify or if the surnames are not similar. The connection between surname and relationship is unsure before the mid-fourteenth century. Most onomasticians agree that surnames became hereditary among all members of society throughout England around the mid-fourteenth century. In the capital, occupational surnames may have become hereditary earlier than elsewhere, but evidence on this, too, is contested, and it is likely that this change among individuals at all levels of society was protracted.[79] Likewise, the nature of the sources prevents one from reconstituting families completely, as only those to whom the testator wished to bequeath goods and property were mentioned. For example, of the 8,411 recipients in the wills enrolled between 1300 and 1500, 1,529 daughters are mentioned as compared with 1,854 sons. Rather than indicating a high sex ratio, this most likely suggests that some daughters had already been provided for outside of the wills.

---

[78] Barron, *London in the Later Middle Ages*, 4.

[79] See Dave Postles, *Talking Ballocs: Nicknames and English Medieval Sociolinguistics* (Leicester: University of Leicester, 2003), 10. P. H. Reaney, *A Dictionary of English Surnames*, 3rd ed. (Oxford: Oxford University Press, 1997), xlviii. Richard McKinley, one of the most well-known scholars of surnames, posits that even by the fifteenth and sixteenth centuries there were people who had surnames that were not hereditary. McKinley pushes the date that surnames became hereditary back to 1500 in urban populations, rather than 1350. R. A. McKinley, *A History of British Surnames* (New York: Longman, 1990), 35–36.

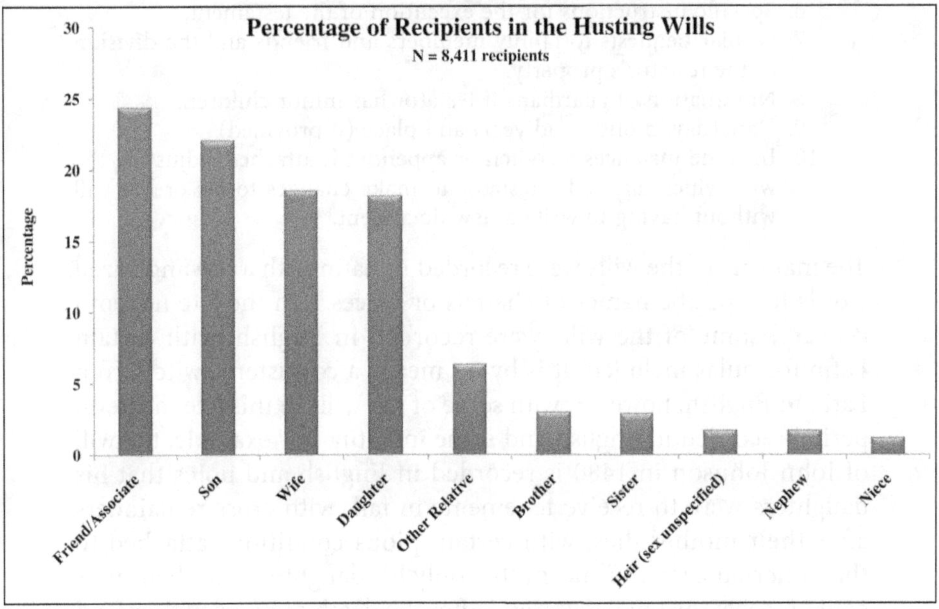

Figure 1.2

These predominantly male testators from the upper echelons of London society enrolled relatively uniform wills, or, what is more likely, the clerks recording the testators' wishes with the Husting Court placed their concerns within a relatively uniform format. The standard formula of the wills enrolled at the Court of Husting is as follows, although not every will contained all of these elements, and the order often varied considerably.

1. Name of testator, occupation (if provided). If the testator was a woman, the name and occupation of her husband, alive or deceased, is given (in most cases).
2. Burial site and requests pertaining to the funeral (for example, limit on the money to be spent or details concerning the distribution of cloth used over the coffin in the funeral).
3. Provisions for the soul and the souls of family members, predeceased or not, such as chantries and masses.
4. Charitable bequests and bequests to churches, including bequests for the construction of roads or parts of churches, bequests to lepers, prisoners, and poor girls for their marriage portions, and bequests of goods, money, or property to specific churches, religious houses, or members of religious orders, such as friars.
5. Directions as to the fulfillment of debts.

6. Specific instructions for the execution of the testament.
7. Secular bequests to family members and friends and the division of the testator's property.
8. Nomination of guardians if testator has minor children.
9. Date (day, month, and year) and place (if provided).
10. In some instances a codicil or appendix is attached, adjusting the will, which allowed a testator to make changes to his or her will without having to write a new document.[80]

The majority of the wills were recorded in Latin with a few anglicized words for specific names of chattels or places.[81] In the late fifteenth century, some of the wills were recorded in English, with certain Latin formulas included. It is by no means a consistent switch from Latin to English, however, with some of the wills in this late medieval period recorded in English and some in Latin. For example, the will of John Johnson in 1480 is recorded in English and notes that his daughters were to receive tenements in tail, with cross remainders after their mother dies, with certain pious conditions attached to that inheritance.[82] This meant that only his daughters and their heirs could receive the tenements, and after the death of one daughter and her heirs, the inheritance would be left to the other and her heirs. In 1488, William Hobbys's will records in Latin that his daughter receive an annuity.[83] This inconsistency in language was probably due to the scribe involved in the enrollment of the wills. Karen Grannum and Nigel Taylor explain that Latin was the language employed for recording wills well into the sixteenth century in practice, and in theory it continued as the written language of the courts until 1733.[84]

---

[80] Grannum and Taylor, *Wills and Other Probate Records*, 5, 78. Compare this formula for London wills with Genoese wills outlined by Epstein, *Wills and Wealth in Medieval Genoa*, 6–7. The formula of the Genoese wills appears to be more uniform than that of the London wills, and they include a few more elements, such as the place where the will was made, sometimes the time of day the will was recorded, and the reason for making the will, such as impending journey or sickness. The Genoese wills were recorded by licensed notaries. Wills recorded in Castile are similar to those of London and Genoa in that they include concerns for pious donation, burial and or masses, and the distribution of their property and goods to family and friends. The makeup of Castilian wills, however, changes radically around the thirteenth century due to cultural and economic changes in Castile. See Ruiz, *From Heaven to Earth*.

[81] The fact that these wills are in Latin runs contrary to Pollock and Maitland, who claim that toward the end of the fourteenth century English wills were recorded in either French or English. Pollock and Maitland, *History of English Law*, II:337.

[82] Corporation of London Records Office, HR 211(20) (hereafter cited as CLRO).

[83] CLRO, 219(15).

[84] Grannum and Taylor, *Wills and Other Probate Records*, 76.

This study examines the 3,081 wills enrolled between 1300 and 1500 in the Husting Court of London both qualitatively and quantitatively.[85] There have been a few very large quantitative considerations of wills including that of Marie-Thérèse Lorcin who considered fifteen thousand testaments in her study, *Vivre et mourir en Lyonnais: à la fin du Moyen Age*, but most are smaller samples. For example, Kristen Burkholder studied 550 selected wills from the Husting Court and the Prerogative Court of Canterbury in her study of material culture in late medieval England, Clive Burgess considered 350 wills from late medieval Bristol, and Philippa Maddern examined 369 wills recorded between 1400 and 1500 in Norfolk. Drawing on a larger sample allows patterns to emerge from the data. The study thus becomes more representative of society, and the content of the wills becomes more significant in a consideration of change over time.

The quantitative part of this study rests on a database built from a consideration of the Husting wills in translation, provided by Reginald Sharpe. In 1889, Sharpe compiled a calendar of the wills, which summarized each will enrolled with the court between 1258 and 1688. His abstracts included the names of people closely related to the testator, burial place, bequests, charitable gifts, and directions for the division of property.

The compilation of the abstracts into a database and statistical study has been complemented by close readings of a selection of the original wills in the predominantly Latin hand of the scribe. I conducted research of the wills themselves using a microfilm collection that includes the wills enrolled from 1252 to 1485. I also examined a selection of the originals held in the Corporation of London Records Office at the Guildhall, London (CLRO), namely those that were difficult to read on the microfilm due to the unkindness of time, and a selection of those enrolled between 1485 and 1500 that were not reproduced in the microfilm collection. This qualitative examination of the wills fills in some of the absences of Sharpe's abstracts, and such close readings add flesh to the numerical bones, so to speak, as the rhetoric used reveals conditions parents placed on their daughters' inheritance, how they sought to determine their daughters' futures,

[85] Marie-Thérèse Lorcin, *Vivre et mourir en Lyonnais: à la fin du Moyen Age* (Paris: Editions du CNRS, 1981); Burkholder, "Material Culture and Self-Presentation," 24; Burgess, "Late Medieval Wills," 31, n. 10; Maddern, "Friends of the Dead." For a study from the Continent, Daniel Smail included 231 notarized testaments in his study of mid-fourteenth-century Marseille. Smail, "Mapping Networks," 95.

boundaries set, and how they provided for their daughters in marriage and occupation. The narrative detail of the wills also lets us test what the statistics suggest.

Sharpe's abstracts, however, are true to their form; they do not include all of every testator's wishes. Sharpe omitted names and details of beneficiaries outside of the testator's family. To elucidate Sharpe's choices in his abstracts and the utility of his work for this study, I have taken a random sample of five wills of the 3,081 total wills enrolled between 1300 and 1500, generated by the statistical software program SPSS. I compared the abstracts of these five wills with the original wills. The comparison, detailed below, shows that Sharpe's abstracts permit a statistical analysis of the wills, without losing meaning, in order to examine trends in inheritance by daughters during this period in London's past.

The first will in the random sample is that of John le Little. Although the will does not include the date, it was enrolled with the court in 1311 or, more likely, 1312. According to Sharpe, this parishioner of St. Ethelburga in Bishopsgate left his two shops in the parish of St. Bartholomew the Less for the support of his two sons, Robert and Simon; he also left a tenement in St. Ethelburga to his wife, Roisia, and to a third son after her death. John also left his wife a portion of land in the parish of Stepney and one of his sons another tenement.[86] Through a comparison with the original, Sharpe left out the names of the executors, William de Pontefract and Richard de Thorp, two witnesses, and the two aldermen, Nicholas Pycot (alderman from 1298–1312[87]) and Anketin de Gysors (alderman from 1312–1336[88]). The original will also specifies that John's wife have custody of Robert and Simon.[89] John le Little's will is relatively short and lacks some of the more elaborate formulae that appear in later wills.

Similarly, the second will from the sample, that of Thomas Wobourne, is brief, although complex. Sharpe's abstract retains the details of the web of legacies specified in the original, which begins

[86] Sharpe, *Calendar of Wills*, I:225–26.

[87] Sylvia Thrupp notes the dates of aldermen and mayors in the Middle Ages in her work, *The Merchant Class of Medieval London* (Ann Arbor: The University of Michigan Press, 1962), 362.

[88] Thrupp, *The Merchant Class*, 345. Sharpe lists him as Anketynus de Gisorz, alderman of the Ward of Alegate in 1319–20. Sharpe, *Calendar of Wills*, I:704. From the service dates of these two alderman, one can see why enrollment during 1312 is more likely than 1311.

[89] CLRO, HR 40(72).

with a relatively simple bequest: Thomas's tenements were to be sold except for funds to pay his sister an annuity.[90] Sharpe's abstract (as in the original will) then goes on to include a dispute over the bequest. Thomas's sister, Isabella, is the only heir mentioned in the will proper. She challenged the will: "venit et reclamat contra legatum praedictum …"[91] She also claimed to be an heir of her parents and argued that the tenements were to be left to her after her brother died. This appears to be the case considering her father's will proved and enrolled roughly fifteen years earlier. William de Wobourne, Thomas and Isabella's father, left tenements and rents to his wife, Juliana, for her life, with remainders to his son and daughter.[92] However, in his son Thomas's will, the one I began with here, the executors note that the tenements were left to son Thomas in a certain form, "sub certa forma," after Juliana's death and that since Juliana did not contest it, "nichil [sic] dicit contra praemissa," the executors supported Thomas's will. Isabella was left, presumably, with her life-long annuity, "annuo redditu," owed to her, "sibi debito," by her brother.[93]

For this will, as with le Little's, Sharpe also left out the names of three executors and two witnesses. Mayor and aldermen are evoked, but not named in the original. Besides these omissions, Sharpe retains a fairly literal translation. The original will notes Isabella's challenge, and Sharpe preserves it in his abstract. The only difference is in presentation. There is no pause in the original between Thomas's will and Isabella's reclamation. In Sharpe's abstract, he sets the two apart, presumably to draw attention to the distinction between the will and the challenge to the will.

John de Colkirk's will is the third in the sample, and Sharpe includes the main recipients of John's property in his summary: Thomas, Adam, William, Elias, and John Jr., the testator's sons.[94] His son Thomas was to receive his tenement in Wodestret, with the remainder to his son Adam, according to Sharpe. Or, according to the Latin original, his son Adam would inherit if the eldest son Thomas was without heirs from a legitimate marriage: "absque herede ab ipso legatimo matrimonio procreato …"[95] Another tenement was to be

[90] Sharpe, *Calendar of Wills*, I:265–66.
[91] CLRO, HR 45(57).
[92] Sharpe, *Calendar of Wills*, I:144.
[93] CLRO, HR 45(57).
[94] Sharpe, *Calendar of Wills*, I:357.
[95] CLRO, HR 58(33).

sold and the money to go to his other three sons; this information appears in the original and in the abstract. This will was dated, unlike the first two, to 1329, and the abstract includes this information as it appears in the original: "Dated London, Sunday next after the Feast of S. Martin in Yeme, 3 Edward III."[96] Like those above, Sharpe left out the name of the Alderman, in this case Thomas de Leyre,[97] the witnesses, John le Chandeler and William le Coupe, and the executors, who—according to the original—are to handle the sale of the one tenement, including one man who might be a relative: Hugo de Colekirk.[98]

Sharpe's abstract of the will of Thomas Curteise, the fourth in the sample, from the plague year 1349, also follows the original closely. The main beneficiary, Alice, Thomas's daughter, received a tenement for her life, "totam vitam," and some trade tools: two leads, "plumba," a cistern, and a "taptrogh," perhaps for brewing. The will also includes numerous pious bequests Thomas made to two churches in London.[99] In reviewing the original, part of which is difficult to read due to poor preservation over time, Sharpe again left out the names of the executors and witnesses, and he did not include the specific details involved with a bequest of a chantry. Sharpe detailed that the testator left a bequest for "the maintenance of a chantry in the aforesaid church of S. Michael."[100] The original will enrolled at the Husting Court specifies a legacy of twenty-four marks to maintain a chantry for about four years.[101]

The last will in the sample is that of vinter, a wine merchant, Thomas Serieant dated 1380. His will is very well preserved in the original, and as is common with later wills in the series, his will is more detailed, both in the original and in Sharpe's abstract. Sharpe includes burial information and pious and charitable bequests, such as for the inmates of Newgate prison. The main and only beneficiary Sharpe includes is Johanna, Thomas's wife, who receives "his leasehold interest in a house in Berebynderesane" with some additional

---

[96] Sharpe, *Calendar of Wills*, I:357. The Latin will also includes "post conquestum" in its dating schematic, which Sharpe does not preserve. CLRO, HR 58(33).

[97] According to Sylvia Thrupp, Thomas de Leyre was alderman between 1327 and 1331; Thrupp, *The Merchant Class*, 353.

[98] CLRO, HR 58(33).

[99] Sharpe, *Calendar of Wills*, I:541; CLRO, HR 76(157).

[100] Sharpe, *Calendar of Wills*, I:541.

[101] CLRO, HR 76(157).

rents in two separate parishes.[102] Without looking at the original, one would not know that Johanna is the sole executrix named in the will or that the date and reign information are included in the first third of the will, rather than at the end, as in Colkirk's will above. Although Johanna is named as sole executrix, at the end of the will Serieant names three men as supervisors, "supervirsores," of his will.[103] This original is longer than the earlier wills in the sample, and it includes more flourishes and formulae more common in later wills, such as the testator's statement that he makes this will in sound mind and body: "sanus mente et corpora ac in bona mea existens memoria ..."[104]

However, aside from these details, Sharpe's abstract adheres to the original in the broad strokes, especially in the details of the main beneficiary, Johanna. The main bequest to her of the leasehold interest in a house of his is in the original as it is translated by Sharpe: "totum terminum venturum domum mee ... vite sue ... in Berbyndereslane in parochia bte Mare de Wolchircheawe ..."[105] The original mentions that this term in this house was acquired from two men who Sharpe does not mention.[106] The original also mentions the rents she was to inherit for her life in the parishes of "Ste Mildrede in Pulletra" and "bte Mare de Wolcherchehawe."[107] Finally, in his abstract, as in the abstract for Curtiese's will, Sharpe shortened Serieant's pious bequests, which comprise the remainder of his original will. For example, while Sharpe mentions the prisoners of Newgate, he leaves out the names of the hospitals inhabited by the poor who were to receive his bequests, such as those of St. Bartholomew of West Smithfield, St. Thomas of Southwerk, and St. Mary without Bishopsgate mentioned in the original will.

In his introduction, Sharpe states: "To have taken note of every name and bequest would have entailed so great a sacrifice of time and money that nothing more has been attempted than a general abstract of each will, noticing more particularly the names of the testators, their place of burial (when stated), the names of those nearly related to them ... on the other hand, names of many beneficiaries

---

[102] Sharpe, *Calendar of Wills*, II:226.
[103] CLRO, HR 110(32).
[104] CLRO, HR 110(32).
[105] CLRO, HR 110(32).
[106] CLRO, HR 110(32).
[107] CLRO, HR 110(32).

outside a testator's own family and bequests of no special interest or importance have necessarily been omitted."[108] In addition to the time, labor, and expense that would have been required to translate all of the wills in full, he justified his edits by stating, "Enough of the wills has been set out in these two volumes to afford the reader an insight into the domestic lives of the families and individuals intimately associated with the municipal history of London ..."[109] He recognized the weakness of this approach but maintained that it was a beginning to providing access to this important primary source.[110]

The random sample of five wills from the 3,081 enrolled between 1300 and 1500 illustrate his expressions. What Sharpe thought important may differ from another's view of important historical information, depending on the goal of the study. For example, it is clear from the five wills in the sample that if a historian wanted information concerning executors and witnesses, and perhaps the social networks they formed, the original wills would be necessary and Sharpe's abstracts insufficient. However, for this consideration of daughters' inheritance of real estate and movable property, Sharpe's abstracts are valuable to analyze statistically, as he consistently notes bequests to daughters as core members of the testators' families.

Inheriting Opportunity in London: A New Framework

This study begins with an exploration of the Husting will testators' backgrounds by considering the types of bequests they included in their wills and how their gender and occupation influenced the legacies—and by extension the opportunities—they left to their daughters and sons. Next, through a consideration of patterns in bequests of property, such as tenements, shops, and rental properties, paired with examples from the wills themselves, daughters' economic opportunities to own real estate will become clear. Chapter 3 will also consider how patterns in bequests of real estate changed over time. The following chapter, chapter 4, considers testators' bequests of movable wealth and how their descriptions of the goods they left to their children illustrate ideas about wealth, value, social status, and culture in the consciousness of late medieval Londoners. This chapter also

---

[108] Sharpe, *Calendar of Wills*, I:xlviii.
[109] Sharpe, *Calendar of Wills*, II:ii.
[110] Sharpe, *Calendar of Wills*, I:xlviii.

explores the extent to which the language of the wills describes the world in which these daughters lived and worked. Throughout the book, both quantitative and qualitative approaches allow an examination of how the factors of religion, occupation, and gender worked to influence testators' bequests and daughters' experiences in late medieval London. Finally, in the last chapter, I place these daughters' legacies within two important contexts. First, I consider the legacies of London daughters in the context of women owning and managing property throughout England and Europe in the late Middle Ages. This context is crucial to entertain ideas of how daughters used the opportunities presented to them in their parents' wills. Second, I consider the findings from the Husting wills in the context of urban women's opportunities in towns throughout England, in an effort to explore the extent to which London was an anomaly. Through this approach I hope to suggest a new framework in which to place our understandings of women's lives in the Middle Ages.

The property a woman in the Middle Ages received from her family, as a daughter, was hers, and it could be substantial, as the Husting wills show. If we explore the opportunities medieval European women, here as daughters, had to own and manage property, we will acquire a much more nuanced understanding of their lives and their historical experiences. Studying women and property in urban settings, specifically as daughters, allows us to ask new questions about women's positions in medieval society, gendered expectations, and avenues open for them to achieve their goals. In the medieval past, not all women married, and those who did often had identities in addition to the one formed by their marriage. From an examination of daughterhood and property in the Husting wills in an urban context, it becomes clear that some medieval women were given significant opportunities to exercise influence in their world.

CHAPTER TWO

TESTATORS AND THEIR INFLUENCE IN LATE MEDIEVAL LONDON

The wishes of parents in late medieval London, expressed through bequests in their wills, shaped the lives of their children. This chapter will explore who testators were and how their characteristics influenced the lives of their daughters specifically. These daughters of London were born into primarily merchant and artisan families, and this background influenced the property, and by extension the opportunities, they inherited. In addition to the property they received, in many instances parents placed conditions on the bequests to their children that determined how those children would use the property. However, as we will see, it was more likely for parents to place specific boundaries on bequests to daughters than to sons about the options they had in marriage partners and professions.

The gender and occupation of the testators affected the types of property they bequeathed to daughters and sons alike, but in different ways. Fathers more equally distributed property, both movable wealth and real estate, to their daughters and sons than mothers did. In terms of occupation, daughters of noble, professional, and artisan testators inherited more real estate than movable wealth, in comparison with daughters of government officials and merchants. However, these indicators need to be placed in context to best understand daughters' life opportunities and living conditions. Necessarily, we need to allow a fair amount of space for daughters' personal situations as well as that of their parents. A nobleman's concerns and holdings were likely to be different from an artisan's and likewise the concerns and needs of their daughters. More real estate does not always equate with the best situation. Yet, while keeping this caveat in mind, an analysis of the factors influencing the testators, such as gender and occupation, does allow us to see the diversity in lifestyles and personal situations of these women.

In the wills proved and enrolled in the London Husting Court, male testators were in the majority. Of the 3,081 wills enrolled between 1300 and 1500, 2,720 were enrolled by men (88%), and only 361 were enrolled by women (12%). Theoretically, anyone who was a citizen of London could enroll his or her will at the Court of Husting, and he or she could modify it as often as desired.[1] In practice, however, only adult males and adult unmarried or widowed women enrolled wills with any frequency.

A married woman, as a *femme couverte*, was under the legal authority of her husband and therefore could not make a will, except with his consent. Infants and individuals not in their right mind (*non compos mentis*) also could not enroll wills.[2] In the seventeenth century, Henry Calthrop explained it in this way: "He which holdeth Tenements joyntly with others, may devise that which belongeth to him, without any other separation; but Infants within age can make no devise, nor women under covertbarn, cannot devise their Tenements by leave of their Husbands, nor in any other sort during the coverture."[3] Calthrop here is using the phrase "under covertbarn," or "under covert-baron," which simply means the condition of being a *femme couverte* or married woman.[4] Common law lawyers argued that a married woman could not bequeath property she did not own. Michael Sheehan explains that in the thirteenth century there was a debate over who could make a will in England. At this time, the church argued that married women and those of the servile class should be allowed to draw up wills. This push by bishops and canonists did not make it into common law, but wives were allowed to make wills with their husbands' consent. Despite the common law resistance to married women making wills, Sheehan argues that there was a "strongly held view that husbands should permit them [to make wills]. And there was in the society an important body of opinion which maintained that the wife's capacity was not a matter of privilege, but of right."[5]

---

[1] Sharpe, *Calendar of Wills*, I:xxxiii.

[2] Sharpe, *Calendar of Wills*, I:xli–xlii.

[3] Henry Calthrop, *Reports of Speciall Cases Touching Severall Customs and Liberties of the City of London* (London: Printed for Abel Roper, 1655), 156.

[4] *Oxford English Dictionary Online*, s.v. "covert-baron," accessed 10.25.2010, http://dictionary.oed.com.

[5] Michael M. Sheehan, *The Will in Medieval England: From the Conversion of the Anglo-Saxons to the End of the Thirteenth Century*, vol. 6 (Toronto: Pontifical Institution of Mediaeval Studies, 1963), 239, 233–39. See also Pollock and Maitland's discussion of the common law's decision that wives could not make wills without the consent of their husbands. Pollock and Maitland, *History of English Law*, 2:428–30. For a recent discussion of the incidence of will-making by married women, see Kettle, "My Wife Shall Have It", 94, and Richard Helmholz's article, "Married Women's Wills in Later Medieval England," in *Wife and Widow in Medieval England*, ed. Sue Sheridan Walker (Ann Arbor: University of Michigan Press, 1993), 165–82.

Only 14 of the 361 female testators in this two-hundred-year period described themselves as married women, and all noted that they had the consent of their husbands to make their wills. Compare this number with the 1,556 male testators, or 50%, who were married or mentioned their wives in their wills. Since women were entitled to dowers, some wives may not have been mentioned in married men's wills. This may explain why the number is lower than what one might expect. Juliana Kelleseye is an example of a woman who described herself as wife of Robert de Kelleseye and left property to her sons and niece.[6] Four of the fourteen women I count here as married mention a previous husband or describe themselves as wife *and* widow—Amycia Burwell, Clarice Clopton, Margaret Holym, and Johan Carre—noting both their present and past husbands.[7] Two women—Emma Wylekyn, around 1307, and Cristiana la Flaoners, around 1291—were married women who enrolled their wills, but they were considered void because they were *sub virga* and did not have the permission of their husbands.[8]

Most of the women among these testators were formerly married and at the moment of their will-making were independent women from a legal standpoint. In all, 248 women, or 69% of the women testators, described themselves either as widows (using the term *relicta* most often) (224), mentioned their deceased husbands in their wills (21), or did not mention their husbands but did mention their children (33). It is not possible to know with certainty how many of the women who enrolled wills were never married. In all, nineteen women described themselves as daughters, although five of these also

Helmholz agrees with Sheehan that wills were indeed made by married women in medieval England, but that these incidences declined in the fifteenth century. For a general discussion of the role of common and canon law in the lives of the women in late medieval London, see Kay Lacey, "Women and Work," 24–45.

[6] Sharpe, *Calendar of Wills*, I:511; CLRO, HR 75(205).

[7] Sharpe, *Calendar of Wills*, II:336, 476, 501, 599; CLRO, HR 127(35), 164(45), 171(35), 225(27). Elsewhere in England, Jenny Kermode has found more married women's wills; about thirty-one merchants' wives made wills in York, Beverley, and Hull. Jenny Kermode, *Medieval Merchants: York, Beverley and Hull in the Later Middle* Ages (Cambridge: Cambridge University Press, 1998), 93. Cf. Ellen Kittel's study of Genoa and Douai. According to Kittel, in Genoa, 23 percent of testators were married women compared with 3 percent in Douai. Kittel, "Testaments of Two Cities: A Comparative Analysis of the Wills of Medieval Genoa and Douai," *European Review of History*, 5 (1998): 47–83. It seems, then, that it was more common in the south for married women to leave wills than with their northern counterparts.

[8] Sharpe, *Calendar of Wills*, I:105, 188. CLRO, HR 21(27), 35(98).

described themselves as widows or wives. Dyonesia Norman, for instance, described herself as daughter and wife.[9] The other four women described themselves as daughters and widows: Agnes Suffolk, Margery Broun, Johanna Osekyn, and Margaret Cruse.[10] Fifty-one women did not mention a husband, alive or dead, in their wills. However, without them explicitly stating their marital status, it is not possible to know for certain if these forty-seven women were never married or if they were widowed.

The wills enrolled at the Court of Husting in the fourteenth and fifteenth centuries also represent people of relatively high social status. One needed to possess £10 worth of land, tenements, or chattels in order to enroll one's will specifying the division of that property with the Husting Court.[11] This was a substantial amount considering the average wage in late medieval London. In the fifteenth century, for example, dyer and blacksmith servants' wages were set at 40s. a year plus room and board, while an unskilled laborer averaged about £3 10s. a year, and craftsmen, such as masons and carpenters, earned from £5–7 per year.[12] Christopher Dyer has found evidence outside of London also that corroborate these estimates; for example, at the start of the fourteenth century, a carpenter, Adam de Chudleigh, earned £2 13s. 10d. for twenty-six weeks of work on Exeter Cathedral, while skilled mason Richard de la Streme earned £4 17s. 2¼d for forty-six weeks of labor.[13] In the fifteenth century, skilled mason Robert Bardolf earned £7 2s. 0d. for forty-one weeks of work on a castle in Leicestershire, while laborer Simon Phelyp recieved £3 0s. 5¾ d.

[9] Sharpe, *Calendar of Wills*, I:170; CLRO, HR 33(59).

[10] Sharpe, *Calendar of Wills*, I:425, II:36, 320, 520; CLRO, HR 64(138), 89(134), 124(118), 180(14).

[11] In London a testator had to possess *bona notabilia*, which is Latin for "considerable goods," of £10 or more; elsewhere it was usually £5 or more. Jeremy Sumner Gibson, *Probate Jurisdictions: Where to Look for Wills* (Baltimore: Genealogical Pub. Co., 1997), 7.

[12] See Christopher Dyer, *Standards of Living in the Later Middle Ages: Social Change in England c. 1200–1520* (New York: Cambridge University Press, 1989), 193–96, 224–25. Sylvia Thrupp, *The Merchant Class of Medieval London* (Ann Arbor: University of Michigan Press, 1962), 114, 152. John Munro offers another estimate of a master mason in London in 1438–1439 who earned eight pence per day, which works out to be about six and a half pounds per annum. See John Munro, "The Consumption of Spices and Their Costs in Late-Medieval and Early-Modern Europe: Luxuries or Necessities?" (lecture, University of Toronto, rev. Nov. 5, 2005), accessed Jan. 21, 2009, http://www.economics.utoronto.ca/munro5/SPICES1.pdf.

[13] Dyer, *An Age of Transition*, 226.

for thirty-one weeks of work.[14] With fifty-two weeks in a year and about one hundred holy days, plus the amount from earnings that needed to be spent on food and clothing, an individual would need to save substantially on these wages in order to amass enough to enroll one's will with the court. In most cases, then, the testators in the London wills were merchants and the upper crust of artisans. Heather Swanson has found a similar situation in York. Through an examination of the 1327 lay subsidy, the wealthiest individuals—those assessed at over £5 of goods—were merchants, including those in the victualling trade, while most artisans were assessed at under £2 of goods.[15]

For London, the nature of the Husting Wills precludes a definitive study of the occupations of these testators, as not every testator mentioned his or her occupation; yet in comparison to the subsidy from York, more artisans are represented in the London wills. Of the 3,081 wills enrolled between 1300 and 1500, 1,658 testators, or 54%, mention their occupation, leaving 1,423 testators' occupations unknown. The frequency of noting occupation increased over time, with very few occupations mentioned in the early fourteenth century, more recorded after the 1330s, and near routine notice by the end of the fifteenth century. This was likely a change in the procedures of enrollment in the court. Another complication with noting occupations is that there may have been a difference between self-identity and popular perception. Kristen Burkholder points this out in her study of wills from the Husting Court and the Prerogative Court of Canterbury: "a man who described himself as a weaver might have also owned a brewhouse and be thought of by his neighbors as a brewer, not a weaver at all."[16] Therefore, the consideration of occupation here deals with self-perception and how testators viewed their own livelihoods and status.

In order to consider how a testator's occupation may have influenced his (or occasionally her) bequests, I organized the 165 different occupations specified by these London testators into six larger occupational categories: artisans, merchants, professionals, ecclesiastics, nobility and gentry, and government officials. Among the

---

[14] Dyer, *An Age of Transition*, 227.

[15] Heather Swanson, *Medieval Artisans: An Urban Class in Late Medieval England* (Oxford: Basil Blackwell, 1989), 151.

[16] Burkholder, "Material Culture and Self-Presentation," 29.

Husting wills, ninety-eight types of artisans were mentioned, thirty-three types of merchants, eleven types of ecclesiastics, ten types of professionals, seven types of nobility and gentry, and six types of government officials.

Of the 54% of testators who mentioned their occupation in their wills, the majority were artisans (48%) and merchants (36%) (see figure 2.1).[17] Artisans were considered as those who worked at a craft and made a product for sale. Included in this category were such craftsmen as bakers, fletchers, and tilers, although it is important to note that among those who processed goods for sale, it was common and arguably necessary for these individuals to be flexible. Numerous scholars have noted that artisans frequently varied their work and rarely limited themselves to one trade; instead, they often engaged in side jobs while pursuing a main occupation.[18] The variety and flexibility are significant if we are to understand the reality of the London economy in which daughters operated.

Londoners who sold goods rather than making them were categorized as merchants, such as cheesemongers, fishmongers, and spicers.[19] Professionals—those individuals who required some amount of formal education and/or literacy—such as lawyers, clerks, and those of the medical fields, consisted of 6% of the testators who mentioned their occupations. Ecclesiastical testators, including priests, chaplains, and rectors (men in major orders, or higher clergy, who committed themselves to a celibate life[20]), also comprised 6%. Less frequent among the testators who mentioned occupation were members of the nobility and gentry—such as earls, gentlemen, knights, and esquires—at 3%,[21] and government officials—including recorders, sergeants, minters, and pleaders—at less than 1%. Government

---

[17] In comparison, the majority of testators in Castile were clerics, but these men were also members of the middling sort of the region. Ruiz, *From Heaven to Earth*, 56.

[18] For two examples, see Swanson, *Medieval Artisans*, 6, 172, and Maryanne Kowaleski, *Local Markets and Regional Trade in Medieval Exeter* (Cambridge: Cambridge University Press, 1995), 123–26.

[19] The standard work on London merchants remains Thrupp's work, *The Merchant Class of Medieval London*.

[20] Joseph Lynch, *The Medieval Church: A Brief History* (London: Longman, 1992), 293–94.

[21] For works on the English nobility in later medieval England, see K. B. McFarlane, *The Nobility of Later Medieval England* (Oxford: Clarendon Press, 1973) and Chris Given-Wilson, *The English Nobility in the Late Middle Ages: The Fourteenth-Century Political Community* (London: Routledge, 1987). For a recent work on the

officials were perhaps a small group, of those included amongst the testators here, but they could hold important posts in the government of the city. For example, as Caroline Barron explains, the office of the recorder by the end of the Middle Ages was "the highest paid and the most prestigious member of the civic hierarchy."[22]

These larger categories are not without their grey areas. Clerks, for example, were technically ecclesiastics; however, sixteen of the testators identified as clerks (of 68 total clerks) left legacies to their wives, and twenty-four left legacies to their children. For example, Hugh de Waltham, clerk of London, left property to his five daughters and three sons, while he specified that he be buried near his wife.[23] I could not consider all of the clerks as ecclesiastics as some were not celibate and since most clerks were in minor orders in the Middle Ages. That is, those in minor orders could marry if they gave up their ecclesiastical privileges.[24] Therefore, I considered clerks as professionals because the nature of their work and their status placed them in line more with the other professional occupations than with the other ecclesiastics represented in the wills. It is worth noting here another grey area when trying to pin down occupation: testators could take up occupations in addition to their duties as clerks. Four of the clerks in the Husting rolls held another occupation, namely fisherman, rector, and mercer. Hamo de Chigwell, a clerk and fishmonger, also held government positions as alderman, sheriff, and mayor. Interestingly, none of these four testators bequeathed any property to wives or children. Only one, a clerk and rector, left legacies to nephews.[25] In the case of clerks, as well as with the other testators, the fluidity of occupation needs to be borne in mind.

---

gentry, see Peter Coss, *The Origins of the English Gentry* (Cambridge: Cambridge University Press, 2003).

[22] Caroline Barron, *London in the Later Middle Ages: Government and People, 1200–1500* (Oxford: Oxford University Press, 2004), 173. Barron discusses London's government officials in detail in this work. See especially pages 173–98.

[23] CLRO, HR 62(110).

[24] Frank Pegues, "The *Clericus* in the Legal Administration of Thirteenth-Century England" *The English Historical Review* 71 (October, 1956): 556. Richard H. Bowers, "From Rolls to Riches: King's Clerks and Moneylending in Thirteenth-Century England" *Speculum* 58 (1983): 60.

[25] Sharpe, *Calendar of Wills*, I:382–83, 426; Sharpe, *Calendar of Wills*, II:385, 539–40; CLRO, HR 61(17), 65(24), 138(1), 188(13).

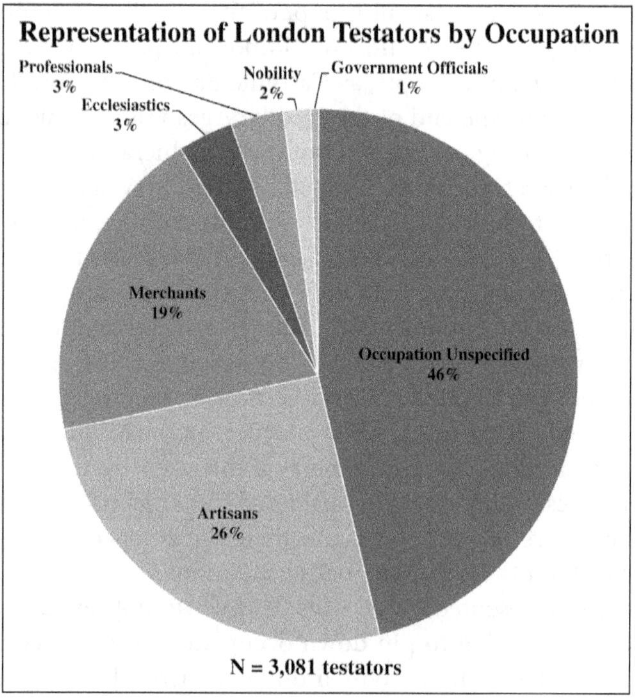

Figure 2.1

The range of occupations in the Husting wills is stunningly wide and not limited to the very elite. The occupations of these testators include those members of the nobility and merchants, but they also dip lower in the social scale, proving that the urban milieu of late medieval London provided opportunities for many individuals to improve their material situation. The Husting wills provide a more diverse population to study than wills from the rural elite. The occupations mentioned in the Husting wills range from pepperers and vinters, who were often wealthy merchants, to fripperers and upholders, dealers in old clothing and furniture. The top five most frequently mentioned occupations between 1300 and 1500 were fishmongers (134), goldsmiths (91), drapers (84), mercers (dealers in fabrics) (77), and clerks (68).

Even though it is difficult to gauge wealth with any precision without inventories, the Husting wills give a very rough indication of those occupations that provided the most comfortable living. Similarly, in her study of artisans in wills from fifteenth-century York,

Heather Swanson found that the testators from the leading positions in York society were in the clothing industry (rather than those involved in piecework), with dyers and drapers most frequently bequeathing more than £20 worth of bequests.[26] Swanson notes that: "at the bottom end come the builders," with very few making wills.[27] As among the York testators, there were few London testators representing the building trades: only five tilers and twenty-one carpenters of the 1,658 testators who mention their occupations. However, as one might expect, there was more variety of trades in London, so we also find among the least frequently noted occupations a hosteler[28] (innkeeper), "maltmongere"[29] (a merchant of malt), "pyebaker"[30] and "tortebaker" [31] (maker of a course brown bread[32]), "netmaker,"[33] "pynner"[34] (a pin- or nail-maker[35]), "chaloner" (a maker of chalons, thick material for blankets[36]), "bokelsmyth" [37] (one who makes buckles[38]), "hakenayman"[39] (rents small horses[40]), "healmer" (helmet maker[41]), "stacioner"[42] (a bookdealer[43]), and tentmaker.[44] Each of these

---

26 Swanson, *Medieval Artisans*, 157.

27 Swanson, *Medieval Artisans*, 156.

28 Will of Robert Whappelode, Sharpe, *Calendar of Wills*, II:452; CLRO, HR 159 (13).

29 Will of John Ruwenhale, Sharpe, *Calendar of Wills*, II:382; CLRO, HR 136(33).

30 Will of Andrew Smyth, Sharpe, *Calendar of Wills*, II:345–46; CLRO HR 129(5).

31 Will of Thomas Kyngeston, Sharpe, *Calendar of Wills*, II:146–47; CLRO, HR 100 (87).

32 Robert E. Lewis, ed., *Middle English Dictionary*, vol. 8 (Ann Arbor: University of Michigan Press, 1996), 940.

33 Will of John Clerk, Sharpe, *Calendar of Wills*, II:562; CLRO, HR 198(28).

34 Will of John Hill, Sharpe, *Calendar of Wills*, II:498–99; CLRO, HR 179(64).

35 *Middle English Dictionary*, s.v. "pinner(e," accessed 10.25.2010, http://quod.lib.umich.edu/m/med/.

36 Will of Hugh Alright, Sharpe, *Calendar of Wills*, II:150; CLRO, HR 100 (127).

37 Will of John Mayner, Sharpe, *Calendar of Wills*, II:357–58; CLRO, HR 133(16).

38 *Middle English Dictionary*, s.v. "bokel," accessed 10.25.2010, http://quod.lib.umich.edu/m/med/.

39 Will of William de Chippenham, Sharpe, *Calendar of Wills*, II:27; CLRO, HR 89 (107).

40 *Middle English Dictionary*, s.v. "hakenei(e" accessed 10.25.2010, http://quod.lib.umich.edu/m/med/.

41 Will of Thomas Canoun, Sharpe, *Calendar of Wills*, I:576–77; CLRO, HR 76(316).

42 Will of John Nicolson, Sharpe, *Calendar of Wills*, II:560–61; CLRO, HR 198 (19).

43 *Middle English Dictionary*, s.v. "stacioner(e" accessed 10.25.2010, http://quod.lib.umich.edu/m/med/.

44 Will of John de Yakesley, Sharpe, *Calendar of Wills*, I:695; CLRO, HR 85(38).

trades was only mentioned once. It is noteworthy that many of these singularly-noted occupations are more specialized victualling trades (rather than bakers and butchers, for example) and pieceworkers in the cloth-making trades. These singular cases likely reflect the size of the capital and diversity of trades there. However, it also may indicate a few lone individuals from the middling to lower groups in London society who amassed enough personal wealth to register their wills with the court.

All but one testator who mentioned an occupation were male. The lone female testator who identified her occupation was Dyonisia la Longe in 1349, a "gildestere," or gilder. A gilder was an artisan who decorated or embellished work by adding a layer of gold or gold leaf. Interestingly, Dyonisia does not mention a husband or children in her will, and thus she may have operated as a single woman, although we cannot know for certain. In addition to her stated occupation, she owned a brewery, which she left to the church of S. Laurence.[45] Except for Dyonisia, women testators did not appear among the more traditionally female occupations of food provision and the textile industry, such as brewing (thirty-seven men), baking (fifteen men), embroidery (four men), or cloth-working (three men). The occupation of spinning, a common one for medieval women, was not mentioned in any of the wills from 1300 to 1500, likely because spinsters would not have had enough personal wealth to enroll their wills with the Husting Court. There is one woman mentioned as a "Thredwomman," which Sharpe determines to be a dealer in thread or yarn, in the will of Margery de Wybourne from 1349. This woman, Isabella de Wybourne, perhaps Margery's mother or relative, is mentioned as the owner of houses and shops that she gave to Margery. Margery is leaving these properties at her death for the establishment of a chantry.[46]

Although women merchants and artisans are absent in the wills, there were a number of female testators whose surnames may indicate their livelihoods. For example, Sabine Taillour, late wife of Philip, may have tailored clothes, and Margery Chaundeler, daughter of Adam, may have been involved in the candle-making business.[47]

---

[45] Sharpe, *Calendar of Wills*, I:575; CLRO, HR 76(306).

[46] Sharpe, *Calendar of Wills*, I:627; CLRO, HR 78(24).

[47] Sharpe, *Calendar of Wills*, I:244; CLRO, HR 42(91); Sharpe, *Calendar of Wills*, I:256; CLRO, HR 44(26).

However, it is difficult to ascertain if an occupational surname for a woman represents her own work or simply that of her husband or father. Johanna le Spicere, with no husband mentioned, may very well have numbered among the spicers of London in the early fourteenth century, but it is difficult to determine with any conviction.[48]

In relatively rare cases (only 2 percent of the wills), testators mentioned the office they held in city government, and the offices mentioned also indicate the relatively high social status of these individuals. Of all the testators, fifty-four are mentioned as aldermen, twenty-three as mayor, and twenty as sheriff, with many of them serving more than one of these offices in their lifetimes. In fact, there were nine men who served in all three roles of sheriff, mayor, and alderman in their lifetimes, like vinter John de Oxenford who served as an alderman, 1324-1342,[49] sheriff in 1323–1324, and mayor in 1341–1342. Oxenford was quite wealthy, as he left over £100 for his funeral expenses and £100 to be distributed to the poor at his funeral, in addition to other bequests of money, wine, and property to convents, churches, building maintenance, and his heirs.[50] This is a trend that spans the entire period. Almost all nine of these men were drawn from the merchant group in late medieval London (a vinter, two grocers, three mercers—one mercer was also a knight[51]—, a draper, a knight, and one with no occupation identified), as were almost all aldermen.[52] Of course, none of these London government positions were held by female testators during this period.

Types of Bequests in the Husting Wills

In the Husting wills, testators dispersed their goods and property widely and for various causes (figure 2.2). The most common bequests were to family members, friends, and parish churches, as well

[48] Sharpe, *Calendar of Wills*, I:249; CLRO, HR 43(17).

[49] Thrupp, *The Merchant Class*, 359.

[50] Sharpe, *Calendar of Wills*, I:460–61; CLRO, HR, 69(93).

[51] Sharpe, *Calendar of Wills*, II: 509-511; CLRO, HR 175(19). See also Thrupp, *The Merchant Class*, 338, who notes William Estfeld was knighted in 1439.

[52] Barron, *London in the Later Middle Ages*, 4. Henry le Galeys is the one man who served in these government positions, but whose occupation is not mentioned in his will. Reginald Sharpe has noted that he served as alderman, sherriff, and mayor, but has not noted his occupation. Henry le Galeys is not mentioned in Thrupp's index of Aldermanic families either.

as for charitable causes, such as for the construction of London Bridge or for poor girls' dowries. Bequests made explicitly for the testator's afterlife or that of his family members were also common, such as masses or chantries. Anniversary masses were a popular provision throughout Europe, and the foundation or endowment of a chantry by will for the commemoration of an individual or family in a set place was likewise popular among burgesses in the late Middle Ages.[53]

It should be noted here that it is difficult to separate secular and religious reasons for bequests in these medieval wills, as testators might today.[54] Charitable efforts such as road maintenance today would be thought of as public works projects supported by the government, whereas in the Middle Ages, maintenance of roads and bridges fell to the owners of the land that those roads and bridges traversed. The tenants of lay and religious lords worked to repair and maintain them, and oftentimes landowners and city planners levied taxes and tolls to help the cause. Likewise, sheriffs taxed those landowners who failed to keep up their roads.[55] Testators left bequests for such maintenance either in an act of self-interest, if they traveled that road or bridge frequently, or piety, as pilgrims traversed those roads and bridges.[56] A bequest to a hospital was similarly intended to aid those residing therein, and although not overtly stated, it was as-

---

[53] See Samuel Kline Cohn, *The Cult of Remembrance and the Black Death: Six Renaissance Cities in Central Italy* (Baltimore: Johns Hopkins University Press, 1992), 81–84; N. P. Tanner, *The Church in Late Medieval Norwich 1370–1532* (Toronto: Pontifical Institute of Mediaeval Studies, 1984), 2–6, 100–106; David A. Postles, "Record-keeping in the Medieval Borough: Proof of Wills," *Archives: The Journal of the British Records Association* 16 (1983): 14; and Joel T. Rosenthal, *The Purchase of Paradise: Gift Giving and the Aristocracy, 1307–1485* (London: Routledge, 1972), 31–52, who speaks about their popularity among the late medieval English nobility and gentry.

[54] J. M. Jennings also makes this point in his study of Husting testators between 1400 and 1450. Jennings, "The Distribution of Landed Wealth in the Wills of London Merchants 1400–1450," *Mediaeval Studies* 39 (1977): 261–80.

[55] J. J. Jusserand *English Wayfaring Life in the Middle Ages*, trans. Lucy Toulmin Smith (Williamstown, M.A.: Corner House Publishers, 1974), 35–36, 80–85.

[56] The church sometimes encouraged such donations through indulgences. C. T. Flower, ed., *Public Works in Medieval Law* (London: B. Quaritch, 1923), 2:xix. Guilds too sometimes took on the task of bridge maintenance, which they viewed as a religious duty. H. F. Westlake, *The Parish Gilds of Mediaeval England* (New York: The MacMillan Company, 1919), 15. See also Christopher Dyer, *An Age of Transition? Economy and Society in England in the Later Middle Ages* (Oxford: Oxford University Press, 2005), 120.

sumed that in return, the inmates would pray for the donor. Bequests to the poor or down-trodden, however, were influenced by the medieval belief that the only worthy, or "deserving," poor were those individuals who had come upon hard times through ill luck, rather than through their own misjudgment or laziness.[57]

Also scattered among the testators' wishes were specific bequests to take care of personal debts, to cover funeral expenses, and to fulfill the details of the testament. Despite some of the uniform features across these 3,081 wills, many of the wills have elements that are individual to the testators' personal situations and reflective of their characters and beliefs. For example, eleven testators in this sample sponsored pilgrimages taken in their name, including Walter de Stokwell, a "peyntour" who in 1348 left "sixty gold *scudi*" to support a pilgrim to the Holy Land in his name.[58] The other ten wills also specify pilgrimages to the Holy Land, Santiago de Compostella, Rome, the Blessed Mary of Suthwerk, and other sites.[59] Three wills more generally aided crusading efforts, like that of Edmund de Suffolk enrolled in 1308–1309, who left ten shillings for the purpose.[60]

---

[57] Barbara A. Hanawalt, "Reading the Lives of the Illiterate: London's Poor," *Speculum* 80 (Oct. 2005): 1067–1086. See also Thrupp, *The Merchant Class*,180; Barron, *London in the Later Middle Ages* 273–78; Jennings, "The Distribution of Landed Wealth," 274; Jamieson Floyd Weetman, "London Wills and the Black Death," 90. For a focused discussion of poverty and medieval attitudes to the poor and charitable organizations, see Sharon Farmer, *Surviving Poverty in Medieval Paris: Gender, Ideology, and the Daily Lives of the Poor* (Ithaca: Cornell University Press, 2002).

[58] Sharpe, *Calendar of Wills*, I:640–41; CLRO, HR 78(225).

[59] See the wills of John de Holegh, hosier, dated 1348, who leaves sums for anyone going on pilgrimage to Jerusalem, the tomb of St. Katherine on Mount Sinai, or St. James of Compostella. William Brangewayn, vinter, dated 1361, for pilgrimages to St. James of Compostella and St. Mary de Walsingham. Hugh Peyntour, dated 1361, for a pilgrimage to Canterbury; William de Brikelesworth, dated 1356, for a pilgrimage to the Holy Land; John de Weston, dated 1373, for a pilgrimage to Santiago; Margery Broun, dated 1376, also to Santiago; John de Guldeford, dated 1382, for a pilgrimage to Rome; Peter Shepeye, dated 1380, for a pilgrimage to the Blessed Mary of Suthwerk; John de Heylesdon, mercer, dated 1384, for two pilgrims to Rome; Roger Crede, draper, dated 1383, also to support a pilgrim to Rome; and John Clerk, dated 1397, for a pilgrimage again to Rome. Sharpe, *Calendar of Wills*, I:657; II:41, 104–5, 107, 163, 221, 234–35, 240, 241–43, 250–51, 335–36; CLRO, HR 80(1), 89(148), 95(158), 96(100), 102(94), 109(89) 111(159), 112(92), 113(1), 114(56), 126(137).

[60] Sharpe, *Calendar of Wills*, I:203; CLRO, HR 37 (60). The other two wills are those of William de Evesham, dated 1351, and Thomas de Useflete, dated 1348, Sharpe, *Calendar of Wills*, I:652–53, II:2; CLRO, HR 79(69), 86(49).

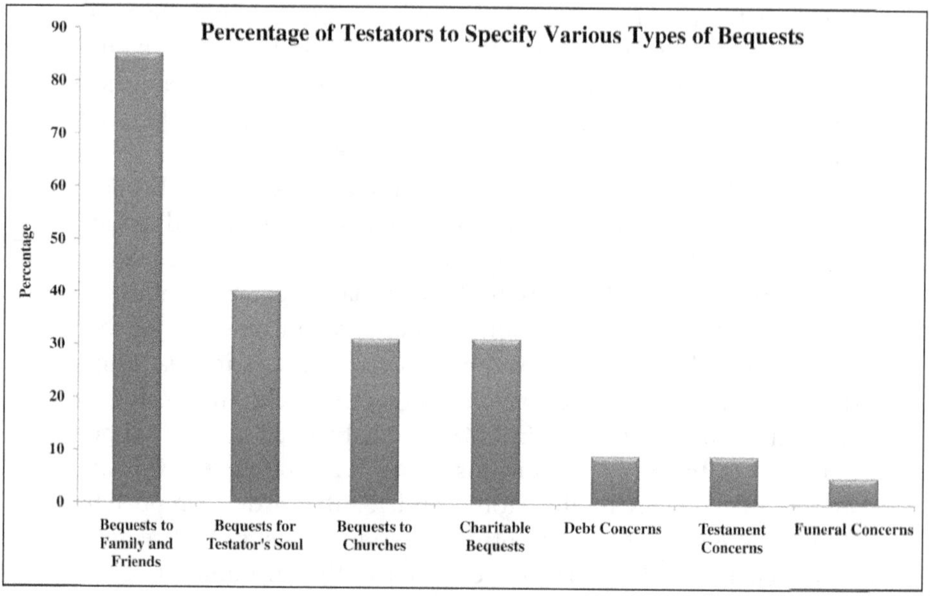

Figure 2.2

Of the 3,081 testators, 2,604, or 85%, included bequests of a secular nature, leaving some amount of property to family and friends. The majority of those testators specified ten or fewer separate secular bequests. For example, 460 testators mentioned only one secular bequest in their wills, 503 mentioned two secular bequests, and so on. Only 198 testators mentioned over ten separate bequests to family and friends.

Legacies denoted as explicitly for the soul of the testator or the souls of his family members were the next most common with 1,217 testators, or 40%, mentioning bequests for the good of their souls and those of their relatives. The majority of these testators mentioned only one or two such bequests. A typical will including a bequest for the good of the testator's soul would read like that of Richard Groom. Groom specified that part of his bequests, 20 marks, should be allocated for finding chaplains to celebrate "for my soul, the souls of my father and my mother, and all my ancestors and benefactors" (*pro anima mea animabus patris mei et matris mee omni perentum et benefactorum meorum*).[61]

[61] CLRO, HR 106(80).

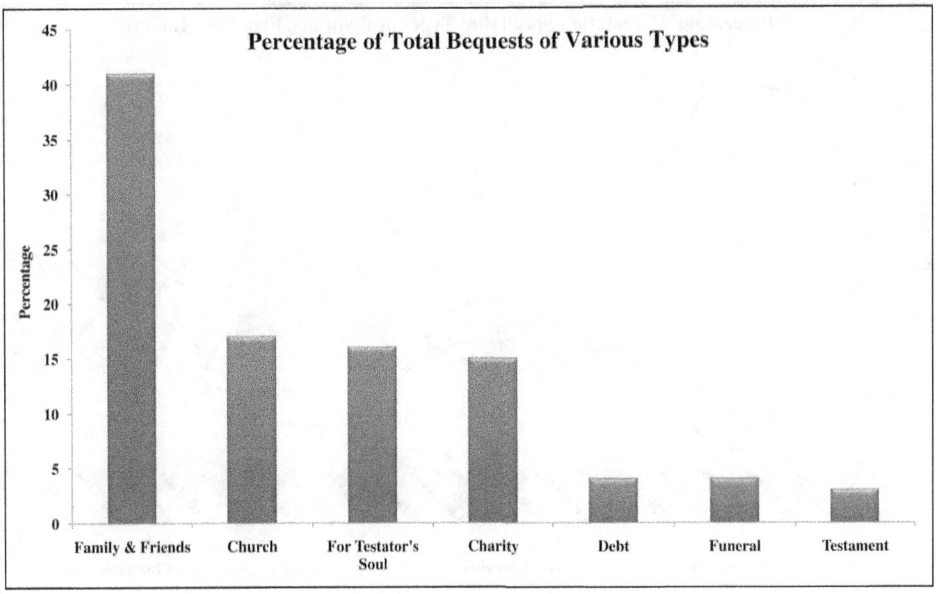

Figure 2.3

Bequests for the sustenance of churches and charitable bequests, also often for religious ends, followed as the next most common type of bequest in the Husting wills from 1300 to 1500, with 965 testators mentioning bequests to churches and 954 mentioning charitable bequests, both at 31% of the total number of testators. For example, in 1349, the will of John de Shenefeld, a tanner, left a messuage, or dwelling, to the Fraternity of the Light of S. Mary in the church of St. Sepulchre.[62] Similarly, the will of William Isyldon specifies that charitable gifts go to a number of hospitals inside and outside London.[63]

Only 287 of all testators mentioned concern for their debts and 273 for the execution of their testament, or 9% each. A total of 158 testators, or 5%, specifically mentioned details about their funerals, like that of vinter John de Oxenford mentioned above. Considered from the view of total bequests in these wills (figure 2.3), rather than from the view of the individual testators, 41% of all seven categories of bequests went to family and friends, 17% to churches, 16% for the

[62] Sharpe, *Calendar of Wills*, I:540–41.
[63] Sharpe, *Calendar of Wills*, I:578–79

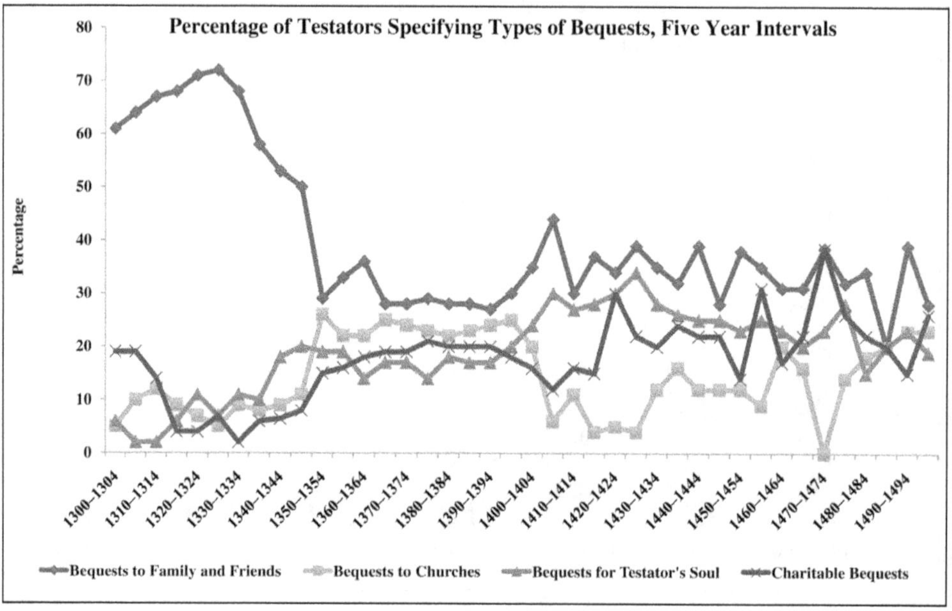

Figure 2.4

testator's soul, 15% for charitable causes, 4% for debt and funeral concerns, and only 3% to carry out the testament of the testator.

The four most common bequests—those to friends and family, to churches, for the testator's soul, and to charity causes—did change over time. Figure 2.4 shows the percentage of testators within five-year intervals that left one or more of those types of legacies in their wills between 1300 and 1500. For example, between 1300 and 1305, 215 testators (or 61%) of 354 total during that period left one or more bequests to family and friends, sixty-six (19%) for charitable causes, twenty-two (6%) for the testator's soul, and twenty (5%) to churches.

Bequests to family and friends remained constant as the most popular type of bequest; however, these bequests dipped during the middle of the fourteenth century, around the time the plague visited London. The Black Death seems to have had a large effect on the allocation of bequests among testators. During the period between 1345 and 1355, the allocation of bequests changed. The percentage of testators who left bequests to friends and family dropped, while the percentage of testators who left bequests to churches and charitable causes rose. The percentage of testators who left bequests for their souls remained roughly the same. It is probable that, faced with the high mortality rate of the plague, testators chose to distribute their goods and property more evenly than they had done before, favoring outlets that might help their souls beyond death.

Among those testators who mentioned an occupation, government officials, merchants, and artisans were more likely to leave property to friends and family than testators of other occupations. For example, 93% of the government officials represented in these wills bequeathed property to secular individuals, as compared with only 59% of members of the clergy. This is perhaps not surprising, as these testators may have been expected to leave property to individuals and institutions within their realm of influence: city government officials to friends and family and church officials to churches, friars, and other religious. For example, 45% of testators who held ecclesiastical positions left property to individual churches, the highest percentage among all of the testators.

Merchants (44%) and government officials (40%) more frequently bequeathed property for charitable causes than individuals of any other occupations. Merchants and government officials were likely among the wealthiest members of London society and thus may have spread their bequests more broadly to include bequests to charitable outlets. Sylvia Thrupp suggests that a number of merchants believed that "maximum safety would lie in the distribution of a maximum number of gifts."[64] For example, in his will enrolled in the Prerogative Court of Canterbury, Philip Malpas, an influential draper, sheriff, and alderman in fifteenth-century London, left over £1,000 spread out among many separate bequests to "the pour people most nedefull," the "pour householders," and the "pour folk" of various parishes in London.[65] Similarly, in the Husting wills, William Estfeld—mercer, sheriff, alderman, and knight—left twenty-eight separate charitable bequests, including bequests to the poor of six different parishes; to the prisoners, lepers, and sick of London; for bridge, highway, and water conduit maintenance and repair; and to the poor box of the Mercers guild of London.[66] Another explanation may reside in other outlets that were available for charitable causes. Many guilds took care of their poorer members through various means,

[64] Thrupp, *The Merchant Class*, 178.

[65] TNA: PRO PROB 11/5, f 210 RH; abstract of Malpas will in Josiah Wedgwood, ed., *History of Parliament, Biographies of the Members of the Commons House 1439–1509* (London: His Majesty's Stationery Office, 1936), 569, n. 9.

[66] Sharpe, *Calendar of Wills*, II:509; CLRO, HR 175(19).

including fines and fees, obviating the need perhaps for some artisans to leave bequests for the poor.[67]

When it came to concern over one's own soul, there was not much difference among the testators. In all, 56% of merchants gave property for such pious intentions compared with 47% of those holding government and ecclesiastical posts, 45% of artisans, 43% of nobility, and 37% of professionals. Such bequests were important to testators of all occupations, considering the pervasiveness of the doctrine of purgatory in late medieval society. In the minds of most of the laity in the later Middle Ages, legacies left for prayers for the soul of the testator, as well as for the testator's family members, could improve one's situation in the hereafter.[68]

Specific concern over personal debt did not rank high among the 54% of testators who mentioned their occupation. In most wills, such concern was articulated as property to be sold directly to cover the testator's debts. For example, fishmonger Salamon Borouhard listed his house to be sold to cover his debts.[69] Of the testators who mentioned their occupation, only between 8 and 11% mentioned a concern over debts. No government officials mentioned a specific concern for debt.

Likewise, only a handful of these testators, between 8 and 13%, mentioned specific concerns for how their testament should be carried out. This type of bequest most often came in the form of specific sums of money left to executors to ensure their last wishes were met. In 1329, pepperer and alderman Simon Corp specified in his will that his tenements in the parishes of St. John and St. Pancras be sold to fulfill the other wishes outlined in his testament.[70]

Also nearly negligible were bequests to cover funerary expenses, with the exception of those testators who listed themselves as noble or gentry—19% of these testators made specific bequests to cover funeral expenses. Such individuals perhaps felt the pressure or desire to conform to expectations for ceremony and spectacle at funerals of the upper crust of London society. There seems to have been a perceived need for members of the nobility or gentry to spend money on

[67] Hanawalt, "London's Poor," 1080–1081.

[68] Westlake, *Parish Gilds*; Rosenthal, *Purchase of Paradise*, 11–30; Michael L. Zell, "Fifteenth- and Sixteenth-Century Wills as Historical Sources," *Archives* 14 (1979), 68.

[69] CLRO, HR 32(83).

[70] CLRO, HR 57(100).

their ceremonious exit from this world, a need that was not reflected in the wills of the others. Artisans and merchants may also have had their burials covered by their guilds and thus would not have needed to specify such coverage in their wills.

Conditions Placed on Bequests

The most direct way that Londoners influenced their daughters' lives through their wills was by placing conditions on their bequests of property to these women. The most common condition placed on the legacies in the Husting Court was a pious one. For example, a testator would bequeath a piece of property under the condition that the recipient used the proceeds of the property to commemorate the testator in some way. As Clive Burgess describes such conditions placed on legacies to spouses, "the bonds of marriage galvanized widows into activity as spiritual lieutenants for dead spouses."[71]

These conditions were likewise typically placed on legacies to daughters, and in this way, testators "pried into other affairs of their heirs" as Samuel Cohn suggests.[72] For example, around the turn of the fourteenth century, Cristina Hurer received a tenement from her father after the death of her mother as long as she burned a wax taper in the parish church.[73] Isabella, with her husband Hamo and daughter Leticia, received from her father a tenement and rents as long as they maintained chantries for his soul and others in St. Botolph parish church.[74] In 1335, Matilda inherited eight shops from her father provided she pay 20s. to the Hospital of St. James.[75]

Pious conditions were attached most often to real estate with only twelve instances of such conditions on movable wealth. Among the categories of real estate, pious conditions were attached to tenements more often than any other kind of landed wealth. Of the bequests of tenements, 249 had pious conditions placed on them, like those noted above, compared with eighty for commercial buildings; seventy-

---

[71] Clive Burgess, "Late Medieval Wills and Pious Convention: Testamentary Evidence Reconsidered," in *Profit, Piety, and the Profession in Later Medieval England*, ed. Michael Hicks (Gloucester: Alan Sutton, 1990), 21.

[72] Samuel Cohn, *Death and Property in Siena, 1205–1800: Strategies for the Afterlife* (Baltimore: Johns Hopkins University Press, 1988), 149.

[73] Sharpe, *Calendar of Wills*, I:157; CLRO, HR 31(39).

[74] Sharpe, *Calendar of Wills*, I:251; CLRO, HR 43(63).

[75] Sharpe, *Calendar of Wills*, I:414–15; CLRO, HR 63(238).

five for houses, dwellings, and halls; seventy-two for rents; and sixty for other types of property including gardens and land.

Sons were more often the beneficiaries of legacies with such conditions attached to them. Of the 536 pious conditions placed on real estate bequeathed to 8,411 recipients, 135 (or 25%) were placed on bequests to sons and 63 (or 12%) on those to daughters. In the larger picture, there were 1,592 instances of bequests of some amount of real estate to sons and 1,194 instances of bequests of some amount of real estate to daughters. Therefore, nearly 9% of all bequests to sons carried a pious condition compared with 5% of all bequests to daughters. Sons were expected to carry out such pious bequests more often than daughters, and, in turn, daughters were less likely to have such limitations placed on their inheritance.

Among the testators who specified their occupation, artisans and merchants attached pious conditions to their bequests of real estate more often than the nobility or the members of professional, ecclesiastical, or government offices. Of the recipients who received legacies of real estate from artisan testators, 47% had pious conditions attached, as did 38% of the recipients who received real estate from merchant testators. Only 7% of the recipients of real estate from testators in professional occupations had pious conditions attached to their legacies, 5% of the recipients of real estate from ecclesiastics, 3% of the recipients of real estate from nobility, and only 1% of the recipients of real estate from government officials. Artisans and merchants, more than others, required their relatives to intercede on their behalf through pious and charitable works above and beyond the direct bequests for such causes also specified in their wills.

Other conditions are represented in the wills, but they are far less frequent than pious conditions. Like pious conditions, these other conditions helped shape daughters' lives and included provisions for the support of relatives and others and stipulations that the daughters use their inheritance of that property for marriage portions. Other testators placed requisites about when and to whom their daughters could marry. For example, Margery Malewayn's father permitted her a married life and a sum for the union as long as it was not to a certain man, a mercer by the name of John Dovy.[76] Johanna Hanampstead, widow of grocer William de Hanampstead, allowed her daughters, Johanna, Cristiana, and Margaret, to marry at sixteen

[76] Sharpe, *Calendar of Wills*, II:38; CLRO, HR 89(144).

"without disparagement," but only with the permission of two individuals—the master of the College of St. Laurence de Pulteneye and her aunt Johanna de Durese. This testator, then, not only required her daughters to seek permission, but also placed an age limit on them and required them to marry men of their social status.[77]

Still other testators placed specifications on their daughters' inheritance that the property be divided in some way (for example, a daughter might have received a portion of a bakehouse), and others instituted requisites that the piece of property in question be used to cover debts. One rare but attention-grabbing will serves to illustrate the potential such conditions could have had on shaping daughters' futures. Around 1300, Agnes Dachet received a house from her father for an eight-year term with the condition that she brew. After the term, Agnes was to have five quarters of malt in order to set herself up for future brewing.[78] Agnes may have been a brewster before her father's death, but either way he determined her livelihood for a period of time if she followed his wishes.

Sons, like daughters, received bequests with conditions to support relatives and to cover their parent' debts. They also received money for apprenticeships or schooling. Of twenty bequests of money with stipulations attached that the funds be used for apprenticeships or schooling, seventeen were for sons and three for daughters. In 1341, goldsmith John de Kenesyngg left forty shillings each for his son Robert and daughter Alice for their apprenticeships,[79] John de Oxen "Spicer" left 100 shillings for his daughter's apprenticeship in 1346,[80] and Robert de Rameseye, a fishmonger, left twenty shillings either for his daughter's marriage or for her apprenticeship in 1373.[81]

This disparity in daughters' and sons' apprenticeship provisions seen in the Husting Wills, in part, reflects the reality that it was more common for sons to pursue both apprenticeships and schooling than it was for daughters. However, it was not unheard of for daughters to be apprenticed in late medieval London. Caroline Barron explains that London custom permitted women, acting independent of their husbands, to take apprentices and that the "practice was even wider

---

77 Sharpe, *Calendar of Wills*, II:127; CLRO, HR 97(64).
78 Sharpe, *Calendar of Wills*, I:145; CLRO, HR 29(37).
79 Sharpe, *Calendar of Wills*, I:445; CLRO, HR, 68(43).
80 Sharpe, *Calendar of Wills*, I:498; CLRO, HR 74(134).
81 Sharpe, *Calendar of Wills*, I:157–58; CLRO, HR 102(11).

than the stated custom allowed."[82] In addition to the wills enrolled with the Husting Court, Barron also notes an early fifteenth-century will enrolled with the Archdeaconry Court in which a draper, Peter Smert, noted two apprentices in his will, both women, as well as four surviving indentures in which four girls were bound to mistresses in London.[83] In short, the evidence detailing daughters' schooling and apprenticeships is more difficult to trace in the records, but the evidence that does survive is suggestive of parents' intentions to provide their daughters with the skills they would need in their future households and businesses.

However, stipulations that attempted to determine a son's livelihood the way Agnes Dachet's father did were nonexistent in these wills, as were stipulations that the inheritance of real estate was contingent in some way on sons' marital plans. Only one son received money, via his guardian, with the stipulation that it be used for his marriage. In 1361, Hugh de Sadelyngstanes, a recorder of London, appointed the mayor of Newcastle as the guardian of his son with the stipulation that the mayor pay two hundred marks for his son's marriage.[84] Compare this with fifty-five daughters who received bequests of money directly for their marriages. No testators attempted to tell their sons through their wills whom they could or could not marry. Of seventy-one bequests of money with stipulations attached that the funds be used for marriage, the majority went to daughters. Other recipients of such earmarked funds were nieces (seven), women whose relationship to the testator is unknown (four), women with the same surname (two), one granddaughter, and one sister. It is clear that through certain conditions placed on bequests, parents attempted to set more boundaries in their daughters' lives than in their sons'.

[82] Barron, "The 'Golden Age' of Women in Medieval London," 52, n. 21. Barron, "The Education and Training of Girls in Fifteenth-Century London," in *Courts, Counties, and the Capital in the Later Middle Ages*, ed. Diana Dunn (New York: St. Martin's Press, 1996), 144.

[83] Barron, "The Education and Training of Girls," 145-146. In this article, Barron explores the Parliamentary statute of 1406 that stated, in part, that "every man or woman, of whatever estate or condition he be, [had the right] to set their son or daughter to take learning at any manner of school that pleaseth them". Quotation at 139.

[84] Sharpe, *Calendar of Wills*, II:57; CLRO, HR 89(242).

The Influence of Gender on Bequests

In addition to the influence that a testator's particular wishes had on a late medieval London daughter, the gender and occupation of her benefactor could shape her inheritance and her future life. It is necessary to examine the wills more closely and to take into account the characteristics of the testators themselves. A testator's gender played a significant role in his or her legacy, both overall and in particular to daughters and sons. Women tended to favor other women in gifts of movable wealth, while men often provided for women also, but these women were in most cases their wives. Fathers were more even-handed in their bequests of real estate to their daughters and sons alike, while mothers were more even-handed in their bequests of movable property to their daughters and sons.

In the Husting wills, female testators more often left some amount and type of property to male recipients than to female recipients (table 2.1). In contrast, male testators were more even in their distribution, only slightly favoring female recipients to male recipients. For example, a typical set of bequests by a woman testator is that of Beatrix Barton, widow of a vinter, who left a variety of household goods, including silver cups and iron spits, to seven men and three women, two of whom were wives of her other beneficiaries.[85] In comparison with Beatrix's will, in the same year, Adam Rous—a surgeon—left goods and property to four men and four women plus additional servants, children, and other individuals.[86] This breakdown can only be superficial and suggestive, however, as in his abstracts Sharpe noted bequests to immediate family members and friends. The picture becomes more nuanced when one considers daughters and sons as beneficiaries specifically, and when one considers the types of property bequeathed in the wills.

Table 2.1. Percentage of Women and Men to Receive Property from Female and Male Testators

Women from female testators	44%
Men from female testators	55%
Women from male testators	50%
Men from male testators	48%
(Women from male testators, wives excluded	30%)

[85] Sharpe, *Calendar of Wills*, II:209–10; CLRO, HR 108 (46).
[86] Sharpe, *Calendar of Wills*, II:207–8; CLRO, HR 108 (13).

When bequests to daughters and sons by female and male testators are compared, there is less discrepancy (table 2.2). In general, both men and women bequeathed property to daughters and sons. When looked at closely, there is less gender difference among children as recipients from women than in the larger population of recipients in the Husting wills. There is only a 2% difference in bequests from women to their daughters and sons, whereas there is an 11% difference in bequests from women to other women and men. In contrast, 5% more men provided for sons than daughters as compared with only a 2% difference in bequests by men to other men and women. Likely, the differences between tables 2.1 and 2.2 can be explained by the fact that both men and women were more likely to leave property to sons than to daughters and to other men than to other women. The exception is that men frequently left property to women, which were their wives. When wives are excluded, as seen in table 2.1, the patterns indicate that male testators favored men as recipients of property. Women, in contrast, did not often leave property to husbands as they would not have had to do so.

Women and men alike considered both daughters and sons as worthy recipients when they made their wills. One might expect female testators to focus their bequests even more on recipients outside the immediate family than these findings suggest, since their husbands would have likely taken care of legacies of property to children in their own wills. However, the statistics suggest that women were just as concerned to provide for children in their own wills, perhaps in addition to provision already made for them in their husbands' wills. For example, a husband and wife pair of wills indicates such a situation of provision for children. John de Mitford, a draper, died in 1375. In his will, he left all his lands and tenements to his wife, Johanna, with his daughter, Juliana, and her heirs to inherit after her mother's death. He mentions a son, but it is not clear that he was still living at the time the will was made.[87] In 1382, in her will, Johanna left a tenement and shops for life to the same daughter Juliana, specified as married.[88] Here is a set of parents, then, concerned to provide for their daughter.

---

[87] Sharpe, *Calendar of Wills*, II:181; CLRO, HR, 201(216).
[88] Sharpe, *Calendar of Wills*, II:235–36; CLRO, HR 111(64).

Table 2.2. Percentage of Daughters and Sons to Receive Property from Female and Male Testators

Daughters from female testators	16%
Sons from female testators	18%
Daughters from male testators	18%
Sons from male testators	23%

When one considers the types of property bequeathed in these wills, the nature of the bequests changes slightly (table 2.3). More female testators left real estate to men than to women and, in contrast, more male testators left real estate to women than to men. Rather than indicating a preference for women over men as recipients of real estate among male testators, these numbers likely reflect the tendency among male testators to leave real estate to their surviving wives for their lifetimes—if they left real estate to their wives for anything besides a lifetime interest, the widow needed to renounce the bequest in court for a lifetime estate instead.[89] For example, Richard de Bretevile left his wife Helewisa all his tenements and a house, and she went to court to formally claim only a life interest in the properties.[90] Likewise, Henry de Lewes left his wife Alice and her heirs his houses in fee. Alice then appeared in court and renounced the fee, opting for a life interest.[91]

Table 2.3. Percentage of Women and Men to Receive Various Types of Property from Female and Male Testators

Women to receive real estate from female testators	49%
Men to receive real estate from female testators	58%
Women to receive real estate from male testators	62%
Men to receive real estate from male testators	55%
Women to receive movable property from female testators	41%
Men to receive movable property from female testators	22%
Women to receive movable property from male testators	34%
Men to receive movable property from male testators	32%

Examining movable property reveals a different pattern of bequests among female and male testators. First, female and male testators both detailed legacies for real estate more often than movable wealth.

[89] Sharpe, *Calendar of Wills*, I:xxxviii.
[90] Sharpe, *Calendar of Wills*, I:141; CLRO, HR 28(29).
[91] Sharpe, *Calendar of Wills*, I:102; CLRO, HR 20(96).

Second, there is a larger gender difference in recipients of movable property from female testators than male (table 2.3). Women, more than men, may have felt that a legacy of movable wealth was more useful to a female recipient than to a male one, or they desired to pass on movable wealth to women over men, or both. Barbara Harris found trends in her study of the bequests of eighty aristocratic widows and their spouses between 1450 and 1550. Aristocratic widows used their wills to add to their daughters' dowries with money and goods, to favor their married daughters over their sons with household goods, and to benefit their sisters and their siblings' daughters. Similarly, Anita Fisher found that of 191 recipients (excluding relatives and servants) mentioned in merchant women's wills in late medieval Bristol, 109 were female recipients of personal property. As Fisher explains of the 246 items bequeathed, "women friends received 60% of them and 40% went to men friends."[92] The "enduring female networks" that Harris found among aristocratic testators appear as well among London testators in their bequests of movable property to female recipients.[93] Alternatively, at least for some types of movable goods, there may have been more practical concerns at work. In her analysis of textile bequests in London wills, Kristen Burkholder suggests that "medieval women preferred to bequeath their clothes to members of the same sex, who could wear them without having to alter them into new types of garments. This may have been for the simple reason that since women were physically smaller, their clothes would have been harder to alter to fit men than the reverse."[94]

When gender is considered in bequests to daughters and sons, the picture is less striking (table 2.4). More female testators left real estate to sons than to daughters. As with the larger population, mothers more often left real estate to their male rather than their female off-

---

[92] Anita Loy Beetham Fisher, "The Merchants of Medieval Bristol, 1350-1500," (PhD diss., University of Oregon, 1987), 321-2.

[93] Barbara J. Harris, *English Aristocratic Women, 1450–1550: Marriage and Family, Property and Careers* (Oxford: Oxford University Press, 2002), 167–74, quotation at 172. Caroline Barron also talks about female friendships among London widows. Caroline M. Barron, "Introduction: The Widow's World," in *Medieval London Widows 1300–1500*, ed. Caroline M. Barron and Anne F. Sutton (London: Hambledon Press, 1994), xxxiii.

[94] Kristen Burkholder, "Threads Bared: Dress and Textiles in English Wills," in *Medieval Clothing and Textiles*, vol. 1, ed. Robin Netherton and Gale R. Owen-Crocker (Woodbridge, Suffolk: Boydell Press, 2005), 139.

spring. There is less of this gendered concern among male testators. In her 1403 will, for instance, Christina Atte Bowe, widow of Thomas, an apothecary (whose will does not appear in the Husting wills), left her tenements to her son John for life. John may have inherited property *inter vivos* from his father, but his mother nevertheless used her will to ensure that her intentions for her property were carried out.[95] In contrast, John de Middleton's will reveals a father concerned to provide for all of his children. In John's will in 1382, he specified that his property be sold after his wife, Isabella, dies and the residue to be divided among his three children, John, William, and Matilda.[96] However, in 1410, Isabella mentions only her daughter Matilda.[97]

Isabella's will recommends that we read the statistics carefully, as they show trends but do not explain every case. There are other scenarios in the Husting wills. For instance, both husband and wife, Thomas and Margery Broun, provided for their children in their wills. Thomas, a woolmonger, made his will in 1357, and after numerous pious bequests including provisions for prisoners, nuns, friars, and work on London Bridge, he left tenements in three parishes to Margery with the remainder to his son Thomas.[98] Nineteen years and two husbands later, Margery left a will rich with detail. After particular detail for her funeral and other pious bequests that mirrored her husband's, with an additional request to hire someone to make a pilgrimage for her after her death, she did not specify tenements for her son Thomas. Instead, she left tenements to her daughter Margaret and goods to another daughter Alice.[99] The tenements in Thomas Sr.'s will may have passed on to his son's heirs leaving Margery to specify inheritances for her daughters instead, who may have been born of her later marriages. In her 1423 will, Agnes Gyffard similarly was only concerned with her daughters, leaving a shop and houses to her married daughter, Johanna, with the condition that she pay an annuity to Cecilia, a second daughter of Agnes. Anything left over was to be divided between her grandchildren of her daughter Johanna and of her son Thomas.[100]

---

95 Sharpe, *Calendar of Wills*, II:355; CLRO, HR 132(8).
96 Sharpe, *Calendar of Wills*, II:228–29; CLRO, HR 111(4).
97 Sharpe, *Calendar of Wills*, II:386–87; CLRO, HR 138(29).
98 Sharpe, *Calendar of Wills*, I:696–97; CLRO, HR 85(73).
99 Sharpe, *Calendar of Wills*, II:220–21; CLRO, HR, 109(89).
100 Sharpe, *Calendar of Wills*, II:450; CLRO, HR 159(33).

Although not in the majority, these last cases suggest mothers who are predominantly concerned with the welfare of their daughters over that of their sons. Although women tended to favor their sons to inherit landed wealth, when we consider the narrative detail of the wills, it does seem that men and women both were eager to provide for their children, whether it was in addition to, or in lieu of, what the other spouse provided. In addition, it appears that women, when able and where appropriate, were concerned to leave details pertaining to their interests regarding their property. All of these families, and the others represented in the wills, are different, and the detail of the wills adds further dimension to the statistics.

There are women's and men's wills, of course, that include no provision for children, yet it is not possible to know from the wills themselves if these individuals had no children or if their children were already provided for outside of the will. What is clear is that provision for children appears to be of paramount concern among mothers and fathers alike. It may have been the case that fathers were expected to take care of both their sons and daughters through bequests of real estate, which left mothers free to bequeath the little real estate they had as they wished. Mothers may have provided for their sons with real estate, more than their daughters, because they had already seen their daughters taken care of by their daughters' fathers. Since men's resources came mostly from his natal family, primarily, whereas a daughter's could come through marriage, mothers perhaps felt a greater need to bequeath real estate to their sons.

These findings stand in contrast to the situation in twelfth- and thirteenth-century Barcelona. In his study of Barcelona, Stephen Bensch likewise considers inheritance and found that it was common for women, more than men, to spread their property in their wills more evenly to their children. Men in Barcelona, especially in the thirteenth century, favored sons more than daughters as heirs of their real estate.[101]

Similar to the patterns seen in bequests to female and male recipients of movable property, daughters were favored over sons to receive such property (table 2.4). While both men and women viewed movable wealth as important legacies for their children,[102] both gen-

[101] Stephen P. Bensch, *Barcelona and its Rulers, 1096–1291* (Cambridge: Cambridge University Press, 1995), 254.

[102] See further discussion on this in chapter 4.

Table 2.4. Percentage of Daughters and Sons to Receive Various Types of Property from Female and Male Testators

Daughters to receive real estate from female testators	60%
Sons to receive real estate from female testators	78%
Daughters to receive real estate from male testators	61%
Sons to receive real estate from male testators	66%
Daughters to receive movable property from female testators	24%
Sons to receive movable property from female testators	12%
Daughters to receive movable property from male testators	22%
Sons to receive movable property from male testators	14%
Daughters to receive both types of property from female testators	16%
Sons to receive both types of property from female testators	10%
Daughters to receive both types of property from male testators	18%
Sons to receive both types of property from male testators	20%

ders seem to have felt that movable property was more important for their daughters than for their sons. Female testators similarly left movable wealth more often to female recipients, within and outside of the family, than male ones, as noted above. This is a trend that has been noticed in other provincial towns, like in Bristol where most of the women testators left more sentimental bequests to female beneficiaries.[103] This pattern can be seen in wills where female testators left goods and money to numerous female relatives and friends with no mention of immediate family members, like Margaret Tonk in 1378 who left goods to her two sisters, female friend, female servant, and niece, as well as to her brother-in-law and a male friend.[104] There were only a few wills in which women included both immediate family members and nonrelatives, like Lucy Wycoumbe in 1340 who left dishware and money to her daughter and household goods and money to her stepdaughter, but no movable wealth to the other recipient in the will, a certain John Lambyn (he received real estate).[105] Margery Broun, mentioned above, also included two women who were not specified as family members in addition to her two daughters, and left them furred gowns and clothing.[106] Those women who had movable wealth to bequeath to immediate family members likely focused on their daughters, as the patterns show, and left out mention

[103] Fleming, *Women in Late Medieval Bristol*, 20.
[104] Sharpe, *Calendar of Wills*, II:214; CLRO, HR 108(129).
[105] Sharpe, *Calendar of Wills*, I:464; CLRO, HR 69(140).
[106] Sharpe, *Calendar of Wills*, II:220–21; CLRO, HR 109(89)

of their sons and others entirely. Mothers likely favored their daughters as heirs of the goods they brought to their own marriages and of their paraphernalia: clothing, house wares, bedding, and so forth.

In contrast, male testators distributed movable wealth, such as commercial goods, more evenly to other family members and nonrelatives, while within the immediate family they focused their movable wealth on their daughters more than on their sons. For example, William Box provided for all of his children with movable wealth: all six daughters and three sons received money, yet two of the daughters also received dishware while the sons received no goods.[107] Both women and men bequeathed movable wealth to their daughters, likely as a way to provide for their future households. Men often had more and diverse movable wealth to bequeath, and so were more likely than women to spread these bequests to other family members and nonrelatives than concentrate them solely on their daughters.

A third category of property, bequests of *both* real estate and movable property, can be examined here with interesting results (table 2.4). Among these testators who left both types of property to their children, more men than women left both types of property to their sons and a near equal percentage of male and female testators left both types of property to their daughters. Men, it seems, viewed their offspring of both sexes worthy of legacies of landed and movable wealth. Women, on the other hand, perhaps perceived that their sons would be provided for more so than their daughters through their husbands' wills and in their wills sought to rectify that by more often favoring their daughters with these mixed bequests than their sons.

As recipients, women inherited property at the same rate from both female and male testators. Women gained more real estate from male testators, predominantly as their wives. Women also received more movable property from female testators, which supports other scholars' work that traces legacies among women to other women relatives and friends.[108] For example, Kristen Burkholder suggests that lay men would have been more concerned with bequests of real estate in their wills and with movable goods of great value, leaving women to bequeath less valuable, and perhaps more movable goods such as textiles. In her study, she finds women left four times as many household textiles as lay men.[109]

---

107 Sharpe, *Calendar of Wills*, I:499; CLRO, HR 74(174).

108 Harris, *English Aristocratic Women*, 167–74.

109 Burkholder, "Threads Bared," 138.

Daughters inherited real estate from both their mothers and fathers, although they inherited less real estate than sons did.[110] Daughters who inherited from their fathers were slightly more likely to receive real estate than those who inherited from their mothers, and they were slightly more likely to receive movable property from their mothers than from their fathers. Parents of daughters yet to marry perhaps provided for their marriage portions with legacies of movable property in order to outfit their new homes.[111] Fathers left legacies of both types of property, real estate and movable wealth, to their sons and daughters at near equal percentages, while mothers more often left legacies of both types to daughters than to sons.

It is clear from these wills that both fathers and mothers viewed their daughters as viable heirs of their wealth and competent inheritors of real estate, fathers perhaps more so than mothers. Therefore, depending on her economic, social, and personal situation, a daughter in late medieval London stood a good chance to inherit valuable real estate from her father and arguably equally valuable movable wealth from her mother. Yet, if one considers the numbers rather than the percentages, the gender of her benefactor was more likely to be male than female since a greater number of daughters were affected by the wills of their fathers than their mothers (as male testators made up the majority of the wills in the Husting Court).

The Influence of Occupation on Bequests

Like gender, occupation influenced the type of property that testators bequeathed to their male and female recipients. The nature of the work of testators as well as social expectations of certain professions had an effect on how testators divided their property in their last wills. Thus, a parent's line of work had the potential to affect a daughter's life through her inheritance as much as that parent's individual wishes.

Overall, members of the clergy bequeathed more movable property than real estate. This may have been because they gave their own inherited landed wealth to their ecclesiastical provider at their admit-

[110] See chapter 4 for a further discussion of the inheritance of real estate by daughters and sons.

[111] See chapter 3 for a further discussion of how bequests of movable goods operate in the Husting wills.

tance into the ranks of the church. Or, the reverse may have been true, that they joined the ranks of the church because they lacked land to establish themselves in business or otherwise. Clergy were more likely to leave women movable property than real estate.[112] Of all women who received some type of property from clerics, 71% received movable wealth compared with 26% who received landed wealth, and 3% who received both types of property. Clergy favored men as recipients of their real estate. Of all men to receive property from clerics, 60% received movable property and 38% received real estate. Like the women, 3% received both types of property.

Artisans, merchants, professionals, and government workers, on the other hand, more often left their landed wealth to female recipients. Indeed, the percentages are almost reversed. This is most likely due to the fact that these testators had wives to whom they trusted real estate (or perhaps even from whom they inherited such property). Artisans left real estate more often to both female and male recipients than testators from the clerical professions. Of all female recipients who inherited property from artisanal testators, 60% received real estate, 22% received movable property, and 17% received both types of property. Of all male recipients who inherited property from artisanal testators, 49% received real estate, 38% received movable property, and 12% received both types of property. Indeed, 672 females received bequests only of real estate from artisans compared with only 467 males. Artisans had more landed wealth to bequeath than clerics, and they left much of this wealth to women, and in particular to wives. For example, in 1308 Geoffrey de Borham, a burser (pouch-maker), left his wife and daughter each half of a tenement (his daughter also received numerous household goods including a seven-gallon brass pot).[113] Of the 672 female recipients of real estate from artisans, 328 of them were wives, or 49%.

When one considers merchants, the picture is less striking. While merchant testators, like artisans, also bequeathed more real estate than movable property, they displayed less discrepancy among their female and male recipients. In all, 467 females received landed wealth

---

[112] Jacqueline Murray also found ties between clerics and lay women in clerics' wills from sixteenth-century London. Jacqueline Murray, "Kinship and Friendship: The Perception of Family by Clergy and Laity in Late Medieval London," *Albion* 20, no. 3 (1988), 375.

[113] Sharpe, *Calendar of Wills*, I:200–201; CLRO, HR 37(10).

from merchant testators compared with 426 males, and 190 of the 467 female recipients, or 41%, were wives.

A woman in late medieval London had a greater chance of inheriting real estate from an artisan than from a merchant, and more of a chance from these occupations than from a member of the church, yet a woman's life-cycle role made a difference. Most of these women recipients were wives, or they were somehow tied to the testator by a family relationship: mother, daughter, sister, niece, and so on. Of the women who received real estate from artisans and merchants, only 124 of 672 (or 18%) were unrelated to artisans (or whose relationship was unspecified) and 114 of 467 (or 24%) were unrelated to merchants.

Testators who held professional occupations, like artisans, more often left real estate to female and male recipients alike. Of all female recipients who received property from testators in professional careers, 68% inherited real estate compared with 22% who inherited movable wealth. Only 9% received both types of property. Of the male recipients who received property from these testators, 63% received real estate, 29% received movable property, and only 5% received both types of property.

Government officials who left property in their wills operated along the same lines as merchants. They left real estate more often than movable property, like artisans and professionals, but the distribution was more equal among female and male recipients. Of all women to receive property from government workers, 48% inherited real estate, 38% inherited movable property, and 14% received both types of property. Of all men, 47% inherited real estate, 26% inherited movable wealth, and 21% received both types of property. Merchants and government officers may have been wealthier citizens in general than artisans and professionals and thus may have had more movable wealth to bequeath.

Testators of the noble class have perhaps the most striking differences in their bequests to women and men. Like the other groups, nobles favored women with landed wealth. Female recipients were more likely to receive real estate than movable property from their noble benefactors. Of all females to receive any property from testators of the noble class, 68% inherited landed wealth, compared with only 22% who received movable property; 8% received both types of property. Again, however, wives played a role; seventeen of the twenty-five women to receive real estate from nobles, or 68%, were wives.

Male recipients of property from these testators, however, equally received landed and movable wealth at 48%. Nobles preferred to bequeath their movable wealth to male recipients rather than female recipients. As was common among the elite in the countryside, it is likely that daughters received movable goods with their dowries rather than through the wills of their parents.

Members of all of the occupations, clerics excepted, favored real estate over movable property as legacies to women. As mentioned above, wives were probably the key factor in the presence of female recipients of real estate from testators. Yet not all women were wives. A consideration of daughters and their brothers as recipients makes the picture sketched above clearer in terms of the influence of occupation on daughters' inheritance.

When one isolates daughters and sons as recipients of real estate, it is clear that all of the sons of these testators, no matter what their occupation, received landed wealth more often than their sisters (table 2.5). Although daughters' inheritance of real estate is certainly not negligible, especially daughters of professionals and artisans, occupation did little to affect the disposition of most Londoners to leave their landed wealth more often to their male offspring.

Table 2.5. Percentage of Children to Receive Real Estate by Occupation of the Testator

	Artisans N=827 total children	Merchants N=770 total children	Nobles N=37 total children	Professionals N=93 total children	Government N=16 total children
Daughters	25%	20%	16%	34%	13%
Sons	34%	31%	65%	44%	44%

When one considers daughters separately from their brothers, however, the occupation of the testator plays a more important role in shaping their children's lives (table 2.6). Daughters of noble, professional, and artisan testators did best in their inheritance of real estate.[114] In all of these categories, over 50 percent of the daughters who

[114] The situation of London daughters contrasts with that found for the daughters of one hundred testators in medieval Marseille between 1337–1362 studied by Daniel Smail. Smail found that testators among the elite, including nobles and wealthy merchants and artisans, were more likely to exclude their daughters from their inheri-

inherited some property from their parents received real estate. Daughters of merchants and government officials did less well in terms of receiving real estate.

Sons of the nobility, of professionals, and of artisans, like their sisters, prospered in terms of inheriting real estate, property like the shops that Edmund de Pountefreit, clerk, left to his two sons William and Roger in 1348[115] or the hostel John Ryvel, knight, left his unborn son in 1361 (if the infant turned out to be female the property was to be sold for her marriage).[116] Among the professional classes and artisans, sons also did well by their parents and inherited real estate more often than movable property. Late medieval children of noble birth, as well as children of professionals and artisans, in and around London, female and male alike, could expect inheritances of real estate, more so than the offspring of members of other professions.

Sons of government officials also did well in terms of inheriting real estate, unlike their sisters. It seems that on the whole, merchants were the stingiest of all occupational groups with bequests of real estate to their children, male and female alike. Looked at another way, merchants distributed their movable property and real estate most equally to their daughters and sons alike. Merchants' sons may have been in business with their fathers and may have received wealth from them *inter vivos* rather than in their wills. Merchants may also have bequeathed real estate to members outside of the family more often than members of other occupational groups.

Children of noble, professional, and artisan testators inherited more real estate than movable property. Daughters and sons of merchants inherited more equal amounts of real estate and movable property. A woman's individual situation as a daughter (married, widowed, never-married, looking to marry, dowry already received, starting a trade, and so on), would dictate whether it was better to inherit from a father who was an artisan or one who was a merchant, as inheritance of real estate would have been better for some and movable wealth for others. Regardless of personal situation, however, the testator's occupation did indeed have the potential to influence the situations of these women.

---

tance. Smail, "Mapping Networks and Knowledge in Medieval Marseille, 1337–1362: Variations on a Theme of Mobility," (PhD diss., University of Michigan, 1994), 98–99.

[115] Sharpe, *Calendar of Wills*, II:83; CLRO, HR 92(28).

[116] Sharpe, *Calendar of Wills*, II:16; CLRO, HR, 89(56).

Table 2.6. Percentage of Daughters and of Sons to Receive Types of Property by Occupation of the Testator

Artisans' Children			
	Real estate	Movable Property	Both
Daughters N=368	55%	23%	22%
Sons N=459	61%	18%	22%
Merchants' Children			
	Real estate	Movable Property	Both
Daughters N=344	46%	31%	23%
Sons N=426	56%	17%	27%
Children of Nobles[117]			
	Real estate	Movable Property	Both
Daughters N=8	75%	0%	25%
Sons N=29	83%	10%	7%
Children of Professionals			
	Real estate	Movable Property	Both
Daughters N=44	73%	18%	9%
Sons N=49	84%	8%	8%
Children of Government Officials			
	Real estate	Movable Property	Both
Daughters N=5	40%	40%	20%
Sons N=11	64%	0%	36%

[117] The percentages for children of the nobility and government officials need to be read with care, as the total numbers are small. For example, there are only eight daughters of noble testators and five daughters of government officials mentioned in the wills.

Conclusions

The testators of the Husting wills were predominantly men of the upper echelons of late medieval London society. There were female testators, but they were predominantly widows or single women rather than wives. Of the 54 percent who mentioned their occupation, there was a wide range of professions represented including artisans, merchants, ecclesiastics, professionals, nobles and gentry, and government officials. Most of these testators diversified their deathbed portfolios, so to speak, and spread their legacies to family and friends, to churches, for their souls and those of their family members, to charitable causes, to cover debts and testament execution, and to cover their funerals. The most consistently popular bequests, that to family and friends, is the focus of this study, and examination of these bequests reveals that the gender and occupation of these Londoners, along with their direct wishes, shaped the lives of their daughters and sons.

Both daughters and sons received property from their parents with certain conditions attached. Stipulations were found in wills to children of both sexes to use their inheritance to support relatives, pay debts, or use their inheritance in a pious manner, for example to burn tapers in memoriam of the testator in the parish church. These conditions set limits on inheritance, because the testators reached from beyond the grave to direct how the child was to use that inheritance. Limitations with even more constricting power were more often placed on daughters' inheritances than on sons'. A few testators used their last will and testament to push a certain trade or vocation on their daughters, and a number of testators in the Husting wills attempted to control who their daughters were to marry and at what age.

At first glance, the gender of the testators played little role in the inheritance of children. Both mothers and fathers were concerned to provide for daughters and sons alike, and they viewed daughters, along with their brothers, as viable heirs of their property. When the wills are examined more closely, differences between mothers and fathers emerge in testamentary patterns. Fathers more equally left real estate to their children of both sexes than mothers did, and likewise left legacies of both types of property (real estate and movable wealth) more equally to their children than mothers. Both parents favored their daughters as recipients of movable property. Overall, a daughter in late medieval London was more likely to inherit real estate from her father and movable wealth from her mother, bequests that might be equally important depending on a daughter's needs and personal circumstances.

Occupation, perhaps more than gender, had the potential to influence daughters' lives through bequests. Most Londoners, except for clerics, left their landed wealth more often to women than to men, but most of these women were wives. Because not all women were wives in the Middle Ages, an examination of testators' bequests to their children by occupation is more revealing. When compared with their brothers, daughters of testators of every occupation inherited less real estate, with the sharpest contrast among the nobility and gentry and the most equal among artisans, professionals, and merchants. Considered separately from their brothers, daughters of noble, professional and artisanal testators did better than daughters of merchants and government officials in their receipt of real estate.

It is likely that the occupational and class situation of the testator, rather than the gender of their children, influenced the shape of their will. Factors such as guild membership and personal wealth influenced a testator's choices for the devolution of their real and movable property. A member of the nobility was perhaps more likely to use the last will to pass on real estate to his heirs than an artisan, who might be as preoccupied to detail bequests of goods as he is to detail bequests of shops and houses. Likewise, a merchant was perhaps more likely than a member of the professional class to bequeath property to a business associate.

As with the characteristic of gender among the testators, the extent to which the occupation of the testator would influence the daughter's life depended on her immediate situation. An unmarried daughter might find a bequest of real estate useful to add to what she could bring to a marriage or as property to own as a singlewoman. Yet, a widowed daughter might find a bequest of real estate a burden rather than a blessing, as she might not desire to remarry, and increasing her landed holdings would likely increase her suitors.

The variety of bequests, diverse conditions placed on legacies, and the gender and occupation of the testators all serve to add depth to our understanding of women's circumstances in this late medieval city. The world that daughters faced in late medieval London looked different depending on their parents' circumstances and occupations. It also depended on their parents' level of interest in their future occupations and marriage choices, or at least in spelling out that interest in their last will and testament.

CHAPTER THREE

PROSPECTS OF POWER: INHERITING REAL ESTATE AND REAL OPPORTUNITY

Perhaps the most dominant gender construct in medieval society was that of a man's activity and a woman's passivity. This even entered the economic sphere, as women in most of medieval Europe were expected to be passive agents in financial affairs. If women were married, their husbands often controlled their property, and in court cases involving sales, debts, and property disputes, women usually needed men to represent them. Yet, this generalization is too broad. An analysis of the wills enrolled in the Husting Court of London reveals women as active economic agents in the real estate market: managing tenements, acting as proprietors, and owning their own businesses, potentially independent of male control. This chapter explores the inheritance of real estate by daughters in the Husting wills and challenges current scholarship that argues that in the Middle Ages, daughters were more likely, even in towns, to receive money and goods and thus were denied an active role in economic matters.

The 3,081 wills enrolled with the Husting Court of London indicate intentions of fathers, and sometimes mothers, for their daughters to own and control domestic and commercial real estate, either on their own or with their husbands. Late medieval Londoners presented their daughters with various prospects of economic power. These daughters often inherited real estate such as houses, shops, and land along with their brothers, and were not always limited to legacies of movable property. From these wills it becomes clear that their fathers and mothers viewed these women as viable heirs to real estate and gave them many opportunities to own, rent, and manage property. In addition, many of these parents equipped their daughters with the tools to conduct business and to pursue a livelihood.

Legacies of Real Estate

Archaeological evidence and property records attest to the continual division of and additions to urban property as well the common practice of subletting. Such evidence reveals a sophisticated medieval understanding of the land market and profits to be gained through property ownership.[1] The high value placed on real estate is likewise reflected among London testators. Since late medieval Londoners outlined in detail in their wills the devolution of their real property, including land, houses, and rental properties, it is clear that such real estate was very significant in the consciousness of Londoners and had the potential to benefit women inheriting in late medieval London.

When one considers all types of property bequeathed in these 3,081 wills, it is perhaps unsurprising that between 1300 and 1500, more moveable property was bequeathed to daughters than to their brothers, while more real property was bequeathed to sons than to their sisters. It was common for daughters to receive movable property; for instance, Isabella Tiffeld received a variety of household goods from her father in 1355, including cups with representations of Saints Katherine and Mary Magdalen, basins and ewers, her father's best blankets, and pewter platters.[2] It was also common for sons, like the three sons of Reginald Conduit in 1344, to receive landed property such as tenements.[3] Despite this general pattern, daughters did receive a remarkably high amount of real property during this period in London. Seventy-eight percent of all daughters represented in the wills received some amount of real property compared with eighty-six percent of all sons mentioned in the wills.

The Husting wills, like all medieval records, are not without their challenges. In most wills, testators did not list the individual pieces of property in their legacies, nor did they include the value of the property. Instead, they bequeathed types of property often in groups. Rare was the will like that of Simon Frank's in 1332 in which he left

---

[1] For a detailed discussion of the medieval land market in England, specifically in London and Winchester, see Derek Keene, "Landlords, the Property Market and Urban Development in Medieval England," in *Power, Profit and Urban Land: Landownership in Medieval and Early Modern Northern European Towns,* ed. Finn-Einar Eliassen and Geir Atle Ersland (Brookfield, VT: Scolar Press, 1996), 93–119. For a comparative view of medieval York, see Sarah Rees Jones, "Property, Tenure and Rents: Some Aspects of the Topography and Economy of Medieval York" (master's thesis, University of York, 1987). For a detailed consideration of rent records in medieval Oxford and Canterbury, see A. F. Butcher, "Rent and the Urban Economy: Oxford and Canterbury in the Later Middle Ages," *Southern History* 1(1979): 11–43.

[2] Isabella Tiffeld also received her father's brewery and utensils; Sharpe, *Calendar of Wills*, I:689; CLRO, HR 84(48).

[3] Sharpe, *Calendar of Wills*, I:498; CLRO, HR 74(173).

to his daughter, Petronilla, *twenty* shops on different sides of a street.[4] Similarly rare was the will of Richard Giffard in 1399 in which he specified that his wife have the interest of *three* tenements in Distaflane and Oldefisshestrete.[5] While these exceptional cases can provide specific illustrations of the different types of bequests of real property, they lack quantitative significance. More often, when a testator had more than one piece of property to bequeath, he simply gave the plural form of the property type and the general area of these properties. For example, in 1350 Thomas Pilk left to his mother, Elena, all his lands, rents, and tenements (*omnia terras redditos et tenementa mea*) in the parish of All Hallows near the Tower.[6] Because of the propensity for ambiguity in their bequests of real property, it is only possible to count the number of times property is bequeathed rather than tracking the specific number of properties in the wills. In the 3,081 wills from the Husting Court between 1300 and 1500, then, it is only possible to enumerate that testators bequeathed landed property 7,160 times.

Throughout this period, the types of real property bequeathed to daughters and sons were various and diverse. Almost half of the property bequeathed in the Husting wills was simply called tenements (46%), followed by commercial property at 14%, "rents" also at 14%,[7] other property at 11%,[8] houses at 10%, and dwellings and halls at 4%. Thus noted, the primary bequest of real estate was in the form of the tenement.

The basic definition of a tenement is land or real property that could "embrac[e] all forms of proprietorship"; it could be an unspecified type of building; it could be a house or principal dwelling place; it could be a portion of a house or a block of apartments; or it could be some type of rental property.[9] Technically, a tenement could be any type of property; for this study, however, this property type has been examined as a separate category because first, this is how the testators themselves described their property, and second, in some

[4] Sharpe, *Calendar of Wills*, I:374; CLRO, HR 60(53).

[5] Sharpe, *Calendar of Wills*, II:342; CLRO, HR 128(41).

[6] Sharpe, *Calendar of Wills*, I:645; CLRO, HR 78(251).

[7] See discussion of rents below.

[8] "Other property" serves as a catch-all group of a more various assortment of property types including gardens, wharves, land inside and outside of London, fountains, stables, wells, and so on.

[9] *Oxford English Dictionary Online*, s.v. "tenement,"10.31.2010, http://dictionary.oed.com.

cases the testator mentioned if the tenement or tenements functioned as another property type. For example, in 1344 John Alisaunder indicated that "his entire tenement … in which he lived"—the only property mentioned in his will—be left to his wife and, after her death, to his son.[10] The way in which Alisaunder described this tenement makes it clear that this tenement was his dwelling place. Since testators were more consistent in noting the other types of property in their legacies—such as shops, houses, or even tenements serving the purpose of housing—the majority of tenements in the Husting wills were most likely rental properties.[11] In his work on medieval Winchester, Derek Keene argues that artisans and merchants often had numerous tenements in the same area and kept these properties together by subletting to relations or individuals in the same line of work. This comparative case further supports the idea that the tenements in the Husting wills operated as rental properties.[12]

Within this distribution of real property, one might expect sons to have predominantly inherited tenements if they did indeed function as rental properties, as daughters may have had more difficulty than their brothers in controlling tenements in the commercial or housing markets. However, managing rental properties may have been easier and less risky for daughters than owning commercial properties in which their direct involvement in business would have been required. In a way the Husting wills support both of these expectations. Of all the tenements bequeathed in the Husting wills, sons received the majority at 29%, only slightly edging out their mothers at 27%, and daughters followed at 21%, with the other 23% left to other family members, friends, and business associates.

Although the numbers were lower for daughters than for sons, it is clear that testators gave tremendous opportunities to their daughters to own rental properties, even though management was an activity that medieval society often gendered male. One father in the

---

[10] CLRO, HR 71(138): "totum illud tenementum meum cum omnibus suus partium in quo inhabito in la Redecrouchestrete …" Because this was most likely Alisaunder's dwelling-place, all property specified similarly has been counted as dwellings rather than tenements.

[11] Although most of these wills were recorded in Latin, one of the primary definitions for *tenement* in the *Middle English Dictionary* is rented property. The wills seem to be compatible with this understanding. *Middle English Dictionary Online*, s.v. "tenement," 10.31.2010, http://quod.lib.umich.edu/m/med/.

[12] Derek Keene, *Survey of Medieval Winchester* (Oxford: Clarendon Press, 1985), I:219.

early fourteenth century, William de Hundesdich, left a tenement to his two daughters, Christiana and Matilda, and their heirs, with a condition that it pass to his son Thomas if they had no heirs. Whereas Christiana and Matilda received a tenement directly, Thomas received a variety of household goods including spoons, cups, pots, and jewelry.[13] In this instance, Christiana and Matilda were presented with a significant opportunity of ownership that was denied in the first instance to their brother. Looked at from the standpoint of heirs rather than tenements, the percentage of daughters represented in the Husting wills who received tenements was quite high at 52 percent, while the percentage of sons was only slightly higher at 59 percent. A difference of only seven percentage points indicates that while male heirs were still favored as recipients of tenements, daughters as recipients were by no means omitted.

Commercial buildings, such as shops, brewhouses, inns, and bakehouses, also appeared frequently in the wills. These were the spaces in which many testators carried out their livelihoods. As with tenements, one might expect sons to have inherited more commercial properties than their sisters. The general patterns in inheritance of commercial property again meet expectations. It was common for sons, like John Fulham in 1406, to receive a shop from their fathers after their mothers died.[14] Daughters more frequently received commercial goods rather than the physical spaces. As explained by Barbara Hanawalt, "Women were trained to deal with rents and property better than they were trained to undertake businesses or crafts."[15] However, once again it is notable that daughters received this type of landed wealth at all, and that they did so in significant proportions.

Commercial buildings, like tenements, were bequeathed by and large to members of the nuclear family: 30% of all commercial buildings went to sons, 23% to wives, and 19% to daughters. All other relatives received only 11% of commercial property, while those in-

[13] Thomas stood to inherit the tenement after his sisters and their heirs died as well as a tenement left to his mother with implements for brewing and tanning should she marry or be unchaste. There is a possibility that Thomas could have received a share in the business *inter vivos*, something not specified in the will. Sharpe, *Calendar of Wills*, I:186–7; CLRO, HR 35(72).

[14] Sharpe, *Calendar of Wills*, II:377; CLRO, HR 135(87).

[15] Barbara Hanwalt, *The Wealth of Wives: Women, Law, and Economy in Late Medieval London* (Oxford: Oxford University Press, 2007), 65.

dividuals who were not related, and who were often business partners or fellow guild members, received 17% of all commercial property in the Husting wills. The fact that the majority of commercial buildings were bequeathed to sons reiterates the point that a son was more likely to carry on his father's business, and thus more likely to inherit the physical space in which to carry out this business. However, it is notable that such a high percentage of commercial property, almost one fifth, was left to daughters. Some daughters did indeed have the means and opportunity to operate businesses in this late medieval city.

Real property called "rents" acted similarly to commercial property. From the thirteenth century, *rent* had a second meaning in London besides our modern understanding of a payment made by a tenant for occupancy of a piece of property. Over time, *rent* also came to mean a shop or small house next to the street.[16] As Derek Keene explains, renting space in a house that adjoined a busy street became very lucrative. Therefore, owners built small trading spaces to let at the front of their properties, and these came to be known as "rents."[17] In fourteenth-century London, in the suburb of Southwark, for example, Martha Carlin notes that numerous landlords exploited the street-front portions of their property by building shops to rent there. She also traces such building in the sixteenth century, by which time they are clearly called rents, such as "West's Rents."[18] Sarah Rees Jones also notes this development of subdivisions of larger burgage plots in other English towns. Jones argues that this creation of smaller shops and houses was happening as early as the eleventh century, and the tenants of these rents were the responsibility of the chartered owner of the larger plot. After around 1300, she explains, as the use of writing increased in urban settings, these units appear more frequently in the records.[19] For example, in London the records from the Ward of Presentments are riddled with references to individuals

[16] The *Oxford English Dictionary* provides both definitions of the term *rent* as "a source or item of revenue or income" and "a separate piece of property, esp. land, yielding a certain return to the owner," with the earliest definition from 1154. See *Oxford English Dictionary*, s.v. "rent," 10.31.2010, http://dictionary.oed.com.

[17] Keene, "Landlords," 98.

[18] Martha Carlin, *Medieval Southwark* (London: Hambledon Press, 1996), 46–47, 58.

[19] Sarah Rees Jones, "Building Domesticity in the City," in *Medieval Domesticity: Home, Housing and Household in Medieval England*, ed. Maryanne Kowaleski and Jeremy Goldberg (Cambridge: Cambridge University Press, 2008), 87–89.

inhabiting rents who are cited for poor upkeep of the property or for expelling filth from the property into the street. In 1421, "the privy in Richard Osberne's rent is indicted for the stench coming out on the highway, which is an annoyance to the people," and again in 1423, "the privy in Richard Osberne's rent is indicted because of the stench of filth" that comes from it.[20] The records also mention property called "Rents of the Swan,"[21] the inhabitants of which were cited for throwing their filth into the street because they had no privies, "the Chamber rent"[22] that belonged to the Guildhall and had defective pavement before it, and a rent of the abbot of Westminster that had defective overhangings.[23]

Though medieval people did, of course, also understand rent as an income (in a more modern sense) rather than as real property, in the Husting wills it appears that testators used the term *rent* (*redditus*) primarily in the sense of real property. In a will from 1366, mercer and alderman Simon de Worstede bequeathed tenements, houses, and rents (*tenementa, domos, et redditos*) in St. Alban to his wife Alice for life, and after her death to his daughter Margery and the heirs of her body.[24] Likewise, in 1368 William atte Halle left to his son, a canon, thirteen shillings and four pence annual rent for his life to be seized of tenements owned by a John of Romeneye in the parish of St. Botolph. He also left thirteen shillings and four pence annual rent to his daughter, a nun of St. Clare Algate, to be seized of tenements owned by a William of the Garderobe.[25] In these instances, as in others in the wills, testators detailed property that brought in a certain amount in rent rather than a monetary legacy. A later fifteenth-century will of John Credy, an esquire of London, also used the term *rent* in the sense of real property. In his will, he specified that "sir John, preest of the charnel, have ii marc out of my part of

---

[20] A. H. Thomas, ed., *Calendar of Plea and Memoranda Rolls, 1413–1437* (Cambridge: Cambridge University Press, 1943), 128, 155.

[21] Thomas, *Calendar*, 118.

[22] Thomas, *Calendar*, 124.

[23] Thomas, *Calendar*, 131.

[24] Sharpe, *Calendar of Wills*, II:95; CLRO, HR 94(105).

[25] CLRO, HR 96(198): "Item lego Thome filio meo canonicum … tresdecim solidatos et quattuor denarrios annum redditos percipiendi … de tenementa …" and "Item lego Katherine filie mee sororum in Abbathania minorissa St. Clare Algate … tresdecim solidatos et quattuor denarrios annum redditos percipiendi de toti illo tenementa …"

the rente called the cowe heed in Chepe yerly ..."[26] Here, then, John Credy owns, in part, a rent that was perhaps a shop with the sign of a Cow's Head above it.[27]

Bequests of rents were common, with 1,166 instances among 8,411 recipients; 262 were bequests of rents to daughters (23%) and 305 to sons (26%). When testators did specify an amount for the rent indicating income rather than real property, which was rare, it was usually either more than thirteen shillings, also often referred to as a mark, or less than that amount. Legacies of rents of a mark or less were more common to children; however, there was a difference in amounts when one compares daughters and sons. Of all rents of a mark or less, 32% were bequeathed to daughters and 22% to sons. It seems that parents were more comfortable bequeathing smaller rents to daughters. Yet, of rents of more than a mark, 17% were bequests to daughters and 19% to sons, not a significant difference, indicating that parents considered daughters and sons as both worthy recipients of such rents.

As valuable real property, because of the income they could produce, rents were predominantly kept within the immediate family. Twenty percent of all rents were bequeathed to wives, 15% were left to other relatives, and 16% to nonrelatives. Between siblings, daughters received rents only 3% less often than their brothers. Such a slight disparity indicates that testators were interested in providing their daughters with profit-producing real estate and with the opportunities to manage such properties and collect paid rent from occupying tenants. Rents would have offered daughters access to and management of commercial real estate, since they were situated on main thoroughfares.

Still another type of real property bequeathed in the Husting wills was domestic property, including houses and dwellings. It has been suggested by some scholars that daughters, widows, and other single women, often were provided with housing in wills. Michael Sheehan

---

[26] Frederick J. Furnivall, ed., *The Fifty Earliest English Wills in the Court of Probate, London, 1387–1439* (London: Trubner and Co., 1882), 75.

[27] Derek Keene found a similar use of the term *redditus* in his study of a piece of property in London in the thirteenth century. In his study of a house with street-front rents in the parish of St. Mary Le Bow, which is near the busy sector of Cheapside, a tenant's son conveyed rent in a land deed to his father that was due from the tenant's main house and "from the property let out (*redditus*) in front of it towards the street." Derek Keene, *Historical Gazetteer of London before the Great Fire* (Cambridge, England: Chadwyck-Healey, 1987), 252.

explains that in wills, "a special concern to provide suitable housing for unmarried daughters and widows is often discernible."[28] He cites a will enrolled in an ecclesiastical court of Exeter in which in 1294 a Londoner left a house to his widow with the provision that the cellar and two solars go to his daughter.[29] In evidence drawn primarily from York, Sarah Rees Jones also comments on a tendency in wills and other property records for testators to provide housing for female relatives: "Indeed, one obvious conclusion to draw from these property arrangements is that the first priority of landowners was to use their property in a functional way to provide their relatives, and perhaps especially their female relatives, whether married or unmarried, with a secure residence, either within or outside the main family home."[30] This argument for provision and support, which reinforces the idea of women as passive participants in the medieval economy, rather than ownership and control of property, is seen to a limited extent in the Husting wills. Yet the wills also show that there were other ways for parents to support their daughters, including bequeathing them direct, active control of housing.

In the Husting wills, a few testators specified that someone, usually a son, should use a piece of landed property to support his sister or sisters while other testators provided their daughters directly with housing. One might suppose that the former type of provision would allow a daughter to receive a space in the house of the one who inherited. However, in the Husting wills it appears that this provision acted more often as a condition on the inheritance. That is, a son might inherit a house, but upon receiving that inheritance, he was to support his sister monetarily in some manner. For example, in 1312 John Blund left his *messuage* or dwelling, *mesuagium meum*, to his son Edward, "charged with an annuity of forty shillings to Ann his daughter until she marry or enter a religious house."[31] We may suppose that it was intended for the daughter to reside with her brother,

---

[28] Michael M. Sheehan, *The Will in Medieval England: From the Conversion of the Anglo-Saxons to the End of the Thirteenth Century*, vol. 6 (Toronto: Pontifical Institution of Mediaeval Studies, 1963), 264.

[29] Sheehan, *The Will in Medieval England*, 264.

[30] Sarah Rees Jones, "Women's Influence on the Design of Urban Homes," in *Gendering the Master Narrative: Women and Power in the Middle Ages*, ed. Mary Erler and Maryanne Kowaleski (Ithaca: Cornell University Press, 2003), 201.

[31] Sharpe, *Calendar of Wills*, I:236; CLRO, HR 41(45). The two other wills also specify a payment of, in one case 40s. to the sister of the son, the main inheritor, and in the other 20 marks to the sister of the daughter, the main inheritor. Sharpe, *Cal-*

but it is not explicitly stated in the will. Under the system of primogeniture in Norwich, Elaine Clark has noted a similar tendency for a sole heir to support unmarried siblings, sometimes monetarily, sometimes with land, which was usually negotiated.[32] In London, of the 1,201 times one or more pieces of domestic property were bequeathed in wills, in only three instances was it specifically stated that individuals were to support the daughter of the testator. In two of these instances, the primary heir was a son and in the third, it was another daughter.

Similar charges of sibling support were placed on inheritance of other types of landed property, most notably tenements. Around 1319, John, son of Walter Wenlok inherited all of his father's tenements after his mother died, but the inheritance was subject to payment of the marriage portions of his two sisters, Alice and Beatrice.[33] In addition to daughters, other dependents were supported, including sons, brothers, wives, fathers, and other individuals, and some of these relatives were provided for with housing rather than monetary support. For example, in 1307, John de Stanford bequeathed a tenement to his married daughter charged specifically with providing food, clothing, and lodging to his wife.[34]

From the Husting wills it does not appear common for testators to provide spaces within houses, or their primary residences, to their daughters, or at least not to explicitly state so. They did appear to provide houses to their daughters, but so too did they to their sons. In the Husting wills, 19% of all domestic property was bequeathed to daughters, while 27% was left to sons. In figure 3.1 different types of landed property are separated into domestic and nondomestic categories. Here, nondomestic property includes commercial buildings, rents, and tenements, primarily, and domestic property includes houses, dwellings, and halls. Figure 3.1 reflects again that sons were favored generally as heirs to real property—in each category they received more than daughters did in comparison. Of all the sons mentioned in the wills, 68% received nondomestic property, 8% domestic, 9% both types of property, and 14% no property, while of all the

---

endar of Wills, I:475; CLRO, HR 71(138); Sharpe, *Calendar of Wills*, I:285; CLRO, HR 48(29).

[32] Elaine Clark, "The Decision to Marry in Thirteenth- and early Fourteenth-Century Norfolk," *Mediaeval Studies* 49 (1987), 507.

[33] Sharpe, *Calendar of Wills*, I:283; CLRO, HR 47(120).

[34] Sharpe, *Calendar of Wills*, I:187; CLRO, HR 35(88).

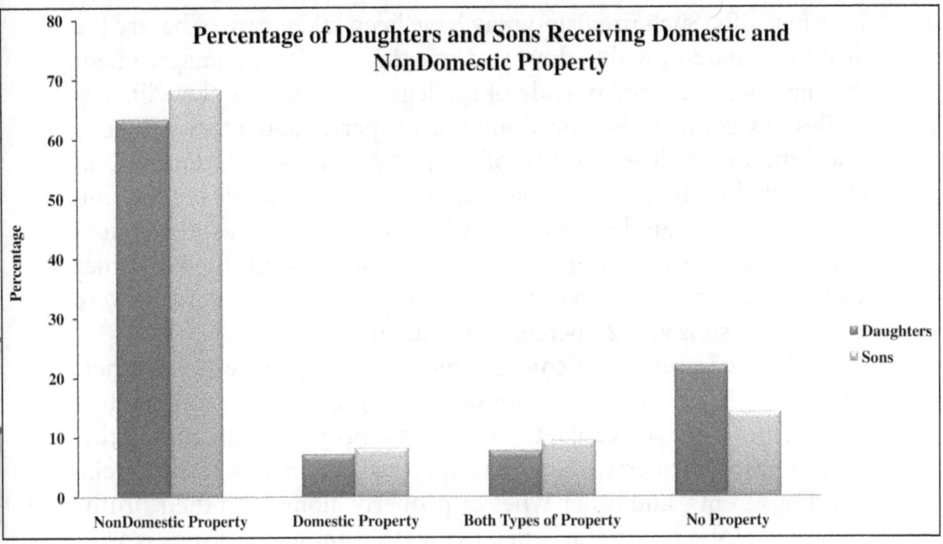

Figure 3.1

daughters mentioned in the wills, 63% received nondomestic types of property, 7% domestic, 8% both types of property, and 22% no property. Yet, in light of the Husting wills, the percentage of daughters who received real estate is certainly not insignificant—78% of all daughters received some type of property. Furthermore, presumptions that daughters might receive more domestic property than sons do not play out in the Husting wills.

Property mentioned specifically as primary dwellings, understood as the principal residence of the testator, more often were bequeathed to sons than to daughters as compared to property referred to only as "houses." Among the 311 times one or more dwellings were bequeathed in the wills, 29% went to sons, while only 13% went to daughters. Among the 844 times houses were bequeathed in the wills, 27% went to sons and 21% went to daughters.

A house might mean a dwelling space for the recipient, as well as rentable property. Through the wills, then, daughters appear less often as dependent on their relatives who required provision. Instead, daughters appear more often as independent individuals capable of managing a house as a piece of property, in which either to live upon marriage or to rent as a singlewoman. For those who did not inherit houses—the majority—their housing provisions are unstated in the

Husting wills. Such provision may have been taken care of before the death of a parent, with a dowry or marriage, or it was an agreement that had been reached outside of the legal document of the will.

Besides commercial and domestic property, daughters and sons also inherited a diverse range of property that was nondomestic in nature, including gardens, wharves, and vacant or arable land within and outside of London. This grab bag of property was distributed almost equally by testators to daughters and sons. Of the 937 times such types of property were mentioned in the wills, 24 percent were bequests to sons and 21 percent to daughters.

Testators were clearly comfortable in leaving real estate to their daughters. In general, more nondomestic property was bequeathed to daughters and sons alike than domestic property, and among this nondomestic property, daughters received tenements, commercial buildings, rents, and other types of property along with their brothers. The largest numerical difference within these categories is with commercial property. While 19 percent of all commercial property went to daughters, 30 percent of it went to sons. This likely reflects more of an expectation among many testators of sons to carry on their businesses, rather than a comfort level among testators for males controlling commercial property. If the bequests of houses are also understood as rentable properties, it appears from the Husting wills of late medieval London that testators placed confidence in daughters as owners and managers of real estate. These wills clearly reflect women who were given opportunities to become active economic agents in their worlds.

Types of Inheritance

To further complicate the inheritance patterns, testators often specified exactly how their real estate was to devolve to their heirs. Real property could be bequeathed directly to a daughter, or it could be bequeathed indirectly, for example after her brother and his heirs inherited it. A daughter who inherited a brewery directly from her father held a much more secure economic niche than a daughter who was to inherit after the death of her brother and his heirs. Thus, the types of inheritance of real property in these wills had a great potential to influence daughters' lives.

The type of inheritance in which a piece of landed property was left to a child directly and to the heirs of that child was known as "fee tail". Property bequeathed in fee tail meant that the recipient and the heirs of his or her body inherited that property. If the recipient had no heirs, the property would revert back to the grantor, or it would continue on to another recipient specified by the grantor. This type of inheritance was developed at the end of the twelfth century as a way to get around common law and the 1176 assize of *mort d'ancestor*, under which only a person's descendants closest in relation by blood could inherit that person's property.[35] Mort d'ancestor limited inheritance to children, siblings, nephews, and nieces of the descendant. However, if a grantor only wanted his property to go to one recipient and the heirs of the body of that recipient—not to the recipient's brother, for example—the grantor would need to use a fee tail in the grant of land. With a fee tail, the grantor could exclude the recipient's collateral heirs, like a brother, from succession.[36] Property bequeathed with the condition of fee tail was "entailed: or limited by a fixed line of succession, regardless of general succession of the law."[37] Thus, using the fee tail allowed grantors, or testators, more control over the devolution of their property against the royal, common law rules.[38]

However, until the first chapter of the Satute of Westminster, *De donis conditionalibus* in 1258 there was no legal protection from a recipient of property granted alienating the property against the

[35] Joseph Biancalana, *The Fee Tail and the Common Recovery in Medieval England, 1176–1502* (Cambridge: Cambridge University Press, 2001), 10.

[36] Biancalana, *Fee Tail*, 13.

[37] Henry Campbell Black, *Black's Law Dictionary: Definitions of the Terms and Phrases of American and English Jurisprudence, Ancient and Modern*, 6th ed. (St. Paul: West Publishing Co., 1990), s.v. "fee tail," 616. The entail was "the settlement of the succession of a landed estate, so that it cannot be bequeathed at pleasure by any one possessor," *Oxford English Dictionary Online*, s.v. "entail," 10.31.2010, http://dictionary.oed.com. Another definition explains that *entail* is "a fee abridged or limited to the issue, or certain classes of issue, instead of descending to all the heirs." Used as a verb, *entail* means to create an estate in fee tail. See Black, *Black's Law Dictionary*, s.v. "entail," 530.

[38] Grantors also used the fee tail to get around rules governing grants in "fee simple," in which property granted from A to B and B's heirs could not revert back to A upon there being no heirs, instead it would automatically go on to B's collateral heirs. Biancalana, *Fee Tail*, 14. See also Black, *Black's Law Dictionary*, s.v. "fee simple," 615.

grantor's or testator's wishes, as soon as the recipient had an heir.[39] The idea here was that as soon as the recipient had an heir, the custom of reversion back to the grantor was null and void. Under this statute, the *De donis,* a fee tail was not freely alienable by the recipient.[40] This statute permitted the testator to specify inheritance however he wished with more comfort that his wishes would be followed.[41]

Testators complicated the fee tail with further restrictions following their interests. For example, a testator could bequeath property to an individual and to the male or female heirs only of that individual, or in "tail male/female." In 1344, Reginald Conduit, a vinter, left his daughter Lucy a tenement for her lifetime (another type of inheritance) while his son Reginald received a tenement in tail, and his other son William received a tenement in tail male, meaning that only the male heirs of William would inherit the tenement after William died.[42] Other types of inheritance included "successive tail," which referred to property that was passed on by succession; "several tail," in which two or more recipients inherited separately by halves; and "special tail," which involved inheritance left to a "special class of heirs".[43]

In addition to the direct inheritance of fee tail, other property in the Husting wills was bequeathed to children indirectly. That is, these heirs stood in line to inherit. This type of inheritance was known as the "remainder." For example, in William de Hundesdich's will of around 1307, noted above, he left a tenement in tail to his two daughters, "Christina and Matilda and the heirs of their bodies legitimately procreated," while his son Thomas received the tenement in remainder should his two sisters die without progeny.[44]

---

[39] Frederick Pollock and Frederick Maitland, *History of English Law before the Time of Edward I* (Cambridge: Cambridge University Press, 1924), 2:17; J. H. Baker, *An Introduction to English Legal History*, 2nd ed. (London: Buttersworths, 1979), 231–232.

[40] Baker, *Introduction,* 232. See also Biancalana's more nuanced discussion of the development of *De donis*, Biancalana, *Fee Tail,* 21–33.

[41] Claire de Trafford argues that with *De donis* came the reduction of women's power, as before the statute a widow had full control of her maritagium and could grant it as she wished. De Trafford, "Share and Share Alike? The Marriage Portion, Inheritance and Family Politics," in *Studies on Medieval and Early Modern Women: Pawns or Players?*, ed. Christine Meek and Catherine Lawless (Dublin: Four Courts Press, 2003), 47–48.

[42] Sharpe, *Calendar of Wills*, I:498–9; CLRO, HR 74(173).

[43] *Oxford English Dictionary Online*, s.v. "several," "successive," "tail," accessed 10.30.2010. http://dictionary.oed.com.

[44] CLRO, HR 35(72): "heredibus earum de corporibus suus legitime procreatis."

Testators could place further restrictions on remainders, specifying that an heir inherit indirectly in tail or for life, or inherit second, third, fourth, and so on, in the line of succession. In 1335, John de Bricheford left a tenement to his son Henry after his wife Alice died, and after Henry's death, the tenement was to revert to his other son, Thomas and Thomas's heirs, thus "remainder in tail," and then, thirdly, to Osbert, John's brother.[45] The devolution of property in wills could be quite complicated, combining all types of inheritance, as the testator wished. In 1349, Laurence de Braghayngg left his tenements, shops, and wharves to his wife for life, and only some of those properties to his son Laurence in tail, with remainder to his son John in tail. Meanwhile, to John, his second son, he left another set of tenements with a tavern, with remainder to his first son, Laurence. Margaret, his daughter, was to receive all of the above property if her brothers died without heirs.[46] "Cross remainder" was yet another type of inheritance, which specified that two or more heirs "has reciprocally a remainder in the share of the other."[47]

There were yet more types of inheritance that guided the legacies of real property. For example, instead of inheriting a piece of property for one's lifetime, which was common for widows,[48] the recipient could inherit it for a limited time only, the length of which was sometimes specified. In other instances, the testator specified that the property was to be sold and the recipient was to gain the profits of the sale or a portion of the profits, sometimes after debts were paid and pious requests met. This portion was called the "residue."[49] In other wills, recipients were themselves given the power to sell the property and collect the profits if they so chose. Generally, the latter type was reserved for property bequeathed to widows, with only one

---

[45] Sharpe, *Calendar of Wills*, I:406–7; CLRO, HR 63(88).

[46] Sharpe, *Calendar of Wills*, I:619; CLRO, HR 77(238).

[47] Herbert Newman Mozley and George Crispe Whiteley, eds., *A Concise Law Dictionary*, (London: C. Roworth and Sons, 1876), 104. Black's dictionary describes such heirs as "tenants in common." Henry Campbell Black, *A Dictionary of Law* (Clark, NJ: The Lawbook Exchange, 1991), 304.

[48] Sharpe explains that by the *Statute of Wills*, a husband could not "devise to his wife any tenements within the City for higher estate than the term of life." Whenever a husband bequeathed property to his wife for more than a life estate, she came to court and renounced the inheritance, and expressed her desire for only a life estate. If she did not, she risked losing all of the inheritance. Sharpe, *Calendar of Wills*, I:xxxviii.

[49] Black, *Black's Law Dictionary*, s.v. "residue," 1310.

will in the sample in which a married daughter was given the power to sell. This suggests that widows needed the husband's permission to alienate land that had belonged to him; otherwise she would only receive a life interest in that land, per London custom. It also suggests that married daughters, as covered women, needed such permission. All of these different types of inheritance affected the lives of daughters; where they stood in line to inherit real property influenced the course of their lives, determining their level of independence and control over that real property.

The freedom of the recipient to use her legacy as she chose was at times restricted. For example, in 1305–1306 Walter de Reylegh, a cordwainer, left an indeterminate amount of shops to his wife for life, with remainders to his daughter Isabella, *for her marriage*, and to his son Simon, with no similar restriction.[50] *Maritiagium*, like that of Isabella, was a bequest or gift of land provided for the support of a new union. This property would then continue to the children of this union, if there were any.[51] Isabella, then, received land, but it was specifically to be used for her marriage.

Unfortunately, the nature of the source material precludes an examination of dowries. In only 71 (2 percent) of the 3,081 wills did testators mention dowries for their daughters (or only 5 percent of all daughters).[52] However, we may presume that many daughters received dowries before the death of their fathers. If the daughters of the Husting wills did receive dowries that are not mentioned in the wills, their inheritance of real property along with their brothers is even more striking. Rural daughters most often received landed property as part of their dowries, handed over to their husbands at the time of their marriages. Yet, even in this case a woman's control of that property was nonexistent because her landed inheritance moved from her father's control to that of her husband.[53] In contrast,

[50] Sharpe, *Calendar of Wills*, I:176–7; CLRO, HR 34(30).

[51] Biancalana, *Fee Tail*, 7.

[52] One son did receive a marriage portion in 1361. Hugh de Sadelyngstanes specified that the guardian of his son pay his wife two hundred marks for his marriage. This is the only example in the Husting wills, in this sample, in which a marriage portion is specified for a son. Sharpe, *Calendar of Wills*, II:57; CLRO, HR 89(242).

[53] S. F. C. Milsom explains the obstacles to women's independent control of landed property in rural areas in his article on female inheritance in the twelfth and thirteenth centuries. He argues that a father could not give his daughter land before her marriage; instead he had to hold it for her in *custos* until she married. Milsom, "Inheritance by Women in the Twelfth and Early Thirteenth Centuries," in *On the*

London daughters may have received landed property in addition to their dowries and would have had direct control over this land if they were single.

A last type of inheritance, jointure, permits a consideration of dowry from another angle. Heirs could inherit property in jointure, combining all of the conditions explained above. For example, two individuals could inherit jointly in tail, for life, in remainder, or for a limited time. Inheritance in jointure is reflected in the Husting wills and suggests yet another way that parents provided opportunities for economic agency to their daughters. However, before turning to the wills, some explanation of how jointure operated legally is in order.

Joseph Biancalana explains that there was a change beginning in the thirteenth century in the provision for marriages in which the bride's father paid a marriage portion in money rather than land (*maritagium*), and the groom or his father settled a joint fee tail on the bride and groom, rather than giving a dower. The marriage portion and maritagium were synonymous with dowry or *dos* common throughout Europe.[54] Maritagium, given to a woman at her marriage, remained her property after her husband's death. It operated in law as a gift to the wife and "was an estate created for the benefit of the grantor's daughter and her descendants."[55] By common law a widow was entitled to a dower, which was a gift made by the husband to the wife at their marriage, but which she collected only after her husband died and which she held for her lifetime; thus it was not limited to her heirs. Dower was an obligatory gift that entitled a widow to one third of the lands of the husband. Land held jointly by the husband and wife, on the other hand, would revert to her upon her husband's death and would be the legacy of the children of their union. This land was the common right of the two beneficiaries rather than the

---

Laws and Customs of England: Essays in Honor of Samuel E. Thorne, ed. Morris S. Arnold, et al. (Chapel Hill: University of North Carolina Press, 1981), 60–61.

[54] Biancalana, *Fee Tail*, 9, 142–60; Baker, *Introduction*, 231. Biancalana explains that a myriad of factors is responsible for the switch to money portions from land. These factors include increased use of money in the twelfth and thirteenth centuries, the ability of individuals to prevent the devise of their landed estates by giving property to sons and money to daughters, and the increased debtedness of landholders. Biancalana, *Fee Tail*, 143, 145.

[55] Margaret Ruth Kittel, "Married Women in Thirteenth-Century England: A Study in Common Law" (PhD diss., University of California, Berkeley, 1973), 81–82.

right of only the wife, as would be the case of bequests of land to her directly in inheritance or in maritagium.[56]

The change in how parents provided for their sons and daughters at marriage, from a maritagium of land to a money portion and from dower to jointure, can be seen to a limited extent in the Husting wills. There were sixteen instances of marriage portions to daughters of real property versus fifty-five instances of marriage portions in the form of movable property, most often money but sometimes annuities and movable goods. These proportions support the first part of Biancalana's argument of a shift from maritagium of land to a marriage portion of money.[57]

Unfortunately, the nature of the Husting wills prevents an examination of the second part of his theory as the wills do not detail dower arrangements for daughters.[58] In some wills the testator bequeathed real estate to his daughter and her husband, and other times, the testator mentioned that his daughter was married, but he only mentioned her and not her husband as the recipient of the property. For example, in 1307 William de Asschingdone bequeathed a shop with a solar to his daughter Margery and her husband Edmund Heyroun together, whereas a year earlier Emma Faversham bequeathed a tenement with houses to her daughter Custance, specified as wife of John Vigrus.[59] The wills also inconsistently note marital status. Only 113 of 1529 daughters are mentioned as married, or 7 percent, while only six sons are mentioned as married out of 1854, less than 1 percent. Daughters who were married may not have been so labeled in

[56] Kittel, "Married Women," 90. Jointure differed from dower in the sense that the widow did not have to fight for dower land in court. Instead, since she held it with her husband during his lifetime it transferred to her without question upon his death. Peter Fleming, *Family and Household in Medieval England* (Palgrave, 2001), 40.

[57] Jenny Kermode also cites the existence of money and goods provided *ad maritagium* to daughters of merchants in late-fifteenth- and early-sixteenth-century York, Hull, and Beverly. Kermode, *Medieval Merchants: York, Beverley and Hull in the Later Middle Ages* (Cambridge: Cambridge University Press, 1998), 100.

[58] For a discussion of dower arrangements for wives rather than daughters in the Husting Wills, see Hanawalt, *Wealth of Wives*, 63. Hanawalt points out that dower arrangements for wives are sometimes difficult to see in wills, as it was not necessary since they were arranged at marriage.

[59] Sharpe, *Calendar of Wills*, I:194; CLRO, HR 36(46): "Item lego Edmundo Heyroun et Margerie filie mee uxori sue illam schopam cum solario …"; Sharpe, *Calendar of Wills*, I:180; CLRO, HR 34(82): "Item lego Custancie uxor John Vigrus filie mee totus illud tenementum cum domibus …"

the sources, and it is not possible, unfortunately, to analyze the impact of marital status on inheritance.

Even though the wills prevent a thorough consideration of dower and the influence of marital status on inheritance, a consideration of jointure is possible. Among the 8,411 recipients in the Husting wills from 1300 to 1500, there were 571 instances of landed property bequeathed in jointure. There were only eight instances of testators bequeathing property explicitly to sons and daughters-in-law in jointure, and three in joint fee tail. A number of scholars have considered jointure in terms of the son's family and inheritance. Biancalana claims that a father tended to settle a joint fee tail on his son and his son's wife. Likewise, in her dissertation on dower and jointure, Andrea Dianne Bessac Maxeiner suggests that jointure allowed greater flexibility for the son's family to specify which property was to remain to the wife and which would stay within the family if she remarried. The joint estate was a way "to control family property, to create estates that would last for generations yet ensure each family member a sufficient income."[60]

The fact that only in eleven instances were sons and daughters-in-law granted property in jointure in the Husting wills seems at odds with the claims of Biancalana and Maxeiner for heavy use by the grooms' parents, but this may be because of the nature of the source material. There may have been bequests intended for sons in support of their marriages, but the sons may not have been mentioned as married in the wills, or their wives may not have been mentioned. Also, there may have been grants of land in jointure to sons and daughters-in-law before the wills were written, thus understating the total number.

There were seventy-three instances of bequests of jointure to daughters and sons-in-law, of which thirty-seven were in joint fee tail, compared to the eleven for sons and daughters-in-law. The disparity here may be due to the fact that this is an urban area, rather than a rural one. Sarah Rees Jones has suggested that in urban areas, maternal and paternal families alike made jointures after marriage.[61] The other 490 instances of jointure in the wills were used in bequests

[60] Andrea Dianne Bessac Maxeiner, "Dower and Jointure: A Legal and Statistical Analysis of the Property Rights of Married Women in Late Medieval England" (PhD diss., Catholic University of America, 1990). 3. Fleming, *Family and Household,* 40–41.

[61] See Jones, "Women's Influence," 200, n. 46.

of land to individuals other than married sons and married daughters, for example to wives and daughters, married or unmarried friends, and so on.

The proportionally higher number of bequests of land in jointure to daughters and sons-in-law is suggestive of testators who wanted to provide for their daughters both during their marriage and into their widowhood, as a widow could enjoy the landed property held in jointure since it reverted to her after her husband's death. Jointure could have provided more comfort to the widow than dower, the third of the property her husband held during their marriage, depending on the market and the management of the lands by her husband during her marriage.[62] Through an examination of property held by women in the countryside, Maxeiner found that "women with jointures held more property than women with dower or with inheritance alone."[63] In her study of aristocratic women, Barbara Harris argues that fathers often "negotiated jointures for their daughters because they knew that most aristocratic estates would not support adequate common-law dowers for them."[64] Late medieval London fathers may have had similar thoughts of provision for their daughters.

Women were also aware of their influence over land held jointly with their husbands. Scholars have noted instances in early modern England in which women used their jointures to negotiate their financial and political positions. For example, Nancy Wright and Margaret Ferguson describe a seventeenth-century aristocratic woman who sold the land she held jointly to help out her husband financially. Then, she turned around and explained her situation to the king in order to secure financial support for herself while her husband was serving the king. Similarly, Mary Chan and Nancy Wright cite another seventeenth-century aristocratic woman who negotiated her jointure in order to secure a larger inheritance to which she had

---

[62] Erickson, *Women and Property in Early Modern England*, 25.

[63] Maxeiner, "Dower and Jointure," 163–64.

[64] Harris, *English Aristocratic Women, 1450–1550: Marriage and Family, Property and Careers* (New York: Oxford University Press, 2002), 23. Dower may have been a better provision for daughters than jointure, if the jointure was smaller than one third of the husband's estate, but it is difficult to know and there has been no systematic study conducted of such a comparison. Harris, *English Aristocratic Women*, 24. See also J. C. Ward, *English Noblewomen in the Later Middle Ages* (New York: Longman, 1992), 26, who argues that jointure "gave [a woman] wealth and greater security than widows had previously enjoyed."

legal rights as sole heir. These were women who exercised agency and who were very aware of their legal rights in jointure.[65]

Originally, land held in jointure could be alienated by the husband during the marriage, as could land inherited directly. A woman who brought land to a marriage as part of her inheritance was limited in her control over that property. As a *femme couverte*, a married woman relinquished all legal access to that inheritance. Her husband could do with it as he saw fit as the legal guardian of her property. Guardianship meant he could enjoy the profits from that property and could alienate the property if he chose, and contemporary legal opinion expressed that the wife's place was to accept his decisions:

> For since legally a woman is completely in the power of her husband, it is not surprising that her dower and all her other property are clearly deemed to be at his disposal. Therefore any married man may give or sell or alienate in whatever way he pleases his wife's dower during her life, and his wife is bound to consent to this as to all other acts of his which do not offend against God.[66]

The guardianship lasted only the duration of the marriage or until the husband died, and indeed he could only alienate the land for his lifetime, not permanently.[67] Yet before the thirteenth century, land held jointly could be alienated permanently, thereby defeating the jointure. The writ of *cui in vita* was adapted by the thirteenth century to land held in jointure so that a woman's interest in that land would not dissolve upon alienation. That is, "a widow could use the writ to set aside her husband's alienation of land given to him and to her as jointure."[68] This writ was also applied to the marriage portion that she received at her marriage, so that she could recover it should she survive her husband.[69] The existence of such a writ mitigated the re-

[65] Wright and Ferguson, "Introduction," in *Women, Property, and the Letters of the Law in Early Modern England,* ed. Nancy E. Wright, Margaret W. Ferguson, and A. R. Buck (Toronto: University of Toronto Press, 2004), 6–7; Chan and Wright, "Marriage, Identity, and the Pursuit of Property in Seventeenth-Century England: The Cases of Anne Clifford and Elizabeth Wiseman," in *Women, Property, and the Letters of the Law,* 166–67. For a discussion of the development of jointure in early modern England, see Susan Staves, *Married Women's Separate Property in England, 1660–1833* (Cambridge: Harvard University Press, 1990), especially chapter 4.

[66] Glanvill, *A Treatise,* 60.

[67] Kittel, "Married Women," 93. See also Amy Louise Erickson, *Women and Property in Early Modern England,* 24; and Mavis Mate, *Daughters, Wives and Widows,* 77–78.

[68] Biancalana, *Fee Tail,* 159.

[69] Biancalana, *Fee Tail,* 159.

strictions placed on land ownership and control by women once their husbands' guardianship ended, especially on land held in jointure.

Legal protection of widows aside, land bequeathed in jointure to a woman operated similarly to land bequeathed to a woman directly, or as maritagium for her marriage: she was still a *femme couverte* during marriage and thus relinquished direct control over that land. Yet, the number of parents who left property to their daughters directly far outnumbered those who left property to their daughters in jointure. The question remains, then, as to why fathers would leave land jointly rather than directly to their daughters.

Since the provision of land in jointure to daughters would not have bestowed more control over the property than direct inheritance or land granted to her in maritagium, it is possible that jointure operated in these wills as gifts of additional land. That is, it was land bequeathed to married daughters in addition to what the daughter had already received in maritagium or as a dowry. Margaret Kittel, who studied married women's rights under thirteenth-century common law, notes that land held in joint tenancy was most commonly acquired by purchase by the couple while married.[70] Gifts of joint tenancy in the Husting wills to established couples fits into this pattern of land acquisition after marriage. Unfortunately, due to the nature of the source material, it is impossible to know whether the bequests of jointure to daughters in the wills were in addition to earlier gifts of land. For whatever reason, it remains clear that jointure provided testators with an alternative option to a direct bequest of land to their daughters. That jointure was used in 490 other instances of bequests of land indicates that it allowed testators to spread responsibility of land ownership and to provide for more than one person with one parcel of real property.

It is also likely that testators used jointure as a way to fulfill their desire for landed property to remain with the daughter and that daughter's heirs, not other heirs of her husband. Only real property bequeathed directly or jointly would provide such security. The land held jointly by husband and wife was left to the heirs of their bodies only, and not to children of the groom's earlier or later marriages, as would be the case with the groom's other lands granted in dower.[71] Real property bequeathed directly or jointly was also likely used by testators as a way to ensure support for that daughter in widowhood.

[70] Kittel, "Married Women," 90.
[71] Biancalana, *Fee Tail*, 144.

The nature of inheritance in late medieval London was complex. The many types of, and conditions placed on, inheritance allowed flexibility of the devolution of property, highlighted the individuality of the testators, and benefited or restricted the situation of the recipient. Other scholars have commented on the creative use of inheritance by the late medieval landed elite. Peter Fleming notes that most noble or gentry family did not only employ the entail to exclude female heirs, rather, "for many, concern for the future of all their children, not just sons, outweighed their desire to maintain the integrity of the patrimony and the survival of the family name."[72]

Among all of the real estate bequeathed directly to daughters and sons—the most popular type of inheritance in the Husting wills—20% of it went to sons in tail and 13% of it went to daughters in tail, a difference of seven percentage points (figure 3.2).[73] Among other types of direct inheritance of real property, including successive and several tail, the numbers are closer still with 7% to sons and 5% to daughters. This is a bit unexpected. One might assume inheritance in fee tail to be almost exclusively reserved for sons, as it was often in the countryside, because this type of inheritance meant that the property descended to the heirs of the body of the recipient, thus remaining in the family in a society commonly operated by the rules of a male primogeniture system. Yet a relatively sizable amount of all real property bequeathed in tail in the wills (13%) was left to daughters to pass on directly to their children. Testators in London, then, as an urban area, did not display the same concern over parceling up patrimony that was visible among the elite members of society in rural areas. Such division of property in London perhaps suggests that Londoners conceived of "family" differently than their countryside counterparts. Or, if they did not conceive of "family" differently, perhaps Londoners were faced with concerns less relevant to those in rural regions. Daughters in London seem to have been considered,

---

[72] Fleming, *Family and Household*, 120.

[73] These figures were derived from the database of 3,081 wills that was compiled using Sharpe's abstracts. In his abstracts, Sharpe was fairly consistent in noting inheritance types. For example, for over 3,832 times tenements were bequeathed, Sharpe noted 3,154 times when tenements were bequeathed directly (for example, in tail, successive tail, several tail, and so on), indirectly (in remainder), for a limited time, or when they were to be sold. However, in 678 instances within the category of tenements, Sharpe did not note specifically the inheritance type. Because of the predominance of direct inheritance in the wills overall, in these instances I have presumed the inheritance type was direct.

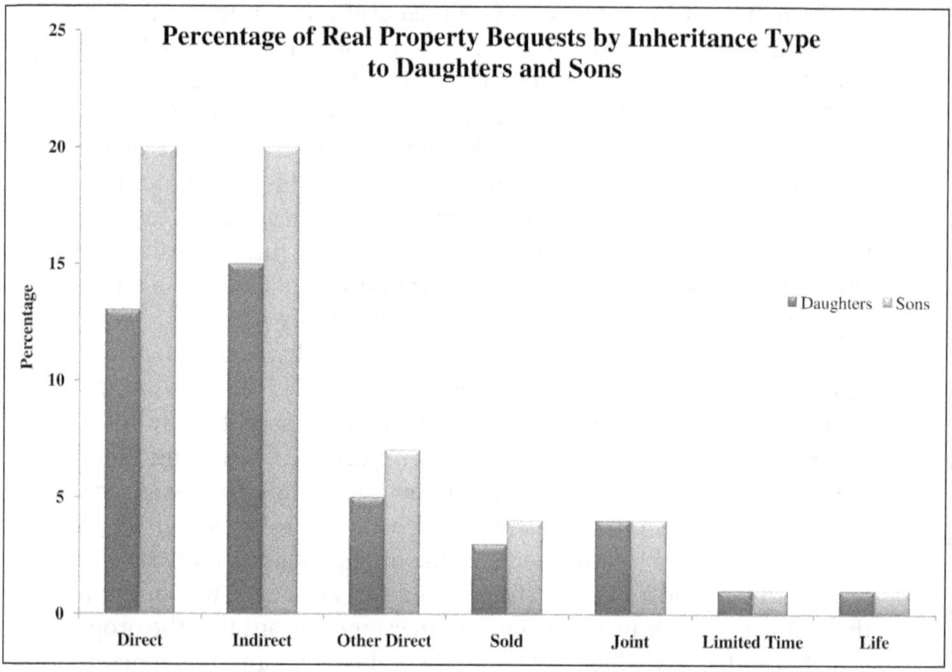

Figure 3.2

along with their brothers, as key components in the devolution of family property.

These London daughters may have been viewed as crucial actors in the preservation of family property from urban creditors. Daniel Smail argues that women's dowries in medieval Marseille, since they belonged to the wife by law, "could serve as a primitive trust, a legal shelter from rapacious creditors in the late medieval culture of debt."[74] The significant inheritance of real property by daughters, not specified as dowries but no less protected by law from alienation by their husbands (at least not permanently), may be a similar indication of fathers securing property from creditors or third parties. Such property would remain in the first instance to the daughters, unless

[74] Daniel Lord Smail, "Mapping Networks and Knowledge in Medieval Marseille, 1337–1362: Variations on a Theme of Mobility," (PhD diss., University of Michigan, 1994), 111, for full discussion, see 111–26; Jenny Kermode also notes the role of women as "agents for transmission through their own blood-line" in her work on late medieval York, Hull, and Beverley, Kermode, *Medieval Merchants*, 91.

of course they contracted a debt on their own, and they could protect the property for the inheritance to the future descendants of those daughters.

One might also expect daughters overall to have inherited property more often indirectly, in remainder, standing in line perhaps behind their brothers to inherit. Again, though, the wills enrolled in the Husting Court show a different pattern. Of all the property bequeathed to daughters and sons in remainder in the wills, 20% was left to sons and 15% to daughters.

The usages of the other types of inheritance, as seen in the Husting wills, are again somewhat surprising. When real property was bequeathed to sons and daughters for life terms, they received this type of inheritance in equal portions: 1% of all property bequeathed to daughters and sons for life went to sons, and 1% went to daughters. The numbers overall are lower here because most property bequeathed for life terms went to wives, rather than to children. Among the properties bequeathed for limited amounts of time, a type of inheritance perhaps similar to a life term, the percentage was the same to daughters at 1% as to sons at 1%.

Finally, when one considers real estate bequeathed to daughters and sons in jointure often, but not always, as provision for marriage, the percentages are again the same. Of all real property bequeathed to daughters and sons in jointure, 4% went to daughters and 4% to sons. In cases where the testator specified that the property was to be sold and the profits or a portion of the profits were to be left to his children, again the percentages are strikingly close. Of all real property left to daughters and sons specified by testators to be sold, 3% went to daughters and 4% to sons.

In a society that in other areas of life and law displayed a discomfort with women inheriting and owning property, one might expect that daughters in London would have inherited real property indirectly, or would have received the proceeds after the sale of property. Yet these data on types of inheritance reveal a different picture. They reveal a city in late medieval England in which daughters inherited landed property alongside their brothers. These women could then, in many cases, pass it on to their heirs, allowing them to be more active agents in the real estate market.

The economic opportunities and authority of these London daughters is even more remarkable when compared with inheritance of daughters elsewhere in Europe, especially southern Europe. In Italy, women's primary source of wealth came with the dowry, and in some towns they were excluded from inheritance with their dowry.[75] When daughters in Venice, for example, were included in the wills of their fathers, it was only when they had no brothers.[76] More often in Venice and in the towns of Northern Italy, Provence, and Catalonia, a daughter's share in the patrimony often came with her dowry.[77] In these regions, from the twelfth century onward there was a distinct preference for cash dowries rather than dowries of real property, as fathers feared precious real property would be alienated from the family by a gift to the daughter. Thus, real property was reserved for the male line.[78]

---

[75] For example, see the *Statuti di Perugia* (1342), in *The Towns of Italy in the Later Middle Ages,* trans. and annot. by Trevor Dean (New York: Manchester University Press, 2000), 198. In Venice, daughters were entitled to inherit a dowry, a right called *exclusio propter dotem*, but their brothers received the bulk of the estate. Linda Guzzetti, "Women's Inheritance and Testamentary Practices in Late Fourteenth- and Early Fifteenth-Century Venice and Ghent," in *The Texture of Society: Medieval Women in the Southern Low Countries,* ed. Ellen E. Kittel and Mary A. Suydam (New York: Palgrave Macmillan, 2004), 82. See also Shona Kelly Wray, "Last Wills in Bologna during the Black Death" (PhD diss., University of Colorado, 1998), 273; Christine Meek, "Women, Dowries, and the Family in Late Medieval Italian Cities" in *The Fragility of Her Sex?: Medieval Irish Women in their European Context*, ed. Christine Meek and Katharine Simms (Dublin: Four Courts Press, 1996), 136–52; and Laurent Mayali, *Droit Savant et Coutumes: L'exclusion des filles dotées XIIème Siècles* (Frankfurt: Klostermann, 1987). See also the work of Patricia Skinner, who found that although not explicit, in Apulia in southern Italy in the early Middle Ages, married daughters were excluded from their fathers' property with their dowries unless they had no brothers. Skinner also found that many early medieval southern Italian fathers preferred to bequeath movable wealth to daughters rather than lands in the patrimony. Skinner, "Women, Wills and Wealth in Medieval Southern Italy," *Early Medieval Europe* 2(1993): 138–39, 146, 152.

In northern Europe, the situation for women was closer to that of London. The custom in Ghent, for example, was partible inheritance, as it was in many English towns. David Nicholas, *The Domestic Life of a Medieval City: Women, Children and the Family in Fourteenth-Century Ghent* (Lincoln: University of Nebraska Press, 1985), 26.

[76] Guzzetti, "Women's Inheritance and Testamentary Practices," 82.

[77] Donald E. Queller and Thomas F. Madden, "Father of the Bride: Fathers, Daughters, and Dowries in Late Medieval and Early Renaissance Venice," *Renaissance Quarterly* 46, no. 4 (1993): 690. Such dowries have been called premortem inheritance. John R. Goody and S. J. Tambiah, *Bridewealth and Dowry* (Cambridge: Cambridge University Press, 1985), 64. Diane Owen Hughes, "From Brideprice to Dowry in Mediterranean Europe," *Journal of Family History* 3 (1978): 278–79. With their dowries, these daughters were often not only excluded from the estate of the one who dowered them, but from the estates of others in their family as well. Hughes, "From Brideprice," 280.

[78] Hughes, "From Brideprice," 281. See also Noël Didier, "Les dispositions du statut de Guillaume II de Foralquier sur les filles dotes (1162)," *Le moyen âge* 56

Thomas Kuehn questioned the application of the theory of *exclusio propter dotem* to practice, with a look at some Florentine cases, arguing that women sometimes inherited even though the legal norms suggest otherwise.[79] Despite this objection, many more scholars have argued for the exclusion of daughters from the patrimony in southern Europe. In Barcelona, for example, under Visigothic law women could inherit along with their brothers, but in practice in the twelfth and thirteenth centuries, testators were leery of leaving all of the family property to a female heir and thus breaking the continuity of the family property through the male line.[80] Furthermore, although they should have been able to claim an equal share in inheritance, daughters in Barcelona received less in inheritance than their brothers. For unmarried daughters, England's customs and laws were decidedly different from southern European countries in that never-married women of age (and widows) operated as legal individuals, not covered by a husband.[81] These London daughters, if they were unmarried, not only inherited landed property directly along with their brothers, but they also enjoyed full control of that property.

(1950): 258; and J. Maillet, "De l'exclusion coutumière des filles dotes à la renunciation à succession future dans les coutumes de Toulouse et Bordeaux," *Revue historique de droit français et étranger* 30 (1952): 514–45. Ellen Kittel also explains that in Genoa, unlike in Douai to the north, it was common for testators to specify that land be kept in the family. Kittel, "Testaments of Two Cities: A Comparative Analysis of the Wills of Medieval Genoa and Douai," *European Review of History* 5 (Spring 1998): 47–83. Likewise, Epstein has argued that Genoese testators more often listed sons as heirs than daughters. Steven Epstein, *Wills and Wealth in Medieval Genoa, 1150–1250* (Cambridge: Harvard University Press, 1984), 74, 111.

[79] Thomas Kuehn, *Law, Family and Women: Toward a Legal Anthropology of Renaissance Italy* (Chicago, 1991), 238–57. Daniel Lord Smail also challenged the works of scholars like Didier in his dissertation. Smail, "Mapping Networks," 87. Smail argued against what he called the "sweeping pronouncements [made by certain scholars] concerning the centrality of female disinheritance to medieval society." Instead, in medieval Marseille he found daughters who inherited real property from their fathers. However, this happened more often in his case study when daughters were only children than when they had to compete for such inheritance with their brothers, whereas in London, the Husting wills indicate that daughters less often competed with their brothers for inheritance. See further discussion below. Smail, "Mapping Networks," 90, 92, 94. Also see Smail's article, "Démanteler le patrimoine. Les femmes et les biens dans la Marseille médiévale," *Annales - Histoire, Sciences Sociales*, 52, no. 2, (1997): 343–68.

[80] Stephen P. Bensch, *Barcelona and Its Rulers, 1096–1291* (Cambridge: Cambridge University Press, 1995), 246, 248–49, 253–54.

[81] Amy Louise Erickson, "Coverture and Capitalism," 2–3.

Presence of Siblings

Over three-quarters of all daughters mentioned in the Husting wills received real estate—tenements, shops, houses, and land—along with their brothers. In a society that followed the laws of primogeniture outside of the cities, one might assume that these daughters received real property only when they did not have brothers with whom to compete. In fact, when considering how the presence of opposite-sex siblings affected the inheritance of real property as a whole, the findings are surprising: daughters were slightly *more* likely to get landed property if they had a brother, 79% to 77%, whereas sons were slightly *less* likely to get landed property if they had a sister, 85% to 88% (figure 3.3). Daughters, then, were not disadvantaged in inheriting landed property when they had brothers; indeed, it was an advantage for daughters to have brothers. In times not plagued by fluctuating demographics, about 20% of couples will have only daughters at the time of the father's death,[82] and so perhaps it is not surprising to see daughters mentioned in wills along with their brothers. Furthermore, these small differences in percentages are not statistically significant, but they do alter the way we view daughters' inheritance in late medieval London. Although the difference is narrow, the fact that daughters inherited when they had brothers indicates that testators viewed these female recipients as worthy and capable property managers.

When one considers how having same-sex siblings affected children's inheritances, the results are less surprising. For both daughters and sons, chances of inheriting real property improved if they did not have siblings of the same sex. A daughter without sisters inherited real property 5% more often than a daughter with sisters (81% to 76%), while a son without brothers inherited 2% more often than a son with brothers (87% to 85%). Again, the differences in percentages are small, but they suggest that testators found it easier to bequeath real property to single heirs or to one son and one daughter rather than to divide up urban property among many children.

---

[82] Erickson, *Women and Property in Early Modern England*, 63. For a detailed exposition of heirship and family demographics in theoretical situations, see R. M. Smith, "Some Issues Concerning Families and Their Property in Rural England 1250–1800," in *Land, Kinship and Life-Cycle*, ed. R. M. Smith (Cambridge: Cambridge University Press, 2002), 40–46.

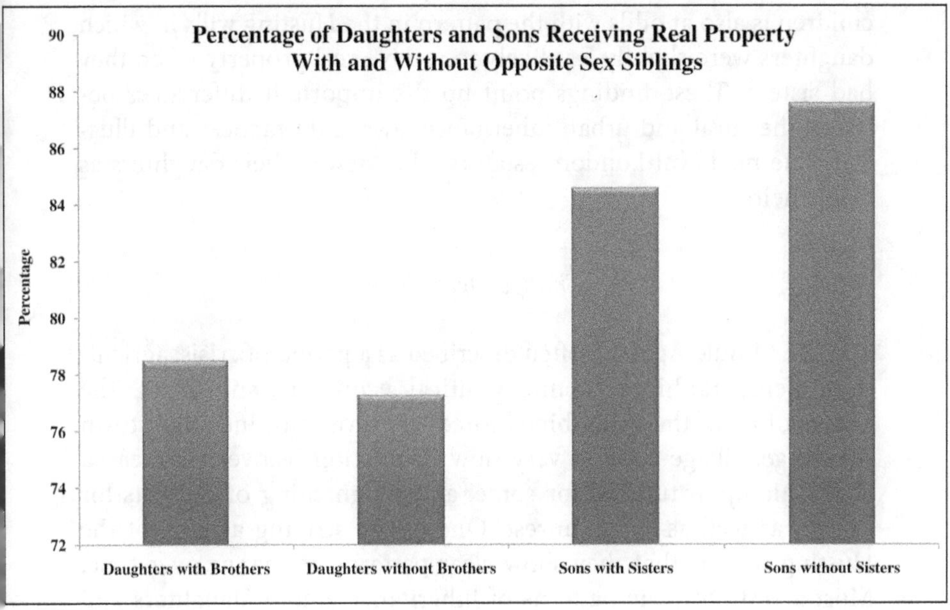

Figure 3.3

These findings illustrate that among testators who mentioned children of both sexes in their wills, there was a concern specifically to provide their daughters, along with their sons, with real property. Although the difference in percentages is slight, sons did not benefit from having sisters who received property, as it may have detracted from the total inheritance they could have received. This pattern runs counter to the common law of primogeniture, or inheritance by the eldest son, which predominated in medieval England, where landed property was left to the male heir and his descendants.[83] In the rural inheritance scheme, if daughters were to receive landed property they did so as a part of their dowries. In the countryside, when there were no male heirs, the landed property was divided equally among the daughters.[84] This phenomenon of dividing property among female

[83] There were areas in which ultimogeniture was practiced, and some areas in which partible inheritance was practiced, most notably in Kent, where it was called *gavelkind*. See Pollock and Maitland, *History of English Law,* 2:270–72, 2:262–69; and George Caspar Homans, *English Villagers of the Thirteenth Century* (Cambridge: Harvard University Press, 1941), 109–20.

[84] Pollock and Maitland, *History of English Law,* 2:260.

children is also at odds with the pattern in the Husting wills in which daughters were slightly less likely to receive real property when they had sisters. These findings point up the important differences between the rural and urban inheritance laws and practices and illustrate late medieval London testators who viewed their daughters as viable heirs.

Change Over Time

The late Middle Ages are often described as a period of crisis: agricultural, demographic, epidemic, political, economic, and social. The results of all of these combined forces were various, including town shrinkage, village stasis, a very slow population recovery, increased economic opportunities for some, and a tightening of markets for others, as well as social unrest. One of the striking aspects of the Husting wills is that they show clear patterns of change over time. Most arrestingly, the patterns of inheritance among daughters and sons do indeed indicate the impact of some of the late medieval crises. Inheritance among daughters and sons in general declined sharply around the time of the Black Death and shortly thereafter (figure 3.4). From around 1335 to 1370 there was a steady decline in the percentage of real estate they were bequeathed. As one might expect, during the period of the first outbreak of the plague, and directly thereafter, there was a great increase in the numbers of wills enrolled in the Husting Court (figure 3.5). Between 1300 and 1347, on average twenty-seven wills were enrolled each year. In 1347, the year before the Black Death, twenty-six wills were enrolled. In the following two years, when the plague was ravaging England, a total of 400 wills were enrolled. It should be noted that while some wills include dates, many do not, and many more were enrolled many months or even years after they were first dictated.[85] In this study, because the dates were often absent from the wills, I went by the year they were enrolled as noted by Sharpe in his *Calendar of Wills*. Rather than the historical year, Sharpe appears to have followed the practice in vogue in the late Middle Ages, that is, dating the start of the year to Lady

[85] Megson notes an exception to this trend: during the plague, "the interval between dating and probated [was] diminishing." Megson, "Mortality among London Citizens," 127.

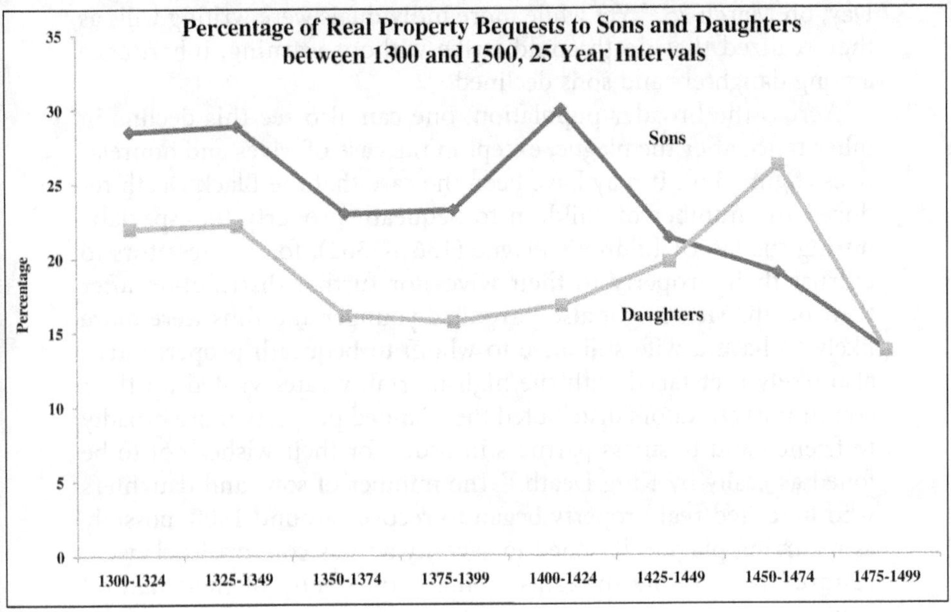

Figure 3.4

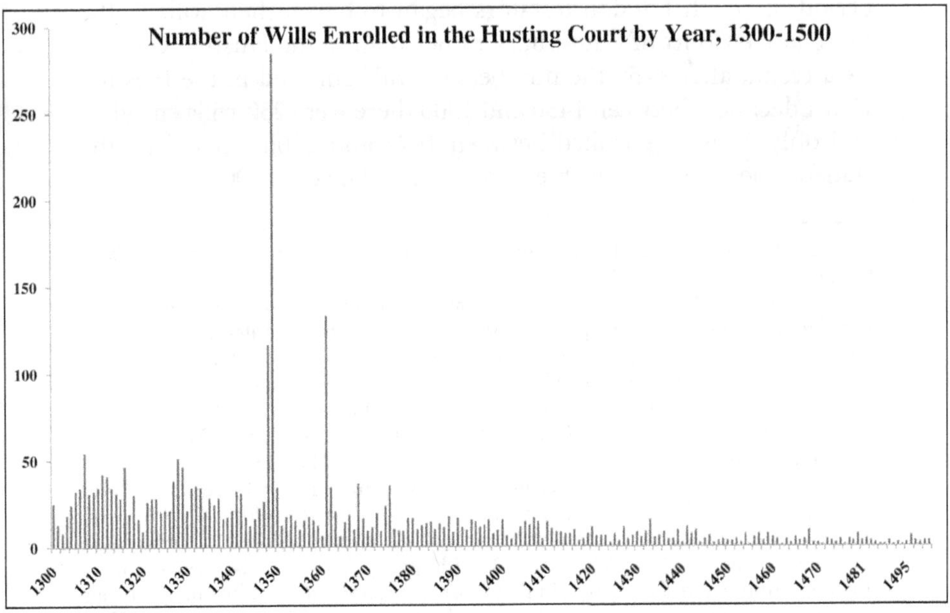

Figure 3.5

Day, on March 25.[86] Yet while more individuals were writing wills as they realized that death could strike without warning, inheritance among daughters and sons declined.

Across the broader population, one can also see this decline in inheritance after the plague, except in the case of wives and nonrelatives (figure 3.6). It may have been the case that the Black Death reduced the number of children to bequeath property to, especially during the later Children's Plague (1361–1362), forcing testators to entrust their property to their wives for further distribution after their death. Men might also have died younger and thus were more likely to have a wife still alive to whom to bequeath property. It is also likely that faced with the high mortality rates visited on their community, testators distributed their landed property more broadly to friends and business partners in order for their wishes not to be foiled as easily by King Death.[87] The number of sons and daughters who inherited real property began to recover around 1400, possibly as recurring plagues lessened in severity and as comfort levels were restored to testators in terms of the survivability of their natural heirs.

Around 1460, inheritance for both daughters and sons in London began to decline again significantly. This coincides roughly with a period in which London testators began to enroll their wills in the Prerogative Court of Canterbury rather than in the Husting Court.[88] As a result, after 1450 the numbers of wills enrolled in the Husting Court declined: between 1450 and 1500 there were 232 wills enrolled, and only 76 were enrolled between 1475 and 1500. Therefore, the statistics become less reliable as one nears the year 1500.

[86] C. R. Cheney and Michael Jones, *A Handbook of Dates* (Cambridge: Cambridge University Press, 2004), 12.

[87] Shona Kelly Wray notes a similar situation in Bologna during the Black Death. Faced with the ravages of the plague, testators more often appointed daughters and other female relatives as principal heirs, whereas prior to the epidemic, they designated only their sons as principal heirs. Wray, "Last Wills," 276–77. See also Shona Kelly Wray, "Women, Family, and Inheritance in Bologna during the Black Death" in *Love, Marriage, and Family Ties in the Later Middle Ages*, ed. Isabel Davis, Miriam Müller, and Sarah Rees Jones (Turnhout: Brepols, 2001), 211, 213–14.

[88] The Prerogative Court of Canterbury began to enroll wills in 1383. Peter Walne, *English Wills: Probate Records in England and Wales with a Brief Note on Scottish and Irish Wills* (Richmond: Virginia State, Library, 1964), 37. Concerning the wills surviving at the PCC from 1383 (despite a few originals surviving from 1484) Grannum and Taylor explain that most "are clerks' copies of the original wills and only exist if the executor paid for the will to be registered." Grannum and Taylor, *Wills and Other Probate Records*, 26.

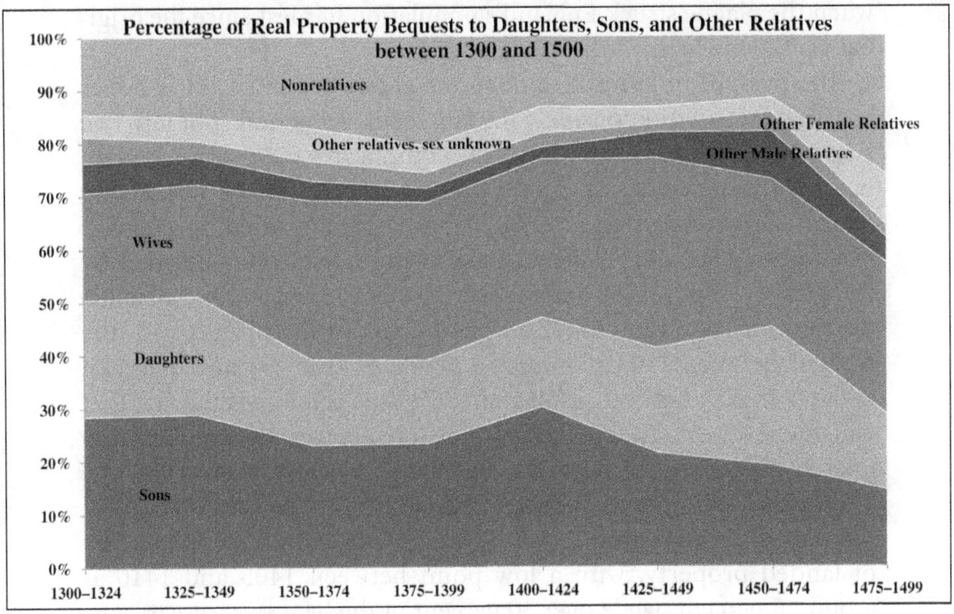

Figure 3.6

If one accounts for the periods of natural disasters, the inheritance patterns look slightly different (figure 3.7). This graph is an attempt to isolate natural disaster periods. Therefore, as the time periods are not equal, it is important to focus on the distinct periods rather than continuous change over time. The period of the Great Famine (1316–1322) seems to have had little effect on inheritance of landed property among daughters and sons. There is a very slight decline in inheritance among sons, but it recovers quickly. This is most likely due to the fact that these urban dwellers would have been less affected by crop failure and cattle disease, especially since they were the wealthier landholders of London who could afford the attendant rise of food prices.[89] In this view of the trends in inheritance patterns, one can again see the decline during the Black Death. Except for the peak in inheritance among daughters around 1355, inheritance to children of both sexes declined, with an ultimate low between 1361 and 1375

[89] Barbara Hanawalt argues that the less fortunate of London did not survive the Great Famine as well as these wealthier Londoners in the Husting wills. Hanawalt, "Reading the Lives of the Illiterate: London's Poor," *Speculum* 80 (October 2005), 1077–78.

when the plague struck England's population hardest since the original visit, namely in 1361–1362 and 1369.

The peak in inheritance among daughters around 1354 is better explained when one considers the late medieval period split into five year intervals (figure 3.8). This view complicates the graph based on natural disasters and one can see that the peak in inheritance among daughters that occurred around 1355 was accompanied by a similar peak among sons. This peak was also preceded and succeeded by troughs for children of both sexes. By this more even and detailed distribution, one can clearly see the impact of the plague, with the troughs between 1349 and 1359, a period of recovery and life, then another trough between 1360 and 1365. This reinforces the fact that daughters were considered practical heirs of real estate; even in times of crisis they were considered as heirs along with their brothers.

Trends in inheritance began to change around the year 1400. After this date, daughters appear to have fared less well in their inheritance of landed property, with a low point between 1405 and 1410 at around 5 percent, while over 30 percent of the bequests were to sons (figure 3.9). After 1420, the trends become more sporadic with daughters surpassing sons for a time between 1430 and 1434. These trends suggest more uniformity among testators in their bequests of landed property to their children in the fourteenth century, and less uniformity in the fifteenth.

Less uniformity in the fifteenth century among inheritance patterns is perhaps due to a change in marriage patterns brought about by economic changes. Daughters may have begun to marry younger in the fifteenth century as the recession hit London's economy after the plague and limited work opportunities for women. If this is the case, these daughters then were receiving their dowries earlier and not inheriting any more real property. Jeremy Goldberg argues for a recession in the mid-fifteenth century that reversed the initial economic opportunities that the plague gave to women.[90] For London in particular, Caroline Barron argues for an "erosion of economic opportunities open to women" and argues that the recession adversely

[90] See P. J. P. Goldberg, *Women, Work, and Life Cycle in a Medieval Economy: Women in York and Yorkshire c. 1300–1520* (Oxford: Clarendon Press, 1992). Judith Bennett argues along similar lines of a tightening of labor opportunities in the case of brewsters. Bennett, *Ale, Beer and Brewsters: Women's Work in a Changing World, 1300–1600* (New York: Oxford University Press, 1996).

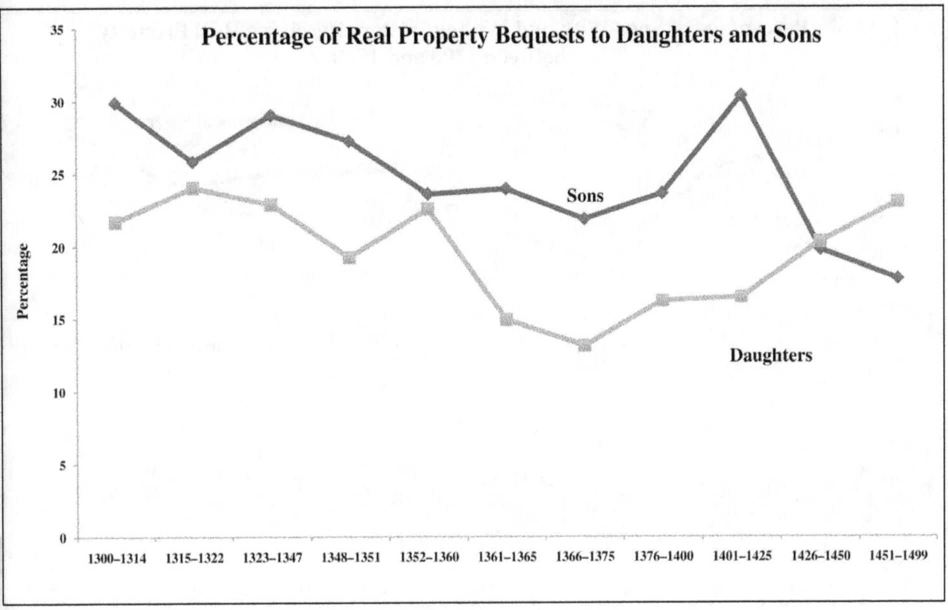

Figure 3.7

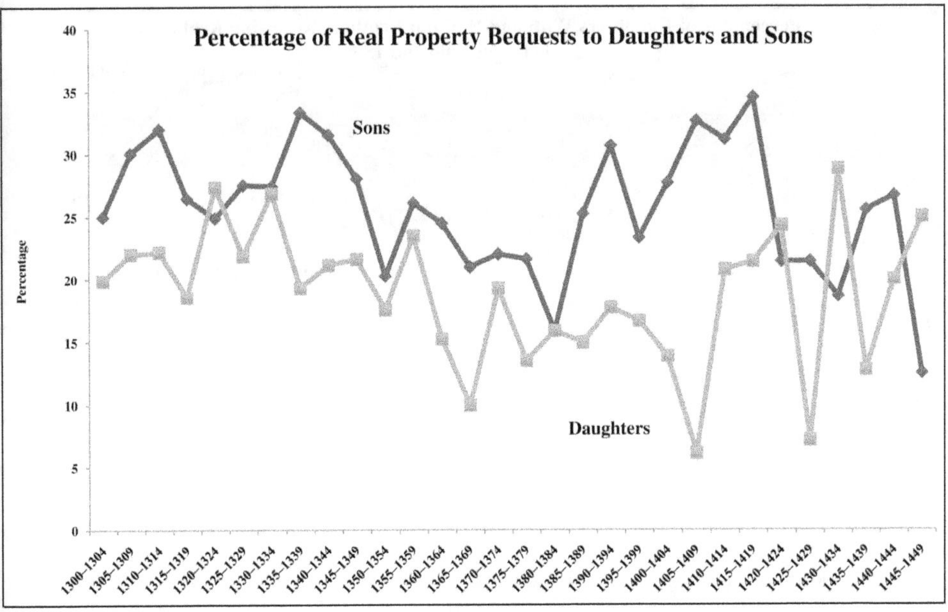

Figure 3.8

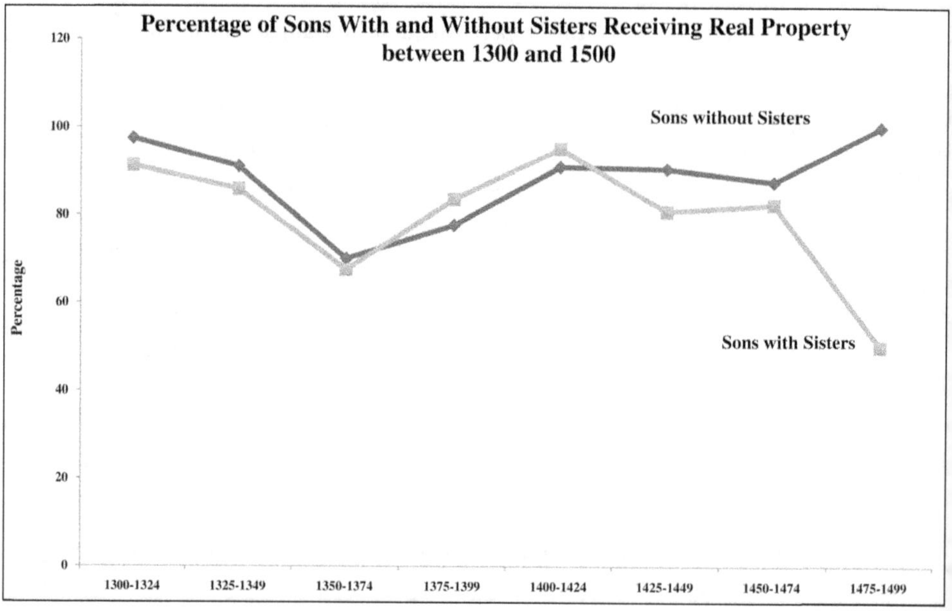

Figure 3.9

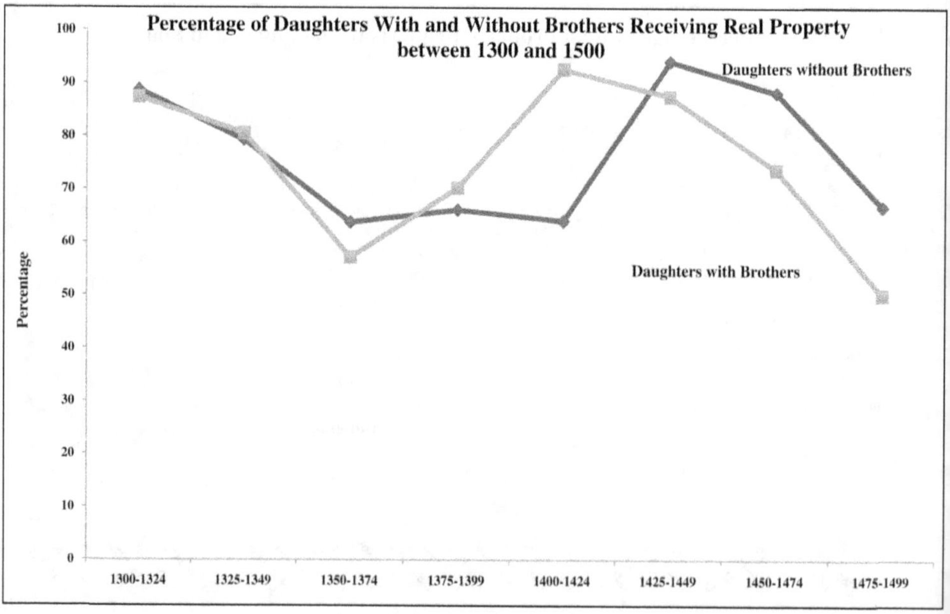

Figure 3.10

affected women's work opportunities. However, she asserts that the economic recession did not hit London until the sixteenth century, because of its size, whereas it hit other cities earlier.[91] By contrast, in terms of inheritance of real property outside of the city, women appeared to have fared the best in the fifteenth century. Maxeiner found in her study of individuals who held property from the king that women held a higher percentage of property by inheritance in the fifteenth century than in the fourteenth, while property held by men by inheritance declined from the thirteenth to the fifteenth centuries.[92]

In terms of the Husting wills, one must remember that the evidence becomes less statistically significant as one nears the end of the fifteenth century. While the theory of a recession's impact on dowries and inheritance is suggestive, more sources from this century would need to be explored in order to suggest a more definitive cause for this change. What is remarkable is that the main body of the wills indicates some significant opportunities for women to own and manage property in medieval London.

Trends in inheritance to children with and without siblings similarly reflect the impact of the Black Death and the recovery afterward (figures 3.9–3.12). Inheritance among daughters and sons with and without same and opposite sex siblings declined in the fifty-year period surrounding the plague. Following the plague, there was a steady increase from 1375 to around 1425, especially among sons with and without same and opposite sex siblings (figures 3.9 and 3.11). As stated above for the overall trend, daughters with brothers generally inherited more landed property than those without brothers, peaking between 1400 and 1425 (figure 3.10).

Inheritance by daughters without sisters and daughters without brothers peaked between 1425 and 1450, twenty-five years later. This may indicate that during this fifty-year period, there was a slight preference for single heirs, as the numbers among all categories without same or opposite sex siblings reached their highest, or near highest, points during this period. A slight preference for single heirs may have been due to recovery from the reoccurrence of the plague in 1399–1400, as testators felt slightly more secure about placing their real estate with one principal heir. Another possibility is that there

---

[91] Caroline M. Barron, "The 'Golden Age' of Women in Medieval London," 48.

[92] Maxeiner, "Dower and Jointure," 162. Maxeiner analyzed the *Calendar of Inquisitions Post Mortem* and the *Year Books* in this study.

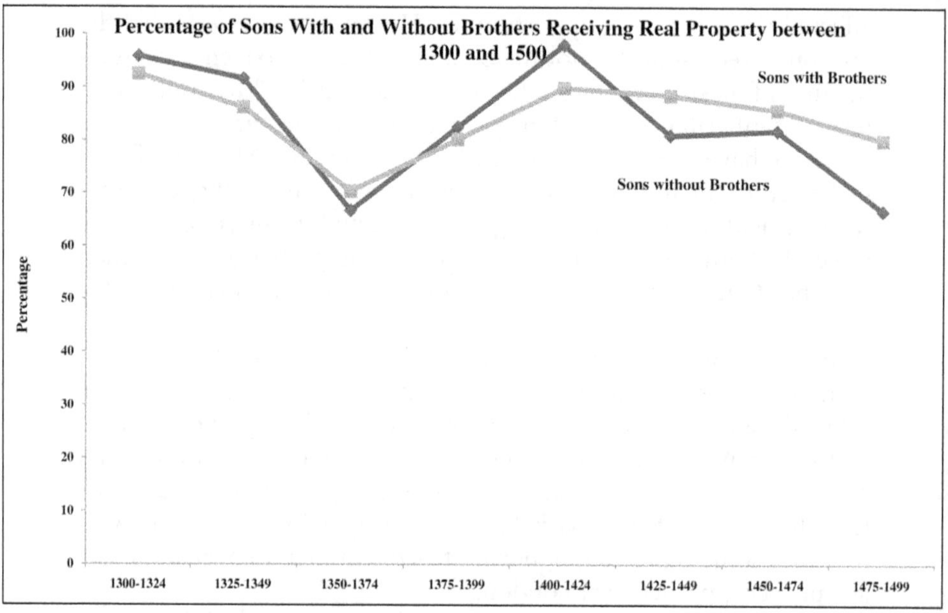

Figure 3.11

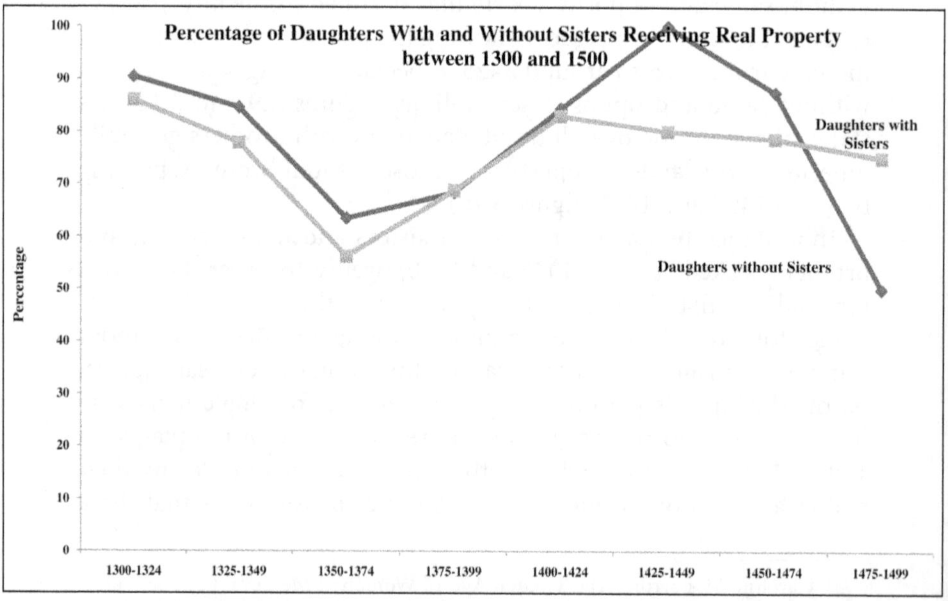

Figure 3.12

may have been more instances of single children inheriting because they had no siblings, as the plague may have reduced the number of heirs that were more typical in pre-plague families.

Conclusions

Natural disasters like the Black Death and the recurrences of the plague negatively affected daughters' inheritance, but so too did they adversely affect that of sons, as many faced the sudden countenance of death. The Husting wills reveal Londoners who adapted by spreading their legacies more thinly. Throughout the entire period from 1300 to 1500, there is consistency in that daughters inherited property along with their brothers, and indeed, in a number of instances, benefited if they had brothers. Through periods of natural disaster, daughters remained viable heirs to real property.

The evidence in the Husting wills also shows a distinct urban aspect of inheritance among the elite of London. The situation among daughters in London runs contrary to the situation in rural areas in which the patrimony was left to the first son, and daughters, if they received landed property, received it with their dowries. In the Husting wills, of all the real property bequeathed, 20 percent of it descended to daughters. In comparison, in a study of English aristocratic women from 1450–1550, Barbara Harris found that of the estates of noblemen, only 12 percent were left to women and 7 percent of the estates of knights who sat in Parliament.[93] London daughters benefited from the custom of burgage tenure in London and from the lack of the custom of primogeniture followed elsewhere in the country.

As many scholars have warned, wills have their limitations as historical sources. Wills can potentially skew research because they often privilege one social stratum, they place intention before action, they are silent on all other gifts or grants outside of this time-specific event, and they were contested by individuals who appear as well as those who are hidden from view. Yet, while wills may not tell the entire story, a detailed examination of testators' wishes over an expanse of time can reveal useful information about daughters' lives. While daughters' voices are absent from these sources directly, it is possible indirectly to reconstruct the world they lived and operated within.

---

[93] Harris, *English Aristocratic Women*, 22.

Daughters inheriting substantial amounts of real property were not rare in late medieval London. Londoners were eager to provide for their daughters with real property—domestic, commercial, and rental property—and indeed viewed them as viable heirs. Parents desired to see to the futures of their daughters with marriage portions and joint fee tails. The image thus emerges of women in late medieval London, equipped, upon the death of their parents, with opportunities to own land, rent properties, and pursue a trade; they appear as potentially active economic agents in a world that often consigned them to passive roles.

CHAPTER FOUR

ENVISIONING DAUGHTERS' LIVES THROUGH MOVABLE LEGACIES

Houses, shops, tenements, and other types of real estate are important in understanding the shape of the world in which medieval daughters lived and worked. Yet, inheritance of real estate only presents part of the picture. A portion of daughters in the Husting wills inherited no real estate, and a portion inherited both real estate and movable wealth. It is necessary to explore movable legacies to entertain all of the possible opportunities presented for these women. As with real estate, in the wills we find that parents provided equally for the futures of their daughters and sons with bequests of money and annuities. This support is important in understanding the variety of opportunities with which daughters were presented.

Real estate gives us a very physical construct, an idea of the material shape of the world for London daughters. To complement this image, testators' cherished belongings help transform those spaces into homes—real inhabited spaces that speak of daughters' potential experiences. The descriptions of daughters' possessions, some of which were detailed in the wills of their parents, were imbued with practical, sentimental, social, and cultural meaning. These precious possessions and their descriptions reveal the values of daughters in late medieval London and the function and meanings of the domestic and commercial spaces in which they operated. These goods and chattels give depth and dimension to daughters' houses and workshops, allowing us to better understand their lived experiences.

A qualitative and quantitative examination of the movable legacies included in the Husting wills reveals that there was a gendered division of space within which these daughters lived and worked. The goods bequeathed to daughters allowed for a substantial amount of flexibility in their lives, which would have been required as most of these women married and pursued occupations supplementary to that of their husbands. Yet, this gendered division of space within the home suggests that the domestic space as a whole was not only a feminine space.

Tracing trends in bequests of movable goods is a thorny matter, because in late medieval London custom held that upon a testator's death, his goods were to be divided among his wife and children. There was no limit to how often a citizen of London could make and alter his will. However, in regard to his personal estate, that is, his property that was movable, he was required to follow the custom of the city and leave one third to his wife, known as the *legitim*,[1] and a third to his children. The last third was to be reserved for "the dead, to be distributed for his almes [*sic*]."[2] The widow's *legitim*, unlike her dower, was hers absolutely.[3] This custom was possibly established as early as 1100, and was widespread and not particular to London.[4] Glanvill, a twelfth-century legal treatise, sets this custom of thirds into writing, specifying that the general custom across the realm was that the testator was permitted to distribute one third of his movable wealth as he chose, with the remaining two-thirds reserved for his wife and heirs.[5] If the testator had no children, then he was to leave one half of his personal estate to his wife, with the other half at his disposal.[6]

---

[1] *Legitim* was abolished around the year 1700 in London. Erickson, "Coverture and Capitalism," 4. Pollock and Maitland explain that by the seventeenth century in the south of England, *legitim*, or "legitimate part," was denied to wives and children, allowing testators to dispose of their goods freely. Pollock and Maitland, *History of English Law before the Time of Edward I* (Cambridge: Cambridge University Press, 1924), 2:349–56; Michael M. Sheehan, *The Will in Medieval England: From the Conversion of the Anglo-Saxons to the End of the Thirteenth Century*, vol. 6 (Toronto: Pontifical Institution of Mediaeval Studies, 1963), 289–93; Albert Kiralfy, "Wills of Personality (Movables) in England from 1066–1500 A.D.," in *Actes à cause de mort* (Bruxelles: De Boeck Université, 1993), 35–45. Kiralfy explains that *legitim* is similar to the "dead part" in Continental law.

[2] Henry Calthrop, *Reports of Speciall Cases Touching Severall Customs and Liberties of the City of London* (London: Printed for Abel Roper, 1655), 161. See also Sheehan's discussion in *The Will in Medieval England*, 289–90; and Barbara Hanawalt, *Growing up in Medieval London: The Experience of Childhood in History* (New York: Oxford University Press, 1993), 91.

[3] Caroline M. Barron, "Introduction: The Widow's World," in *Medieval London Widows 1300–1500*, ed. Caroline M. Barron and Anne F. Sutton, (London: Hambledon Press, 1994), xvii–xxi.

[4] Sheehan suggests that this custom—one third of a testator's chattels was his own to bequeath as he liked—was established as early as the eleventh century, as he finds evidence of it in the late eleventh-century charter of St. Werburgh's Abbey in Chester, as well as in some other eleventh- and twelfth-century charters around England. Sheehan, *The Will in Medieval England*, 290–91.

[5] Glanvill, *A Treatise on the Laws and Customs of the Kingdom of England*, ed. G. D. G. Hall (London: Thomas Nelson Ltd., 1965), 80.

[6] Sharpe, *Calendar of Wills*, I:xxxiii. Glanvill notes that if the testator dies without leaving a wife, then half of his movable goods are at his disposal, rather than a third. Glanvill, *Treatise*, 80. On the other hand, the compilers of *De Legibus et Con-*

This means that the Husting wills may only reveal part of the full picture as testators could have relied on this custom of thirds to have been followed by their executors without having to specify details in their wills. It is also feasible that goods were distributed to family and friends before death, and it is likely that certain goods did not make it into a will. Not every possession would have been noted in a testator's will. For example, a testator might note a movable legacy that held personal or material value, such as a robe or book, and might not mention daily table ware. As a result, in the Husting wills there were far fewer bequests of movable property, especially goods, made to children than real estate (see figure 4.1). This makes a direct comparison between inheritances of real estate and those of movable property unfruitful. Furthermore, in about five hundred wills, testators simply state that their goods should be divided among their wife and children per the city custom. Hence, this custom of thirds does appear to have been followed by Londoners.[7] Reginald Sharpe himself noted that where there is detail in the wills, "it will be found that the widow's and children's portions usually follow near as possible the division of a deceased person's personal estate at common law."[8]

Even so, many of the wills enrolled with the Husting Court do carefully detail bequests of movable goods—there is detail included in over three thousand instances. That is, within the 3,081 wills enrolled in the Husting Court between 1300 and 1500, testators mentioned bequests involving movable property in detail over three

---

suetudinibus Angliae, commonly attributed to Henry of Bracton, a thirteenth-century judge, substitute the word *children* for *wife* so that if the testator has no children, then half should remain to the testator and half to his wife: "Si autem liberos non habuerit, tunc medietas defuncto et alia medietas uxori reservetur." Bracton, *De Legibus et Consuetudinibus Angliae*, ed. George Woodbine (New Haven: Yale University Press, 1915–1942), 2:180, accessed August 22, 2005, http://hlsl.law.harvard.edu/bracton/Unframed/English/v2/180.htm. This text also states that in London in particular, if a widow is given her dower, she cannot claim anything else unless her husband, the testator, agrees. The children must also not take any more than what is left to them, unless again the testator agrees. Bracton, *De Legibus*, 2:180–81, accessed September 20, 2005, http://hlsl.law.harvard.edu/bracton/Unframed/English/v2/181.htm.

[7] Sylvia L. Thrupp, *The Merchant Class of Medieval London* (Ann Arbor: University of Michigan Press, 1948), 177; Hanawalt, *Growing Up*, 91. Since it was a custom that applied to freemen, however, widows and married women writing wills were not hindered by this custom and could bequeath their chattels as they wished. Sheehan, *The Will in Medieval England*, 263.

[8] Sharpe, *Calendar of Wills*, I:xxxiv.

thousand times. It appears that even though the custom existed, many testators still felt it necessary to record their particular wishes for their personal items. It is clear that movable goods—chattels and money predominantly—were important to medieval Londoners, a point made by other scholars working with wills more broadly in England. Elsewhere in England, the distinction between movable and immovable property was quite clear by the thirteenth century, and testators were careful to note their concerns for their movable goods, including women and serfs, where they could.[9] Hence, the detail concerning movable property in the Husting wills remains valuable not only for what it can disclose about the lives of the testators and the 8,411 recipients of movable property, but especially for what it can disclose about the lives of daughters in late medieval London. Furthermore, this detail is important in that it reveals the flexible nature of living spaces for daughters and their brothers and the sense of how movable wealth operated in the consciousness of late medieval Londoners.

Money and Annuities

The testators of the 3,081 wills enrolled between 1300 and 1500 bequeathed movable property 3,378 times. This category was broad and included money, annuities, and otherwise unspecified bequests, along with goods. Within this extensive category of movable property, there was an almost equal distribution of these property types among daughters and sons. Daughters received some amount of movable property 604 times, and sons 605 times, if I count each bequest of movable property as one instance. Of all the instances in which movable property was bequeathed in these wills, 18% went to daughters and 18% to sons. Almost one half of all movable property (47%) bequeathed in the wills was left to members of the immediate family.

Of this movable property, a sum of money was a common bequest to children. Monetary bequests ranged from 10s. given equally to a

[9] Sheehan, *The Will in Medieval England*, 257, 287, 305. By comparison, in medieval Genoa, Stephen Epstein explains that despite the existence of *donation inter vivos* and the frequent exclusion of women as principle heirs, testators did frequently provide for relatives with money and goods in their wills. He examines such types of bequests to explore the differences in will making among men and women. Epstein, *Wills and Wealth in Medieval Genoa*, 13–14, 120–21.

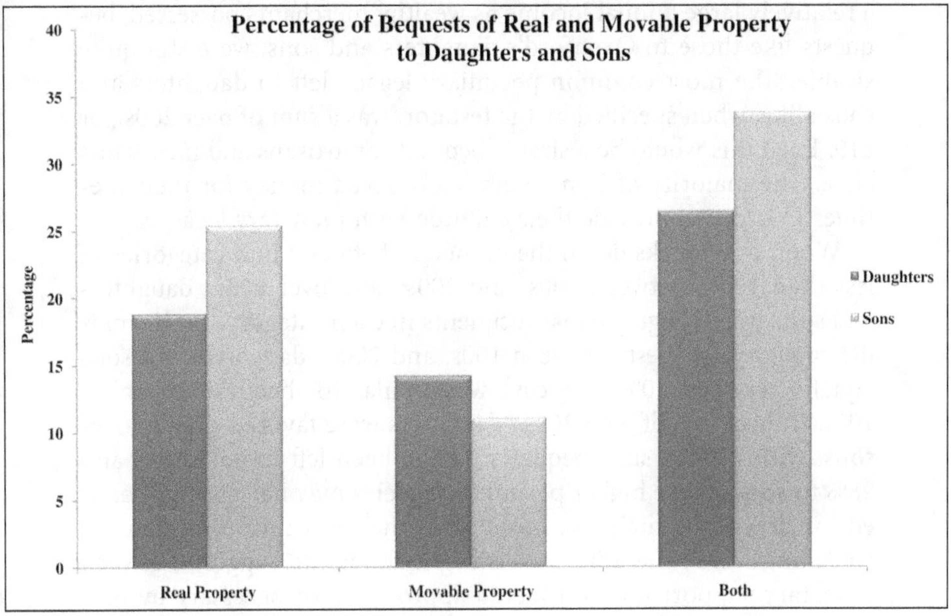

Figure 4.1

son and daughter in 1329 by Walter de Bedefonte, to the 2,000s.—or about £100—John de Oxenford, a vinter, gave to his three daughters and three sons each in 1342.[10] To place these figures in perspective, in the late Middle Ages some well-to-do merchants, perhaps like John de Oxenford, made over £100 per year. For example, a Winchester vinter combined profits from his trade and the rents he controlled to amass over £126 per year.[11] However, most merchants likely had an annual income of less than £10,[12] while the average worker earned a much smaller wage. For example, a mason, Robert Steynforth, was paid in the late fifteenth century £7 5s. 0d. for his work, 290 days worth, on a manor house in Leicestershire, and much further down the social scale, a broiderer working in London for a vestment-maker earned 20s. per annum, plus board.[13] Even with such

[10] Sharpe, *Calendar of Wills*, I:352 and 1:460; CLRO, HR 57(133) and 69(93).

[11] Dyer, *Standards of Living in the Later Middle Ages: Social Change in England c. 1200–1520* (New York: Cambridge University Press, 1989), 194.

[12] Dyer, *Standards of Living*, 194.

[13] Dyer, *Standards of Living*, 227; Thrupp, *The Merchant Class of Medieval London*, 115.

a relatively large annual income as wealthy merchants possessed, bequests like those to Oxenford's daughters and sons, were still quite sizable. The most common pecuniary legacy left to daughters and sons alike, when specified by the testator, was a sum of over 200s., or £10. Even this would be a sizable bequest for artisans and merchants alike. The majority of Londoners likely saved money for their lifetimes in order to provide their children with monetary legacies.

When one breaks down the monetary bequests into categories of less than 100s., between 100s. and 200s., and over 200s., daughters and sons were roughly equal recipients in each category. In the middle category, bequests between 100s. and 200s., daughters and sons equally received 30%. The case was similar for bequests of under 100s. In bequests of over 200s., daughters were favored slightly over sons, with 33% of such bequests having been left to daughters and 28% to sons. These higher pecuniary legacies may have been intended for dowries, which was more often than not unspecified in the wills, but overall the difference is slight enough to suggest that such monetary support was considered appropriate or necessary by parents for their children of both genders.

In some of the Husting wills, children received sums of money with conditions attached, such as for a dowry (*ad maritagium*) or for an apprenticeship fee. Parents, at times, were very particular about how the monetary bequest was to be used. In 1361, for instance, Margery received £200 from her father John Malewayn provided she marry with his executors' consent and specifically *not* marry a mercer named John Dovy. If she acted against her father's wishes, she would lose the £200.[14] Similarly, the daughters of William de Tonge in 1389 received 100 marks for their marriages, but only if they married well. If they did not use good judgment in choosing a marriage partner, the sum was reduced to 100s. Their brothers received 100 marks apiece with no similar condition attached.[15] More often, when money for a dowry was indicated, the testator simply stated that the sum was to be used for marriage without any further conditions.

It was more common for sons to receive money for apprenticeships than daughters (sixteen sons received money for apprenticeships, three daughters, and one unborn child), but daughters do appear as recipients of such funds. In 1347, Alice received 100s. for

---

[14] Sharpe, *Calendar of Wills*, II:38; CLRO, HR 89(144).
[15] Sharpe, *Calendar of Wills*, II:278; CLRO, HR 199(15).

her apprenticeship along with some commercial goods from her father John de Oxon, a man called "Spicer" in the will.[16] In a rare instance, Robert de Rameseye allowed his daughter Elizabeth to choose to use his monetary gift for marriage or for an apprenticeship.[17]

Besides the more common conditions testators placed on bequests for support of marriage and apprenticeship were other, less frequent conditions pertaining to their children's future professions. Two testators left money to a son and godson to cover the expense of schooling,[18] while five daughters were bequeathed money for their profession into nunneries. In 1349, John Syward, a "stokfisshmongere," left £40 to his daughter Dionisia for either her marriage or her advancement into religious life, whatever her choice, within one year after his decease.[19] Likewise, William Wyght, also a "stokfisshmonger," bequeathed £50 to each of his four daughters, Agnes, Margaret, Beatrix, and Alice, for their marriages or entrances into a religious house.[20]

Eileen Power comments on the "dower-like nature" of bequests like these to girls for entrance into religious houses. She cites three examples of girls from outside of London, namely Warwick, Lincoln, and Brompton, who were provided with legacies for their profession into nunneries, like the daughters of Syward and Wyght. However, none of these bequests were from parents providing for their children; instead they were from more distant relatives or perhaps were from unrelated persons. Two of the bequests were made by clerics, one to a niece and another to girl whose relation is not specified, and the third bequest was made by the Countess of Warwick, again to a girl of unknown relation.[21] In her book, *Wayward Nuns in Medieval Literature*, Graciela S. Daichman asserts that wills like those of Syward and Wyght are evidence of a broader trend among parents of coercing their daughters into convent life through their wills.[22] Rather than evidencing coercion, I would argue that these two instances

[16] Sharpe, *Calendar of Wills*, I:498; CLRO, HR 74(134).

[17] Sharpe, *Calendar of Wills*, II:157; CLRO, HR 102(11).

[18] Sharpe, *Calendar of Wills*, II:322; CLRO, HR 125(41); Sharpe, *Calendar of Wills*, I:403; CLRO, HR 63(43).

[19] Sharpe, *Calendar of Wills*, I:588; CLRO, HR 77(54).

[20] Sharpe, *Calendar of Wills*, II:299; CLRO, HR 121(200).

[21] Power, *Medieval English Nunneries* (Cambridge: Cambridge University Press, 1922).

[22] Graciela S. Daichman, *Wayward Nuns in Medieval Literature* (New York: Syracuse University Press, 1986), xiii, 14.

of such provision for daughters out of 3,081 wills enrolled in the Husting Court between 1300 and 1500 instead indicate a desire among parents to provide for the futures of their daughters, with Syward even leaving the choice up to Dionisia herself. This desire for provision fits into the broader trend among parents to grant pecuniary legacies for the general needs of their children, whether it was for vocation or for sustenance, in general.

Another less frequent provision, sometimes in the form of a direct bequest and other times in the form of a condition placed on a monetary legacy, was for the clothing of children. In two separate instances, a daughter and son were left money from their fathers specifically for clothing. Around 1308, Henry le Hodere bequeathed money for clothing to his daughter Mabel. Over a century later in 1483, John Stok, a skinner, left his son Thomas money to be given to him "percelmele," or piecemeal, to clothe himself.[23] While this provision appears only on rare occasions in the wills, it speaks to the desire of parents to provide for their children in their wills, even if in the most basic sense of protection from the elements. All of the conditions in the wills suggest a desire among parents to reach beyond the grave to influence their daughters' choices later in life, but simultaneously, they also suggest a concern to support their daughters in their lives beyond the natal family home.

Annuities, or annual payments of a sum of money, were less common than monetary bequests, with only seventy-three instances among the 8,411 recipients of the 3,081 wills. The average annuity, when specified by the testator, was 59s., with daughters more frequently having received annuities than their brothers (thirteen instances of daughters receiving annuities to seven instances of sons), and among these daughters, 38 percent were nuns. Annuities, then, were the less popular choice of support for daughters, possibly because of their ultimate expense as compared with a one-time pecuniary bequest. Yet, annuities were a way to provide a stable income, especially for someone who had chosen a life within convent walls.

[23] Sharpe, *Calendar of Wills*, I:201; CLRO, HR 37(31); Sharpe, *Calendar of Wills*, II:587; CLRO, HR 214(34).

The Legacies of Movable Goods

The movable goods situated within the real properties bequeathed in the wills were as diverse and sundry as those who bequeathed them. They range from goods one might expect to be present in a last will, such as bowls and featherbeds, to the unexpected, including grain still growing in the field.[24] Besides demonstrating the individuality of testators, these goods are also indicators of the relatively high social status of these London artisans and merchants, as compared with other Londoners. The goods included dishware that was often silver, silver gilt, or silver plated, and these pieces often served as elaborate decorations for various rooms within the house. Furthermore, goods that were specially designated, such as a cup marked with the testator's sign[25] or goods of certain foreign craftsmanship,[26] and thus expensive, served to communicate the social status of the testator to the recipient. Yet, these wills reveal more than the wealth and status of the testators: they also allow one to envision the medieval domestic space in which daughters lived and worked; they illuminate the meanings of these goods to recipients, specifically to daughters and sons; and they reveal the function of this space in late medieval London.

We can examine goods as part of the movable property bequeathed in the wills in even more detail than other types of movable bequests. To make the variety of goods bequeathed in the wills more manageable for analysis, I have grouped the goods into multiple main categories. These categories include: armor, bedding, books, chamber (goods found within the bedchamber[27]), clothing, commercial goods, cookware, dishware, other domestic goods, grain, jewelry, livestock, religious goods, sailing vessels, timber, and unspecified goods.

As stated above, movable property was bequeathed in 3,378 instances in the Husting wills. Of this movable property, goods were bequeathed 2,533 times in the 3,081 wills. It was more viable to record the 2,533 instances of the giving of goods, rather than the precise amount of goods given, because the precise quantity is often unknowable from these sources. It also was more effective to analyze

---

[24] Sharpe, *Calendar of Wills*, I:479; CLRO, HR 72(75).

[25] CLRO, HR 74(174).

[26] Such as goods made in Dynaunt, Reims, and Tours. CLRO, HR 33(108) and 72(75).

[27] See further discussion of the term "chamber" below.

such bequests in categories rather than counting individual items. For example, around the year 1312, Agnes received bedding, cookware, dishware, and jewelry from her father Richard de Welleford. Rather than record each of the twelve spoons she received, the spoons along with the cup comprise one event of the giving of movable goods, specifically dishware.[28] All together, although Agnes inherited a gold brooch, a pot, a pot for cooking specifically, a bowl, a featherbed, twelve silver spoons, and a mazer cup, she was the recipient of four giving events: bedding, cookware, dishware, and jewelry. Heirs received any combination of goods (there were 157 combinations among the 8,411 recipients), and each category was counted once per recipient.

I analyzed these bequests of goods and chattels using both Reginald Sharpe's abstracts and the original wills themselves. At times, the abstracts left out detail about individual goods bequeathed, as Sharpe was not always interested to note each domestic good bequeathed, so I examined the original wills to obtain that detail. In 447 instances, the clerk simply noted a testator's wish for the "residue of all my goods and chattels" to be divided among his heirs. In these cases, the goods were noted as "unspecified." Table 4.1 illustrates the frequency with which each category of goods was bequeathed. Dishware was the most popular item for testators to leave in their legacies, with 456 instances. The categories of unspecified goods, other domestic goods (that is, household goods that do not fit into the other categories of dishware, bedding, or cookware), and clothing round out the top four, all bequeathed over 300 times.

Table 4.1. Frequency of Types of Goods Bequeathed

Dishware	456	Chamber	75
Unspecified Goods	447	Livestock	65
Domestic Goods	392	Armor	50
Clothing	355	Books	41
Bedding	248	Grain	41
Jewelry	117	Sailing Vessels	23
Commercial Goods	113	Religious Goods	4
Cookware	105	Timber	1

All the goods bequeathed that could have been intended to outfit a house (including bedding, chamber, cookware, dishware, and domes-

[28] CLRO, HR 41(63).

tic goods) comprised half of the total bequests of goods, making these items the most popular type of goods to leave to one's heirs. Dishware and cookware combined were bequeathed 561 times, domestic goods 392 times, and bedding 248 times. Goods intended for personal array, such as armor, clothing, and jewelry, were the second most frequent type of goods in these legacies, bequeathed 522 times. Commercial goods, bequeathed 113 times, were not as common as one might expect to find in medieval wills. This could be due to an assumption of the testator that the heir of a workshop or an apprentice might inherit the tools of that workshop and trade, making it unnecessary to mention them in detail as bequests.

Overall, sons collected goods in slightly more instances than their sisters. Sons barely edged out daughters receiving movable goods 497 times to daughters' 487 times. Daughters received proportionally more dishware, domestic goods, bedding, and cookware, while sons received more commercial goods, as is visible in figure 4.2. These numbers, while indicating a difference, are close and it could be argued that there is only a slight gender differentiation in the distribution of goods among children. If one considers all household goods bequeathed to daughters and sons, including dishware, bedding, cookware, chamber, and other domestic items, there was a difference of eight percentage points between the percentage of all instances of such household goods bequeathed to daughters and sons. That is, of 1,529 daughters, there were 340 instances in which household goods were given to daughters (22 percent), and of 1,854 sons, there were 251 instances in which household goods were given to sons (14 percent). Daughters received more household goods, yet the wills show that sons were by no means passed over as recipients of these goods.

Beyond daughters and sons, beneficiaries of movable goods ran as much of a gamut as the goods themselves. Testators named individuals within their immediate and extended families, as well as those outside of familial bonds. Illegitimate children were considered along with legitimate ones, godchildren with natal children, nieces with nephews, sisters with brothers, servants with apprentices. However, when one considers which types of goods were bequeathed to whom, a division becomes clear. Household goods often went to members of the nuclear family, while goods beyond the kitchen and immediate living quarters, such as books and clothing, were often left to nonrelatives. The appearance of these nonrelated recipients, which in-

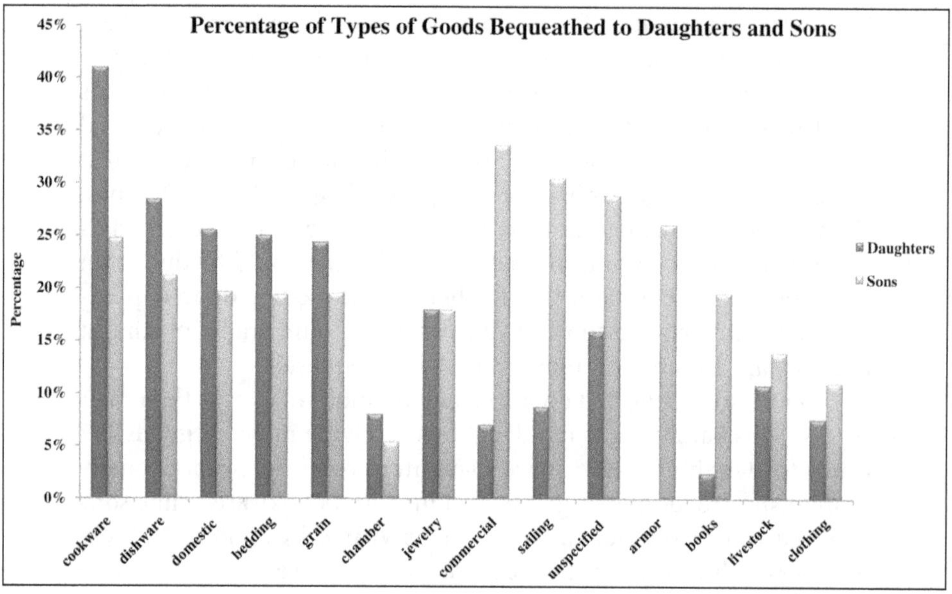

Figure 4.2

cluded apprentices, servants, and individuals whose relationship to the testator is unknown, is not surprising, as they would have been more likely included in bequests of movable goods rather than real estate. Such bequests of goods may have served to recognize service, loyalty, and other personal bonds.

Among children, household goods were a popular legacy. Daughters and sons most frequently received goods to outfit their homes. Together they received 66% of all cookware bequeathed in the wills, 49% of all dishware, 46% of all other domestic goods, and 45% of all bedding. As with monetary bequests, gender seems to have made little or only a small difference in the bequests of these goods. Indeed, in 143 instances of the 3,081 wills, testators mentioned children or heirs but did not specify sex. In fifty-five instances, the testator left bequests to unborn children, sometimes described as "infante in utero."[29] These individuals, whose sex was unknown, received household goods including bedding, cookware, dishware, and domestic

---

[29] CLRO, HR 91(159). Sharpe translates the phrase in his volumes as "en ventre sa mère," *Calendar of Wills*, II:81. In another will, the testator left property to his unborn child if his wife was pregnant, "si contingat quod praedicta Isabella sit pregnans et peperit filium vel filiam ..." CLRO, HR 97(103).

goods, all in very small amounts. Six unborn children received a share in goods and chattels. For example, Geoffrey de Chelchehethe, a tanner, left to his unborn child a share in household and commercial goods with his brothers and sister, and Thomas Atte Vyne, a woolmonger, left his unborn child a share of cups and pots, along with money, with his other four sons.[30]

The largest category of goods that was bequeathed to wives was the chamber. Of all chambers bequeathed in the wills, 83% were left to wives. This is an expected finding, as it was city custom for husbands in late medieval London to leave their wives their "chambers." Legacies of chambers were sometimes physical spaces and other times, as it seems in most of these wills, the goods within a given physical space. Henry Calthrop, a seventeenth-century lawyer and Recorder of London, noted that a "widow's chamber" consisted of the hall (main open room in the house[31]), main chamber, and cellar of the tenement that she shared with her husband, as well as the use of oven, stable, privy, and yard;[32] at the least, a widow would receive her chamber as dower.[33] Sara Rees Jones explains that by the late Middle Ages in English towns, this type of complex was common: in a large timber-framed house, one could expect to find a hall with several smaller rooms, like a chamber or parlor, with the addition of a kitchen or yard.[34]

Chamber could also mean the goods therein, rather than the physical space itself. Sharpe notes that "The *widow's chamber* was a name given to the bed-chamber, furniture, and personal apparel, which it was customary in the City of London to set aside for the widow before proceeding to distribute the effects of one who had died intestate."[35] Ann Kettle notes that the widow's "chamber" in London

---

[30] Sharpe, *Calendar of Wills*, 1: 249, 552-3.

[31] Jane Grenville, *Medieval Housing* (London: Leicester University Press, 1997), 192; Schofield, "Urban Housing in England, 1400–1600," in *The Age of Transition: The Archaeology of English Culture 1400–1600*, ed. David Gaimster and Paul Stamper (Oxford: Oxbow Books, 1997), 135.

[32] Calthrop, *Reports*, 165.

[33] Hanawalt, "The Widow's Mite," in *Upon My Husband's Death: Widows in the Literature and Histories of Medieval Europe*, ed. Louise Mirrer (Ann Arbor: University of Michigan Press, 1992), 24.

[34] Sarah Rees Jones, "Building Domesticity in the City," in *Medieval Domesticity: Home, Housing and Household in Medieval England*, ed. Maryanne Kowaleski and Jeremy Goldberg (Cambridge: Cambridge University Press, 2008), 69–71.

[35] Sharpe, *Calendar of Wills*, I:174, n. 1.

was the equivalent to the common law paraphernalia, which literally meant "the clothes on her back and the ornaments of her body."[36] Instead of bequeathing a bedchamber within a house, it is likely that many of these testators bequeathed the goods within that chamber, as one definition of *chamber* in the Oxford English Dictionary notes, "the hangings or furniture of a chamber." [37] Janet Loengard, who has studied women and the law in great depth, explains that husbands often went well beyond the legal definition of paraphernalia and left their wives all of their clothing and bedroom furnishings.[38] In his work on the laws of England over a century ago, Henry Stevens also explains that the widow's chamber meant the widow's apparel and bedroom furniture.[39]

In the Husting wills, both definitions seem to operate. For example, in a will from 1428, it is clear that Richard Gosselyn left his children a physical space: "a large painted chamber with panelled ceiling (*cum tabula cilurata*), and a small chamber called 'Porteres chambre.'"[40] However, in other wills, "chamber" as a physical space is less clear and likely is a formulaic term that came to mean the goods within rather than the room itself. For example, in the early fourteenth century, Juliana Russel left her daughter Juliana "her entire chamber of Doningtone," which was likely her widow's chamber in the sense of goods within that room, as otherwise it would be one room in a manor outside of London. Likewise, Alan de Suffolk, a potter, left Agnes his wife "her entire chamber with six silver spoons."[41] In 1375, William de Bury left his wife Johanna her entire chamber and hall with bedding, dishware, and other household goods.[42] Indeed, in most of the other wills, "chamber" appears accompanied by

---

[36] Ann J. Kettle, "My Wife Shall Have It: Marriage and Property in the Wills and Testaments of Later Mediaeval England," in *Marriage and Property*, ed. Elizabeth M. Craik (Aberdeen: Aberdeen University Press, 1984), 91.

[37] *Oxford English Dictionary Online*, s.v. "chamber," accessed 11.01.2010, http://dictionary.oed.com.

[38] Janet Loengard, "'Which May Be Said to Be Her Own': Widows and Goods in Late-Medieval England," in *Medieval Domesticity: Home, Housing and Household in Medieval England*, ed. Maryanne Kowaleski and Jeremy Goldberg (Cambridge: Cambridge University Press, 2008): 162–76.

[39] Henry John Stevens, *New Commentaries on the Laws of England* (London: Butterworths, 1874), 2:212.

[40] Sharpe, *Calendar of Wills*, II:464.

[41] CLRO, HR 36(76): "totam cameram suam cum sex cocleariis argenteis."

[42] CLRO, HR, 103(146): "totam cameram suam cum apparatu suo et totam aulam …"

a list of household goods, items one would find within the bedroom.[43] For this study, then, "chamber" has been considered as the goods found within a bedchamber rather than a part of a piece of real estate.

The other largest categories bequeathed to wives were unspecified, with 47% of all unspecified goods left to wives, and jewelry, with 24% of all jewelry bequeathed to wives. That wives often received goods not specified in the wills is again not surprising, as the husband could have simply followed city custom, which left a third of his goods to his wife, with children present, or a half if they had no children.[44]

Other relatives besides those within the nuclear family appeared in the wills 1,256 times. These individuals include sisters (243), brothers (252), nieces (99), nephews (143), and a larger group including mothers, fathers, grandchildren, cousins, and individuals with the same surname as the testator (519). Again, the norm among these extended family members was to receive predominantly household goods: fifty-five of the 519, or 11%, of these other relatives received dishware; fifty of them, or 10%, received other domestic goods; and thirty-seven, or 7%, received bedding. The exception to this observed rule of bequeathing household goods to immediate and extended family members was in the category of clothing. In all, 7% of the extended relatives received clothing, compared with 2% of sons and of daughters and only 1% of wives. Clothing was most often left to sisters (7% of all sisters), brothers (12% of all brothers), and the larger category of other relatives (6% of all other relatives). According to these patterns in bequests of goods, clothing appears to have been considered an appropriate legacy for those outside the immediate family. The wills indicate that the expenses to clothe children were taken care of outside of the testament, either by the real estate they received or from their guardians as part of that role.

As one might expect, beneficiaries outside the family circle fared well in bequests of movable goods. These individuals were more likely to receive goods as bequests rather than real estate, which was pri-

[43] For more examples, see Sharpe, *Calendar of Wills*, I:194: "her entire chamber with linen and woollen cloths"; Sharpe, *Calendar of Wills*, I:266: "her entire chamber with jewels, cloths woolen and linen, beds, vessels, and all utensils appertaining to his house"; Sharpe, *Calendar of Wills*, II:181: "her entire chamber with jewels, apparel, etc."; and Sharpe, *Calendar of Wills*, II:590: "the best chamber, with all its hangings, bed, feather bolster."

[44] See Sharpe, *Calendar of Wills*, I:xxxiii; Calthrop, *Reports*, 161; Glanvill, *Treatise*, 80; and Bracton, *De Legibus*, 2:180.

marily left to family members. In total, 2,016 nonrelatives, including individuals whose relation to the testator was not mentioned, as well as servants and apprentices, received a large percentage of the goods that were not domestic in nature. These beneficiaries received 56% of all armor bequeathed in the wills, 54% of all books, 50% of all clothing, 49% of all livestock, and 44% of all commercial goods. It is not surprising that so many commercial goods were left to apprentices and perhaps to unrelated business partners. Indeed, 2% of all nonrelatives received commercial goods as compared with 2% of all sons, and 1% of all wives (only 0.5% of all daughters received commercial goods). Clothing, it appears, was also seen as a fitting bequest for nonrelatives as it was for other relatives, perhaps even more so (7% of all other relatives received clothing compared with 9% of all nonrelatives). Extended family members, then, appear to have been seen as a bridge between bequests of household and nonhousehold goods, while individuals outside the bounds of family were almost exclusively bequeathed goods for the workshop, body, entertainment, edification, or farm field.[45]

The Meanings of Goods

As people do today, daughters in late medieval London likely identified with the domestic and commercial goods that they received from their parents.[46] These goods were often a part of their lives while growing up, and many such goods became intertwined with their

[45] Nonrelatives are most likely underrepresented in this analysis, more so than others, as this database is based primarily on Sharpe's 14 abstracts, which were often inconsistent in recording individuals not related to the testator. A more complete analysis of goods received by beneficiaries unrelated to the testator would need to rely on the original 3,081 wills detailed in the microfilm collection. Although the database is to a certain extent deficient in this information, there is enough there to indicate patterns in bequests of movable goods to individuals outside the family.

[46] In studying modern Kodi, from the western tip of the Eastern Indonesian island of Sumba, Janet Hoskins found that she "could not collect the histories of objects and the life histories of persons separately. People and the things they valued were so complexly intertwined they could not be disentangled." She argues that for the Kodi, goods gave a sense of self to the possessor and were used as a way to identify people personally and sexually. Hoskins, *Biographical Objects: How Things Tell the Stories of People's Lives* (New York: Routledge, 1998), 2–4. Although such self-identification with objects can be difficult to pin down, especially in past societies, objects in the Middle Ages could have worked biographically or autobiographically as they do for the modern Kodi.

personalities and livelihoods as they grew older and as a result, carried social and cultural meaning.[47] Through goods, we can glean a better sense of what was important and of value to daughters, what their world around them looked like, and how they understood that world.

In detailing his wishes, the testator often meticulously described the goods he or she was bequeathing to his or her children, relatives, and friends. These descriptions commonly included the material, such as brass—for example, *patellam euneam*—or silk; the size; the quality—for example, the "first," "second," or "third" best; and the trappings of the item, like covers and stands. In addition, testators specified the appellation of an item, such as a cup called "le Horn,"[48] and they occasionally gave a locational description, like "the large caldron which used to sit in the furnace in my house," "my bronze pot at London," or the "Cornercheste."[49] On rare occasions testators specified the value of the goods bequeathed. In 1342, vinter John de Oxenford left twelve silver spoons each to his three sons and three daughters, but those left to his sons were worth 18s. whereas those to his daughters were worth 26s.[50]

[47] This argument is also made for the Low Countries by Martha Howell, see "The Social Life of Pots, Beds and Dresses in Late Medieval Cities" (paper, Center for Medieval Studies, University of Minnesota, Minneapolis, MN, 9 October 2003). Howell considered a series of wills from Douai in depth in "Fixing Movables: Gifts by Testament in Late Medieval Douai," *Past and Present* 150 (1996): 3–45. In this article, she argues that Douaisiens "fixed" movables; in other words, they stored wealth in objects in order to protect them from the instability of the commodity market. Douaisiens saved these movables, imbued them with social and cultural meaning, and thereby "resist[ed] the implicit logic of the commercial world." Howell, "Fixing Movables," 41. It is worth noting that in the Low Countries unlike in England, movable property, which was placed in the common marriage fund, included real estate. For example, in Ghent, town homes—but not the ground on which they stood—would have been considered movable wealth. See Linda Guzzetti, "Women's Inheritance and Testamentary Practices in Late Fourteenth- and Early Fifteenth-Century Venice and Ghent," in *The Texture of Society: Medieval Women in the Southern Low Countries*, ed. Ellen E. Kittell and Mary A Suydam (New York: Palgrave Macmillan, 2004), 83.

[48] Will of William Burton, 1466; Sharpe, *Calendar of Wills*, II:566; CLRO, HR 196(6).

[49] Will of John de Armenters, about 1306; CLRO, HR 34(65). Will of William Cosyn de Sutton, 1340; CLRO, HR 72(75). Will of Richard Groom, 1377; CLRO, HR 106(80).

[50] CLRO, HR 69(93), The Latin here indicate worth or value: "praeter 18 solidi."

This variety of descriptions indicates that the goods bequeathed in the wills held worth to the testator, both monetary and personal. Indeed, if these goods were valueless, they would likely not have been noted at all. The rhetoric employed to describe these goods permits a consideration of how they were appreciated and the impact of such appreciation on the spaces that the recipients and their goods inhabited. Testators used language that communicated the special meaning these goods held for them as well as language that helped divide their movable wealth. This language also reveals that domestic spaces were flexible and were spaces that encompassed both genders.

When making a will, the testator chose to bequeath goods that were valuable for a variety of reasons. Not least importantly, these goods were valuable because they meant something personally to the testator. Goods that were given names, for example a cup named "le Flota" in a 1340 will,[51] indicate that items often held sentimental value, as appellation suggests a special connection, affection, special value, or uniqueness. Sometimes vessels were attached in the writing of the will to a particular life event. In a will from the fifteenth century, William Burton left to his son John the large silver-gilt basin given to him by the Countess of Arundel for his baptism. This is an item that indicates William's social standing, but by bequeathing it to his son, he passed on an item that held special meaning to both father and son.[52]

Aside from imparting special meaning, many other descriptors employed in these wills served the pragmatic function of dividing a testator's goods. Without specifications such as size and quality, it might not have been easy for the survivors to identify one cup or blanket from another. In a will from the early fourteenth century, Juliana Russel carefully described which set of clothing she intended for each of her daughters: her green robe (which referred to a formal, complete outfit rather than a dress[53]) with three garnitures and a furred mantle she left to her daughter Agnes, her scarlet robe with three garnitures and a furred mantle to daughter Amicia, and a mixed robe with silk-lined mantle to daughter Katherine. Juliana Russel had specific intentions for each robe and each daughter, and perhaps did

[51] CLRO, HR 72(75).

[52] CLRO, HR 196(6). Howell also discussed the variety of meanings that dresses could hold, in her presentation, "The Social Life of Pots, Beds and Dresses."

[53] Françoise Piponnier and Perrine Mane, *Dress in the Middle Ages*, trans. Caroline Beamish (New Haven, CT: Yale University Press, 1997), 167.

not trust the daughters to divide the robes among themselves. Her descriptors of color, quality, and material served the practical purpose of implementing her intentions without dispute.[54] Such detail again could have served also to communicate social status. In her study of wills from the Kent towns of Yalding, Greenwhich, and Gravesend, Elisabeth Ellen Salter noticed that dresses and other clothing items were often described by color and fabric, and occasionally by style, texture, and origin (for example, "London russet gown"). Such origin specification, she notes, communicated the social importance for some individuals of proximity to or connection with the capital.[55]

Some testators had more trust in their children to divide the goods themselves, but still desired to specify which of their goods were to be divided. For example, at the start of the fourteenth century, Richard de Bernes stipulated that his goods were to be "divided equally" by his son John and daughter Isabella, and he further incorporated qualifiers in his list of these goods: six of his best silver spoons, two of his best napkins, two tapestries with two of his best linen sheets.[56] Richard was not concerned with who received what, and he trusted them to sort out the details themselves, yet he was concerned with the practical matter of which and how many of his table and house accoutrements should continue to serve his children as they had him. Around 1308, Juliana, daughter of Geoffrey de Borham, received a variety of domestic chattels upon her father's death but specifically the "best of three" featherbeds.[57] Meanwhile Liecia, daughter of Thomas Scot, received his "less desirable cup of silver."[58]

[54] CLRO, HR 33(108). See also Kristen Burkholder's study of the bequests of clothing and household textiles, in which she includes many details about bequests of clothing, such as fabric, color, and style, and argues that many of the wills enrolled in late medieval London reveal that by and large individuals obeyed the sumptuary legislation of the day. Burkholder, "Threads Bared: Dress and Textiles in English Wills," in *Medieval Clothing and Textiles*, vol. 1, edited by Robin Netherton and Gale R. Owen-Crocker (Woodbridge, Suffolk: Boydell Press, 2005), 133–53.

[55] Elisabeth Ellen Salter, "Some Differences in the Cultural Production of Household Consumption in Three North Kent Communities, c. 1450–1500," in *The Medieval Household in Christian Europe, c. 850–1550: Managing Power, Wealth, and the Body*, ed. Cordelia Beattie, Anna Maslakovic, and Sarah Rees Jones, International Medieval Research, vol. 12 (Turnhout: Brepols, 2003), 404, 406.

[56] CLRO, HR 33(53).

[57] "meliorem de tribus," CLRO, HR 37(10).

[58] "ciphum argenti debiliorem," CLRO, HR 40(94).

The material and make of the goods indicated value. Cups of silver and mazer, or maple wood,[59] indicated monetary worth. Cups and bowls of mazer were more valuable than those of brass and lead, and silver plate was very valuable.[60] Details about jewelry and clothing also indicated value. Bedding was expensive as well; a furnished bed[61] was equivalent to anywhere between the price of a cow or a house, and could cost as much as a year's wages.[62] In addition, noting the fabric of the item and its location helped executors with the distribution of testators' goods. In 1340, William Cosyn of Sutton left all of his goods and chattels in the village of Mikelham to his son Thomas and his bronze pot in London to his son Peter.[63] These wills and others reveal that Londoners were concerned with the practical division of their movable wealth and with the separation of the valuable from the less valuable of their possessions.

---

[59] *Mediae Latinitatis Lexicon Minus* (1976), s.v. "murra"; *Revised Medieval Latin World-List from British and Irish Sources* (1965), s.v. "murra"; and *Middle English Dictionary Online*, "maser," accessed 11.02.2010, http://ets.umdl.umich.edu. R. W. Lightbrown explains that *mazer* "originally meant wood with variegated markings, and particularly maple-wood, the favourite material for mazers ..." although that did not mean only maple wood. Rather, *mazer* could refer to the style of cup rather than to the material. As he further explains, "In England the term mazer, originally descriptive of the type of wood, came to be applied to the vessels made of it: this transformation never occurred in France, where the term remained restricted to the wood." Lightbrown, *Secular Goldsmiths' Work in Medieval France: A History* (London: Society of Antiquaries of London, 1978), 20.

[60] David Hinton, *Gold and Gilt, Pots and Pans: Possessions and People in Medieval Britain* (Oxford: Oxford University Press, 2005), 214. Kristen Burkholder notes both the symbolic and utilitarian value that plate had: it could communicate status because of its worth, and it could serve as a savings plan as it could be melted and used as coin. Burkholder, "Material Culture and Self-Presentation in Late Medieval England" (PhD diss., University of Minnesota, 2001), 66.

[61] In medieval and early modern society, types of beds ranged from a simple wooden bed frame with cords strung to support a mattress to a grander bed raised off the floor with bedposts from which to hang bed hangings. There were also trundle beds that could slide underneath the great bed and that were often used by servants. N. J. G. Pounds, *The Culture of the English People: Iron Age to the Industrial Revolution* (Cambridge: Cambridge University Press, 1994), 145–46.

[62] See Erickson, *Women and Property in Early Modern England*, 65; and Martha Howell, "The Properties of Marriage in Late Medieval Europe: Commercial Wealth and the Creation of Modern Marriage," in *Love, Marriage, and Family Ties in the Later Middle Ages*, ed. Isabel Davis, Miriam Müller, and Sarah Rees Jones (Turnhout: Brepols, 2001), 41–42. Although it retained its importance as a household feature, by the seventeenth century bedding became less expensive and such possessions as a bed and its accoutrements began to reach down the social ranks in society, no longer limited to the elite in city and country. Pounds, *Culture of the English People*, 147.

[63] CLRO, HR 72(75).

Yet movable goods in late medieval London were not thought of only in sentimental or monetary terms. Although they had a recognized market value, these goods also served functional purposes. Clearly, domestic goods or furnishings and cookware, such as featherbeds, blankets, napkins, pots, pans, and basins, served the daily functions of sleeping, eating, cooking, and washing. Julianna, daughter of Richard Groom, received equally along with her two brothers and her mother, a quarter of all her father's "vessels, utensils, and instruments of [his] hall relating and pertaining to chamber, storeroom, or kitchen."[64] Richard Groom was not concerned enough to specify which goods went to whom, but his will suggests he was concerned enough to pass on pragmatic tools which he intended all of his family members to reuse.

While some testators grouped their bequests of domestic goods around one activity performed in the house[65]—as Richard Groom did around cooking and eating, or as Gilbert Koo did in 1369 when he bequeathed a set of bed hangings, blankets, a mattress, and sheets,[66] intended for sleeping—other will makers went beyond noting the inventory of the linen closet to indicate the specific uses of common household items. For example, in addition to a dress, the abovementioned Juliana Russel bequeathed to her daughter Katherine "a large brass caldron for melting wax with a large tripod."[67] This caldron was intended specifically for candle making, important to Katherine socially and economically, though not necessarily in a separate candlemaking shop.

---

[64] CLRO, HR 106(80).

[65] Catherine Richardson notes similar patterns in the wills she examines from Sandwich, between 1460 and 1520 and between 1560 and 1600. She notes: "two types of testamentary practice: the bequeathal of individual valuable objects, and the passing on of parcels of several less valuable items. Testators who pursued the latter course can be further divided into those who gave only objects associated with one type of household routine overall, and those who only gave objects relating to a distinct routine to each individual beneficiary. Such groupings show a marked bias towards particular kinds of activity as their organizing principle, rather than the status (in financial terms) of the items given." Richardson, "Household Objects and Domestic Ties," in *The Medieval Household in Christian Europe, c. 850–1550: Managing Power, Wealth, and the Body*, ed. Cordelia Beattie, Anna Maslakovic, and Sarah Rees Jones, International Medieval Research, vol. 12 (Turnhout: Brepols, 2003), 439.

[66] CLRO, HR 99(120).

[67] CLRO, HR 33(108).

Often, then, in these wills the line between domestic and commercial becomes blurred. This is especially true in wills in which separate commercial properties, like a shop, are not mentioned. Similar to Katherine Russel, Alice Curtiese received an assortment of goods from her father including: two leaden vessels ("plumba"), a cistern ("cisterna"), and a "taptrogh," which was most likely a trench made of lead equipped with a tap that could be used for brewing.[68] It was probable that Alice brewed or was to use these tools to brew, an activity that could be both domestic and commercial.

In the legacies of goods to sons, the distinction between domestic and commercial goods tended to be sharper. John, the only child of a pepperer, received from his father a variety of dishware and bedding of different materials and value, along with measuring containers, weights, balances, and "all other utensils of my shop … [and] tables and tressels of my house." The language of this will indicates that John's father recognized the separate physical spaces of "shop" and "house," and presumably John would be using these goods in the appropriate and separate physical spaces.

Testators were clearer in their delineations of commercial and domestic goods to their sons than to their daughters because in many cases sons were to carry on the trade of their fathers. These testators, then, also often bequeathed separate physical spaces in which sons could employ these tools. When one considers commercial goods alone, sons received proportionally more than their sisters (see figure 4.2 above). Of all commercial goods bequeathed in the wills, 33 percent went to sons whereas only 7 percent went to daughters. Daughters did inherit distinct commercial spaces, such as breweries, but fewer of them did than sons.

From the Husting wills, it seems then that parents aimed to provide their daughters with tools to supplement household income, rather than tools with specific occupational uses.[69] Scholars have found that women tended to engage in more than one occupation,

---

[68] *Middle English Dictionary Online*, "tappe," accessed 11.01.2010, http://ets.umdl.umich.edu.

[69] P. J. P. Goldberg supports the idea that multiple commercial activities happened in mercantile households, and he proposes that the wife had a "multi-faceted role" in a "multi-enterprise household." Goldberg, "Household and the Organisation of Labour in Late Medieval Towns: Some English Evidence," in *The Household in Late Medieval Cities, Italy and Northwestern Europe Compared*, ed. Myriam Carlier and Tim Soens (Leuven: Garant, 2001), 65, 69–70.

unlike men, which is supported to some extent by the findings in the Husting wills.[70] In terms of the physical organization of urban housing, commercial space was often set apart from domestic space by passages or floors, although still in the same complex.[71] The legacies of goods to daughters, at least in these wills, suggest this flexible use of space. Although the spaces were often separated physically, daughters were bequeathed goods that could be used anywhere as a means to supplement income. In discussing the household economy in late medieval, northern European cities, Martha Howell likewise emphasizes this flexibility, not only in terms of space but also in terms of women's occupations: "The line between market and subsistence production in these households was further blurred because individual family members easily moved back and forth between the two spheres. In the course of a few days a housewife might brew ale and sell her surplus, make clothing for household members, help her husband in his shop, and teach her daughter how to spin fine woolen yarn for merchants."[72]

Goods also held cultural meaning. Jewelry and clothing serve as examples. Clothing and jewelry in the wills seem to work against a hypothesis that one might expect. Jewelry was bequeathed equally to sons and daughters, as one can see in figure 4.2 above, while sons received clothing more frequently than their sisters. In one will mentioned earlier, from the end of the fifteenth century, skinner John Stok bequeathed numerous domestic goods to his two daughters, including cups and spoons, while his son received money for living expenses and clothing to be doled out to him "percelmele," or piecemeal.[73] In an earlier will, shearman William of Madeford bequeathed a simple coat to his daughter, while to his son he left a party or drinking robe of blue and red.[74] These wills, and others like them, reflect a

[70] For example, Maryanne Kowaleski has found that at least 18 percent of the women she studied in medieval Exeter pursued multiple occupations. See Kowaleski, "Women's Work in a Market Town: Exeter in the Late Fourteenth Century," in *Women and Work in Preindustrial Europe*, ed. Barbara Hanawalt (Bloomington: Indiana University Press, 1986), 157.

[71] Schofield, "Urban Housing in England," 140–41.

[72] Martha Howell, *Women, Production, and Patriarchy in Late Medieval Cities* (Chicago: University of Chicago Press, 1986), 10.

[73] Sharpe, *Calendar of Wills*, II:587, n. 2. CLRO, HR 214(34).

[74] Sharpe, *Calendar of Wills*, II:13; CLRO, HR 87(130).

concern for the proper or particular attire and display of the male figure.[75]

Function and Meanings of Domestic Space

Bequests of movable goods in the Husting wills reveal much about the shape and reality of living space in late medieval London for daughters of all ages. Many of the testators included details in their bequests that allow a glimpse of the kitchen, hall, bedroom, workshop, and other rooms. Numerous wills include both the stuff of luxury and decoration—for example, rich and detailed tapestries for walls, such as that with floral and animal images in the will of Thomas Madefrey,[76] and cushions, or *bankers*, for chairs and benches in the will of Richard Groom, which he left to his daughter Juliana.[77] Wills also detail goods as tools for survival against cold and hunger, such as andirons for the fireplace and pots. Other practical goods included *posnets* (saucepans), like that which Johanna received (a *pocenectum* or *posnet*) from her father Thomas Pourte along with other pots, cups, spoons, and bedding,[78] and frying pans for the kitchen.[79] Furniture in which to store goods abounds in the wills, such as a ship chest, a "spruce desked cofer," a little chest and a great chest, and an armoire.[80] All of these items give physical shape to these domestic spaces where daughters lived and worked. With these details, it is

[75] Susan Mosher Stuard makes a similar observation in her work, for example in her presentation, "Recycling Luxuries in the First Age of Fashion," (paper, 25th Annual Medieval Studies Conference, Medieval Domesticity: Home, Housing and Household, Fordham University, NY, March 12–13, 2005); and in her book, *Gilding the Market: Luxury and Fashion in Fourteenth-Century Italy* (Philadelphia: University of Pennsylvania Press, 2006).

[76] Sharpe, *Calendar of Wills*, II:190; CLRO, HR 104(63).

[77] Sharpe, *Calendar of Wills*, II:199; CLRO, HR 106 (80). In 1371, William Hynelond, a clerk, also left a *banker* with floral and animal details to St. Paul's Church. Sharpe, *Calendar of Wills*, II:151–52; CLRO, HR 100(141). A *banker* was a "covering, of tapestry or other fabric, for a bench, couch, or chair; also, an ornamental hanging for a room, altar, or bed," *Middle English Dictionary Online*, "banker," accessed 11.02.2010, http://ets.umdl.umich.edu.

[78] CLRO, HR 35(77).

[79] For examples, see the wills of William de Thorneye in 1349 and Walter de Tiffeld in 1355. Sharpe, *Calendar of Wills*, I:582, 689; CLRO, HR 79(34), 84(48).

[80] See the will of Alice Colyn in 1477; Barholomew de Bordeslee, a fripperer, in 1348; and of William Cosyn de Sutton in 1340. Sharpe, *Calendar of Wills* II:576; Sharpe, *Calendar of Wills*, I:525–26, 479; CLRO, HR 207(18), 76(84), 72(75).

possible to reconstruct what these living spaces would have looked like, but it is necessary to go further and to consider what these physical spaces meant to their inhabitants.

It is important to note that sons received domestic property, just as it is important to note that daughters received landed wealth. That John, son of the pepperer in the will mentioned above, received both domestic and commercial goods from his father is significant. What is more, his father noted the domestic goods in much more detail than the commercial goods. To his son John, he bequeathed three mazer cups, one with a stand and two without stands; four silver spoons; three pots, namely one best pot, and the other second best pot, and the third best pot after the second best pot; two best beds with sheets; three best chests; twenty-four plates; twenty-four dishes; and so on.[81] Such relative detail suggests a special concern by John's father that John receive these specific domestic goods; such cups, spoons, pots, beds, sheets, and dishes were viable assets to John, and with this variety of domestic goods, John could certainly outfit a house. The domestic space of the house was important to men, as is clear from John's father's movable provisions to him.

When one considers the specific goods in the wills, it is clear that domestic goods were valuable assets to children of both sexes. Items such as chests, basin and ewer sets, cushions, pieces of silver, and andirons for the fireplace were bequeathed to sons and daughters alike. Silver spoons are omnipresent in the wills, with the distinction in numbers as the usual qualifier, anywhere from two to twenty-four.[82] Oftentimes, testators showed a desire to provide spoons to both their sons and daughters if they had them. For example, in 1340 Johanna and Thomas, children of William Cosyn, received ten silver spoons each from their father.[83] One testator left seven silver spoons to be divided equally among his children.[84] The idea of dividing seven

[81] CLRO, HR 79(34).

[82] In his study of Lynn, Norfolk, David Hinton notes that silver spoons had around a value of less than 1s., and no one in Lynn had more than twenty-five spoons. David A. Hinton, *Gold and Gilt, Pots and Pins: Possessions and People in Medieval Britain* (Oxford: Oxford University Press, 2005), 214. In the Husting wills, the testatrix with twenty-four spoons divided them among her daughters. CLRO, HR 78(18). The most common number of spoons in a bequest in the Husting wills was six (thirteen instances), then twelve (eleven instances), with a few testators bequeathing other amounts, such as two, four, seven, and ten.

[83] CLRO, HR 72(75).

[84] CLRO, HR 87(130).

spoons suggests that these legacies of tableware did not necessarily follow the notion of a set to outfit one's table. Instead, these spoons were highly cherished goods themselves. In a will from 1372, while Johanna inherited her father's best pot, bronze bowl, and basin and ewer, it is her brother Simon, a friar, who received four silver spoons.[85] The ubiquity of spoons in the wills suggests that they were valuable in terms of worth and functionality to men and women alike. Spoons were bequeathed outside of the family as well. For example, Thomas Atte Naps left silver spoons not only to his wife and brother, but also to two male nonrelatives and to his church.[86]

Both the statistics and the language in the Husting wills make it clear that domestic goods in late medieval London were possessions important to both daughters and sons. These findings support the argument of Jane Whittle who claims that the material goods that both bride and groom brought to a marriage, gained either by inheritance or purchase, were extremely important to the establishment of a new household. She argues that moveable wealth was more important in England in the late medieval and early modern period than elsewhere in the world, where the couple might reside with either set of parents after the marriage.[87] Martha Howell further argues that movable wealth was responsible for the shift in the medieval period to a modern understanding of marriage. She claims that the increase in movable wealth at the end of the Middle Ages led to increased pressure on conjugality, and that people thence adopted an ideal of love and friendship in marriage.[88] Although this analysis of the Husting wills did not approach the meaning of late medieval marriage, the legacies of household goods in the Husting wills makes it clear that they were significant to daughters and sons and would have aided in their search for a marriage partner, as Whittle points out, and in establishing a new home. These daughters and sons may

---

[85] CLRO, HR 102(21). Such spoon bequests are found in other wills. For example, a will from the Canterbury Court of London includes bequests of "ix spones of silver with woodruffe on the endes, gilt" to the testator's son Thomas. See Claire A. Martin, "Dame Margery Astry," *The Ricardian* 14 (2004): 28.

[86] CLRO, HR 114(120).

[87] Jane Whittle, "Servants in Rural England c. 1450–1650: Hired Work as a Means of Accumulating Wealth and Skills before Marriage," in *The Marital Economy in Scandinavia and Britain, 1400–1900*, ed. Maria Ågren and Amy Louise Erickson (Burlington, VT: Ashgate, 2005), 97.

[88] Howell, "Properties," 17–62.

have worked together with their respective spouses, as Howell suggests, to protect and add to their inherited goods.

Through bequests of goods, the Husting wills show that the household was important to men as well as to women, and the spaces in which these goods resided were gendered both feminine and masculine. There is a tradition of scholarship that focuses on the medieval household as a distinctly feminine space controlled by the wife. Barbara Hanawalt has suggested that space was "very gendered" and argues that respectable female activity in the Middle Ages was confined to such areas as the home or the cloister.[89] Similarly, Felicity Riddy argues for a "bourgeois ethos" among the urban elite that confined the woman's role to the household, as seen in "What the Goodwife Taught Her Daughter." Riddy argues that town fathers desired to control young women entering towns for work by providing them with an ideology that defined a specific femininity to the bourgeoisie, a femininity that emphasized the household as her workplace. Riddy sees a domestic space that incorporated both domestic and commercial activities, but these activities were distinctly separate and gendered, therefore endorsing the public-private sphere split. In a footnote she comments that "modern historians" assume a "separate spheres" ideology, and she cites such scholars as Barbara Hanawalt and Judith Bennett.[90]

While not directly contradicting this scholarship, these wills show that the household was important to men as well as to women. Sons' inheritances of dwellings and the material goods to outfit them reveal that men occupied these spaces and that these spaces were significant to men. This line of reasoning complements recent scholarship by Barbara Harris, Shannon McSheffrey, and Anna Dronzek. These

---

[89] Barbara Hanawalt, "At the Margins of Women's Space in Medieval Europe" in *"Of Good and Ill Repute": Gender and Social Control in Medieval England* (New York: Oxford University Press, 1998), 70–87.

[90] Felicity Riddy, "Mother Knows Best: Reading Social Change in a Courtesy Text," *Speculum* 71 (1996): 66–86. For recent scholarship challenging public-private split, see Barbara Harris, *English Aristocratic Women 1450–1550: Marriage and Family, Property and Careers* (New York: Oxford University Press, 2002), 8; Judith Bennett, "Medieval Women, Modern Women: Across the Great Divide," in *Culture and History, 1350–1600: Essays on English Communities, Identities and Writing*, ed. David Aers (Hemel Hempstead: Harvester Wheatsheaf, 1992), 147–75; P. J. P Goldberg, "The Public and The Private: Women in the Pre-Plague Economy," in *Thirteenth Century England III. Proceedings of the Newcastle-upon-Tyne Conference 1989*, ed. P.R. Coss and S.D. Lloyd (Woodbridge, Suffolk: Boydell and Brewer, 1991), 75-89, esp. 82.

scholars argue that the household was important to a man's identity, and they question the usefulness of the public-private sphere dichotomy that has been present in the popular mind since Victorian times.[91]

The Husting wills reveal flexible, domestic spaces in medieval London, and by considering domestic spaces to have been gendered masculine as well as feminine, we can expand our understanding of both daughterhood and domesticity in the Middle Ages. With a better appreciation of what their living spaces looked like, as well as the importance these spaces held for them and for their brothers and husbands, the fuzzy edges of daughterhood can be smoothed out. Since daughters left the houses of their parents equipped with a variety of domestic and commercial goods, it is possible to have a clearer sense of the spaces they inhabited afterward as both single women and spouses. The stock phrase used by historians of family, that daughters passed from the authority of their fathers to that of their husbands, becomes more nuanced when we examine goods in the wills. Women clearly lived and operated in domestic spaces, bringing additional income to their families, albeit under male authority. Yet, this space was space in which married daughters were not alone; instead, it was also occupied and valued by their partners. In short, by understanding the value for sons of these domestic spaces and the objects that filled them, we gain a richer understanding of the value for daughters.

Through analysis of the Husting wills from late medieval London, a picture emerges of busy domestic spaces that were flexible and that encompassed both men and women. The goods within houses were most often described in the Husting wills by quality, size, or material

---

[91] See Barbara Harris, *English Aristocratic Women*, 8; Shannon McSheffrey, "Place, Space, and Situation: Public and Private in the Making of Marriage in Late-Medieval London," 792; Anna Dronzek, "No Separate Spheres: The Household as Masculine and Feminine Space in Late Medieval England" (paper, NACBS Annual Meeting, Baltimore, MD, November 2002). See also Goldberg, "Household and the Organisation of Labour," 61, who challenges the idea that female servants in England before the late fifteenth century were relegated solely to domestic tasks. John Carmi Parsons also questions the utility of the modern conception of private-public in terms of noblewomen's duties as mothers and daughters. John Carmi Parsons, "Mothers, Daughters, Marriage, Power: Some Plantagenet Evidence, 1150–1500," in *Medieval Queenship*, ed. John Carmi Parsons (New York: St. Martin's Press, 1993), 75, 78.

and less frequently by specific appellation or location. These goods served practical purposes, while still communicating social status as well as personal, social, and cultural meaning. The 1347 will of William Box epitomizes the complex nature of these wills. Box bequeathed to his daughter Agnes a silver cup, with a silver cover, which was marked with his sign, "signo meo signatu"[92]—practicality, monetary worth, and sentimental meaning all have a place in this daughter's legacy.

The rhetoric employed to describe the material goods in the wills elucidates that goods held meaning to givers and recipients. It also reveals insights into the spaces that the recipients and their goods inhabited. Furthermore, in the case of wills in which goods were left to daughters, the line was often fuzzy between commercial and domestic goods, suggesting that some vessels could be used for both purposes. This mobility of goods and their multiple meanings helped create flexible physical spaces, a finding that corresponds with archaeological research that argues for the multifunctional rooms of many medieval urban houses.[93]

Other scholars who have studied wills have reached similar conclusions about the flexibility of domestic space. Elisabeth Ellen Salter, who studied wills from three small towns in Kent, argues that urban buildings and household spaces were dense, and multifunctional.[94] Catherine Richardson likewise makes the argument for flexible domestic spaces based on wills enrolled in Kent and posits that domestic actions and rituals, rather than household spaces, defined personal relationships through bequests of goods. However, she builds on this argument to try to delineate a split between the medieval and early modern periods and asserts that in the later period goods became fixed and domestic spaces less flexible, and therefore the people were more concerned with status markers and private spaces.[95] This is not a very effective argument since goods in the Middle Ages, as seen in the Husting wills, were also thought of as status markers and status communicators. There may have been more material goods available in the early modern period, but individuals in the later time frame were building on a medieval foundation of con-

---

[92] CLRO, HR 74(174).

[93] See John Schofield, *Medieval London Houses*, 1200–1600 (New Haven: Yale University Press, 1995) and Grenville, *Medieval Housing*.

[94] Salter, "Some Differences in Cultural Production," 397–400.

[95] Richardson, "Household Objects and Domestic Ties."

necting goods with personal or family status. The use of space may have changed from 1300 to 1800, but the relative value and conception of goods did not.

Sibling Rivalry?

It has been shown in the case of real estate that the presence or absence of siblings had the potential to affect children's inheritance. Under the common law in most regions of England, if daughters were to inherit the patrimony without sons present, they would do so together, dividing the property among themselves. In London, in the case of opposite-sex siblings, daughters were slightly *more* likely to get real estate if they had a brother, 79% to 77%, whereas sons were slightly *less* likely to get real estate if they had a sister, 85% to 88%. If they did not have siblings of the same sex, daughters and sons inherited real estate more often. A daughter without sisters inherited real estate 5% more often than a daughter with sisters (81% to 76%), while a son without brothers inherited 2% more frequently than a son with brothers (87% to 85%).[96]

In bequests of movable property, the variable of siblings operated differently than in bequests of real estate. In the Husting wills, children with siblings of either sex were more numerous than children without any siblings. There were 1,172 sons with brothers and 921 daughters with sisters mentioned in the wills, compared with only 682 sons without brothers and 608 daughters without sisters. Likewise, there were 1,049 sons with sisters and 1,032 daughters with brothers mentioned in the wills, compared with 805 sons without sisters and only 497 daughters without brothers. Daughters were more likely to receive movable property when they had either same-sex or opposite-sex siblings present, and so too were sons. Of all movable property, 12% was bequeathed to daughters with sisters and to daughters with brothers, while only 6% was bequeathed to daughters without sisters and without brothers. The same is true for sons. Of all movable property, 12% was bequeathed to sons with brothers, and 6% to sons without brothers, while 11% of all movable property was bequeathed to sons with sisters, and 7% to sons without sisters.

---

[96] See discussion in chapter 3.

This finding is puzzling at first. In legacies of real estate, Londoners divided their wealth differently than their rural counterparts, namely by not favoring sons over daughters. However, one might then expect a fairly equal distribution of movable property to children with or without same- and opposite-sex siblings, but this was not the case. What seems to be in evidence here is the work of the custom of thirds of London. Testators appear to have faithfully divided their movable wealth among their children, regardless of their gender. Children without same- or opposite-sex siblings still received movable property by will, but less so than if they had had siblings. In these instances, it is likely that children without siblings received their share of movable property but that this share was not specified in detail in the wills themselves. With only one child existent, the details of the division of movable wealth would not seem to be as crucial as with more than one child.

Change Over Time

From 1300 to 1500, testators consistently left the majority of their movable wealth to their immediate families (see figure 4.3), which coincides with the London custom of thirds. Throughout this two-hundred-year period, daughters, sons, and wives received between 55 and 90 percent of all bequests of movable property in the Husting wills. Other relatives certainly received movable property, especially toward the end of the fifteenth century, but only after testators provided for the immediate families.

If one isolates the percentage of bequests of movable property to daughters and sons, it is clear that Londoners distinguished little between their children by gender as recipients of movable wealth (see figure 4.4). Yet these testators were affected by events during their lifetimes, which influenced the children's inheritances. Children of both sexes received their largest percentage of bequests of movable property from their parents in the early years of the fourteenth century. With the onset of the Black Death, the percentages of inheritances by both daughters and sons dropped to around 12 percent between 1360 and 1380. If one isolates the natural disasters of the thirteenth and fourteenth centuries (figure 4.5), rather than looking at an even distribution of change over time, one can clearly see this drop in the inheritance of movable property by daughters and sons

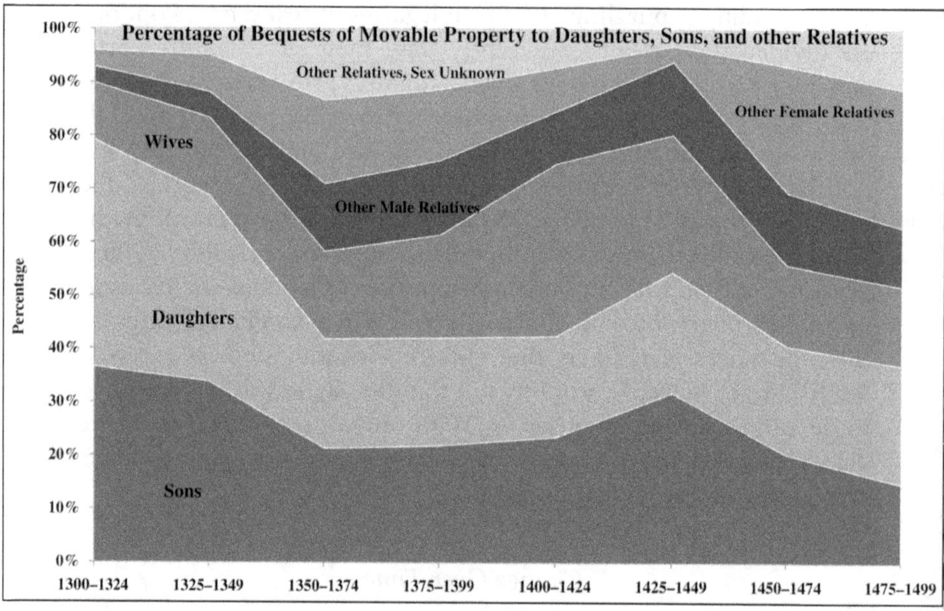

Figure 4.3

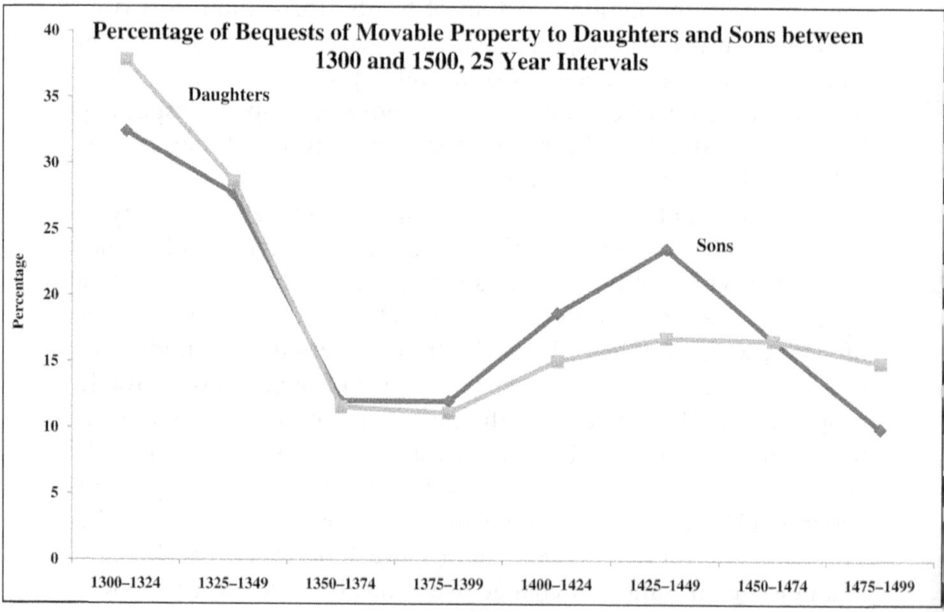

Figure 4.4

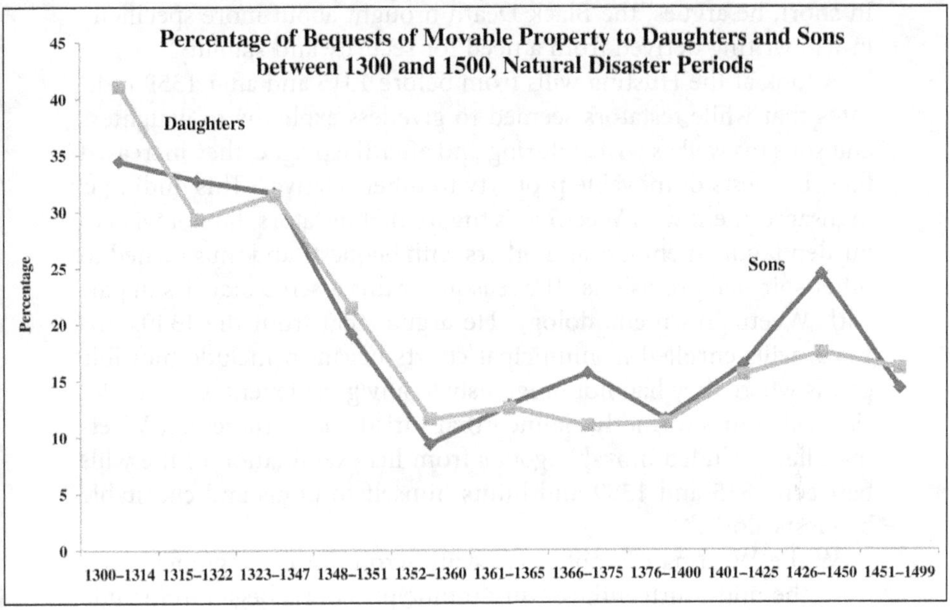

Figure 4.5

at the time of the Black Death. There was very slow recovery after this event, possibly due to reoccurring bouts of the plague until the early fifteenth century.

The sharp decline in inheritance of movable property by daughters and sons following the plague and the subsequent slow recovery may have been due to an even greater assumption on the part of testators that their children would receive their share according to custom. Testators during these years may have been more concerned with the distribution of goods beyond the immediate family, as can be seen in figure 4.3. Jamieson Weetman studied about five hundred of the wills enrolled in the Husting Court between 1315 and 1359 specifically for changes in pious and charitable bequests due to the Black Death. He argues that faced with the plague, testators began to feel uncertain about how their pious and charitable bequests would be carried out past their lifetimes, and as a result they relied on more direct and secure bequests, such as the provision for church lights, and less on bequests to individuals who may not live to carry out such bequests.[97]

[97] Jamieson Floyd Weetman, "London Wills and the Black Death: The Pursuit of Stability in Religious Practise in the Husting Rolls Wills, 1315–1359" (master's thesis, University of Calgary, 1999).

In short, he argues, the Black Death brought about more specificity in will writing derived from a need for security and stability.

A look at the Husting wills from before 1315 and after 1359 indicates that while testators seemed to give less explicitly to daughters and sons (as well as wives) during and after the plague, they increased their bequests of movable property to other relatives. This finding is in disagreement with Weetman's theory that testators did not wish to burden family members and others with bequests and thus turned to other spiritual provisions. The reason for this discrepancy lies in part with Weetman's methodology. He argues that from the 1340s onward, wills enrolled in municipal courts began to include movable goods where they had not previously to any great extent, since ecclesiastical courts formerly claimed that jurisdiction. Therefore, Weetman has excluded movable goods from his examination of the wills between 1315 and 1359 and limits himself to pious and charitable bequests alone.[98]

While Weetman is not necessarily wrong in his argument that from the mid-fourteenth century municipal courts began to include more bequests of movable goods, a consideration of bequests of goods can add depth to his analysis. Indeed, a development parallel to Weetman's main thesis may have occurred with movable property. Faced with the plague, testators may have felt less secure that their movable wealth would remain in their family and consequently may have felt a need for more specificity. Thus, with the third left to their own disposal after their spouse and child(ren) were provided for by custom, testators may have been more detailed in their bequests to other relatives and spread these goods more broadly to family members to ensure that precious goods and money remained in the family rather than going to the market prematurely with the unexpected death of a wife, daughter, or son.

Finally, if one considers change over time in five year intervals from 1300 to 1450 (figure 4.6), remembering that the numbers of wills enrolled in the Husting Court after 1450 dwindled significantly, one can again see the impact of the plague on inheritance. However, more significantly, one can see the fairly even, if at times sporadic, distribution of movable wealth among both daughters and sons from 1300 to 1450. Except for the sharp, and not readily explainable dip for daughters between 1405 and 1409, the fates of daughters and sons

[98] Weetman, "London Wills and the Black Death," 3, 58–65.

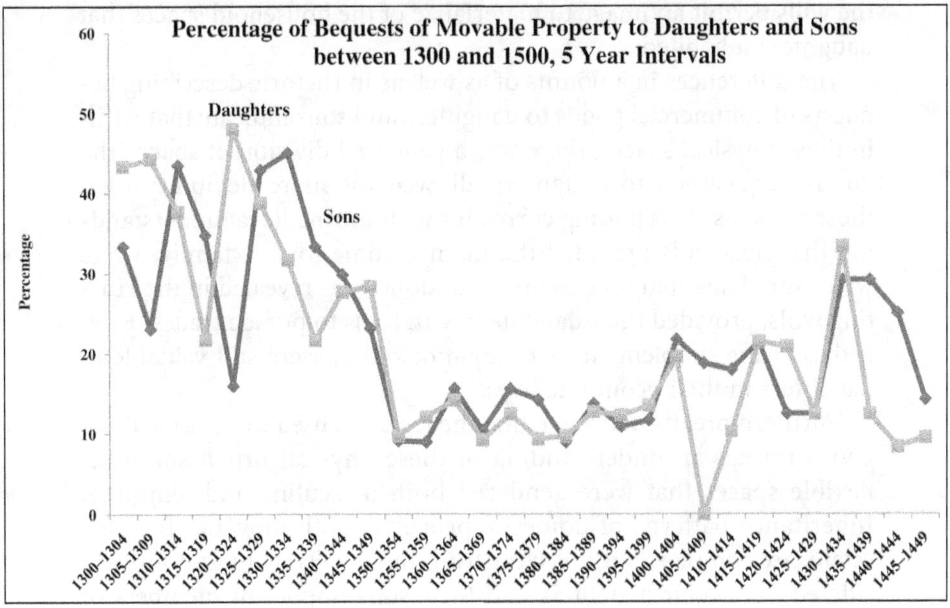

Figure 4.6

are tied together throughout the period under study, regardless of gender, especially between 1340 and 1400. While this relative equality in inheritance of movable wealth by daughters and sons may best reflect the London custom of thirds, it is still remarkable that Londoners adhered to this custom in practice, showing little to no gender preference for daughters or sons. This evidence reiterates the idea that parents believed movable property, including but not exclusive to goods, to be valuable and useful to both daughters and sons alike.

Conclusions

Although movable property is challenging to study in juxtaposition to real estate, because it was often underrepresented in the Husting wills, the inheritance of such property does shed light on daughters and their experiences in late medieval London. Parents provided equally for the futures of their daughters and sons with bequests of money and annuities. Legacies of such movable property suggest a concern to support their daughters, as they did their sons, when they moved away from the family home. Movable goods bequeathed in the wills permit an image to materialize of the household spaces that daughters inhabited.

The differences in amounts of as well as in rhetoric describing bequests of commercial goods to daughters and sons indicate that within these physical spaces, there was a gendered division of space. The goods bequeathed to daughters allowed for more flexibility than those for sons. This finding correlates with the medieval understanding that husbands provided the main income for the family, while wives supplemented that income. Londoners, as revealed in the Husting wills, provided their daughters with tools to pursue trades. Even if these were supplementary occupations, they were still valuable to daughters in their economic lives.

Furthermore, the language that the testators used to describe these goods reveals an understanding of these physical urban spaces as flexible spaces that were gendered both masculine and feminine. Inheritance patterns of domestic property, both movable and real estate, are complex, but it is clear from these wills that testators considered both their daughters and their sons important members of the domestic unit. Such a finding expands our understanding of both domesticity and of daughterhood. The types of goods bequeathed in these wills and how they were described challenge the notion of a predominant feminine domesticity in the Middle Ages. Daughters left their parents' homes equipped with both domestic and commercial goods for their future lives with spouses who shared and appreciated the same physical spaces. Finally, when we examine changes in bequests of movable property, it becomes clear that while the inheritances of both daughters and sons were adversely affected by natural disasters such as the plague, the equal gender distribution of this type of property remained consistent throughout the period under study.

CHAPTER FIVE

REINTERPRETING DAUGHTERS' ECONOMIC POWER IN LATE MEDIEVAL LONDON

In 1352, Isabella de Merwe inherited her father's tenement and all accompanying vessels, while her brothers inherited money and goods;[1] and in 1369, Katherine Koo inherited houses, rents, tenements, and lands from her father, while her brother received money and household goods.[2] Although the first will suggests that Isabella's brothers were younger than she, it is remarkable that she inherited property while she had brothers and indeed inherited before they did. Johanna Ryffawe likewise inherited a significant opportunity from her father. In a codicil to his will, her father specified that his tenements and wharf remain not to his sons, as he had indicated in his original will, but instead to his wife and to his daughter Johanna and her heirs.[3] While perhaps not the norm, the inheritances of Isabella de Merwe, Katherine Koo, and Johanna Ryffawe were not as much of an anomaly in late medieval London as one might first assume in light of the various limitations women faced in medieval society. In fact, the Husting wills reveal daughters who frequently received real estate along with their brothers, a situation that challenges scholarship that argues that even in towns daughters were unlikely to receive real estate and instead were more likely to receive money and goods.

According to the Husting Wills, there were a significant number of women in late medieval London who were given opportunities by their parents to own and manage real estate as well as movable property, and to participate in investment activities to financially support themselves and others. One question that remains is, did they? Were these London daughters active in the capital's economy? To what extent did they invest the property they inherited? A second question is whether or not this situation for these daughters is unique to London. The wills do not allow us to answer the first question, as they

---

[1] Sharpe, *Calendar of Wills*, I:659–60; CLRO, HR 80(115).

[2] Sharpe, *Calendar of Wills*, II:142; CLRO, HR 99(120). Katherine also received household goods.

[3] Sharpe, *Calendar of Wills*, II:494; CLRO, HR 170(16). Unfortunately, the codicil did not mention why or how the sons lost favor, but Johanna certainly benefited.

speak to the intentions of the testators rather than actions of the recipients. However, by first considering scholars' work on women, in general, in late medieval Europe, and second, by turning to scholars' work on women in England, both in town and country, we can come to an understanding of how daughters in late medieval London may have used their inheritance of property. This conclusion, thus, has two aims: to place the study of London daughters' inheritance from 1300 to 1500 in the important contexts of both women's history and urban history. This examination will then permit a reconsideration of how we view women's experiences in the past more broadly.

Studying Women and the Economy

Most work on women in urban economies focuses on women in the workplace. This is a product, mainly, of where women appear in the sources. In some situations, women operated as mistresses independently pursuing their craft, with little or no mention in the sources of their husbands in the same craft. In other situations, widows carried on their husbands' businesses. At times, daughters appear as apprentices and working women. For example, at the end of the fifteenth century in Cologne, Fygen Lutzenkirchen left her silk shop to her daughter Lysbeth, a silk-making master in her own right.[4] Cordelia Beattie has also noted working daughters in some of the tax returns from late medieval England. For example, in the Howdenshire return, Beattie found that 102 of 117 women that the assessors recorded as daughters were also categorized by occupation, such as servants or laborers.[5]

In addition, scholars have considered women's guilds and women-dominated trades and how they changed over time. In Rouen, Paris, and Cologne, guilds developed for women in crafts such as the making and finishing of linen yarn, the spinning of gold thread, and the weaving of silk. Yet, as Maryanne Kowaleski and Judith Bennet argue, while there were women-dominated trades and guilds in medieval Europe, more often guilds were controlled by men, and if

[4] Margret Wensky, "Women's Guilds in Cologne in the Later Middle Ages," *Journal of European Economic History* 11, no. 3 (1982): 642–43.

[5] Cordelia Beattie, *Medieval Single Women: The Politics of Social Classification in Late Medieval England* (Oxford: Oxford University Press, 2007), chapter 3, esp. 92.

women were allowed entrance, they were barred from the main benefits of such organizations.[6] In London, for example, women dominated the silk industry while not belonging officially to a guild.[7] Beyond London, P. J. P. Goldberg found only a handful of female guilds in England, including the silkmakers of London, although he delineates other formal and informal social associations of women.[8] In other cases, it appears from the sources that women worked within the household economy, with husbands in the same craft often securing their wives' raw materials. While most scholars see women in female-dominated guilds or trades as fairly autonomous artisans, Stephanie Trigg argues that the distinction is perhaps too harsh. Through an interdisciplinary exploration of literature and historical source material, Trigg argues that the London silkwomen should not be seen strictly as independent traders but more in the spirit of the medieval household economy.[9]

In line with Trigg's work, many scholars of working women have focused on the household economy. Martha Howell explains that market production in the Middle Ages was rooted in the household economy, a patriarchal structure, and therefore most women's work was completed within that arena. Such work could be high labor status, she argues, but as market production changed to place less emphasis on the family unit, women's work became lower status as they

[6] Maryanne Kowaleski and Judith M. Bennett "Crafts, Gilds, and Women in the Middle Ages: Fifty Years after Marian K. Dale," *Signs* 14, no. 2 (1989): 474–501. See also Margret Wensky, "Women's Guilds in Cologne in the Later Middle Ages," *Journal of European Economic History* 11, no. 3 (1982): 631–50. In London, studies of women in the workplace began with Annie Abram's survey of women's occupations in medieval London. Abram, "Women Traders in Medieval London," *The Economic Journal* 26, no. 102 (1916): 276–85. See Kay Lacey's article for an updated review of medieval London occupations, "Women and Work in Fourteenth- and Fifteenth-Century London," in *Women and Work in Pre-Industrial England*, ed. Lindsey Charles and Lorna Duffin (Dover, NH: Croom Helm, 1985), particularly, 45–56.

[7] Marian K. Dale, "The London Silkwomen of the Fifteenth Century," *The Economic History Review* 4, no. 3 (1933): 324–35; Kay Lacey, "Production of 'Narrow Ware' by Silkwomen in Fourteenth and Fifteenth Century England," *Textile History* 18, no. 2 (1987): 187–204.

[8] Goldberg, "Women in Fifteenth-Century Town Life," in *Towns and Townspeople in the Fifteenth Century*, ed. John A. F. Thomson (Gloucester: Alan Sutton, 1988), 108.

[9] Trigg, "Ye Louely Ladyes with Youre Longe Fyngres,' The Silkwomen of Medieval London," *Studia Anglica Posnaniensia* 38 (2002): 469–84.

lost control over production, consumption, and distribution.[10] Similarly, Judith Bennett has argued that although brewsters dominated the trade in medieval England, as the brewing occupation became professionalized, it became a job for men rather than women due to men's ability to own more capital and to legally borrow money in their own right. Thus by 1600, many women lost the opportunity to earn extra income through brewing, which developed into a mostly male-dominated trade.[11] In medieval Exeter, women had an additional challenge in that they were barred from the town's "freedom," an economic and political organization. This was a limitation that often pushed them into lower-paying retail trades and prostitution.[12] Despite the abundance of examples of working women throughout the Middle Ages, scholars have found that women possessed a weak work identity in comparison to men, often working multiple jobs at lower wages.[13] This focus, then, on women in the

---

[10] Martha C. Howell, "Women, the Family Economy, and the Structures of Market Production in Cities of Northern Europe during the Late Middle Ages," in *Women and Work in Preindustrial Europe*, 198–222, esp. 215–16.

[11] Judith Bennett, *Ale, Beer, and Brewsters in England: Women's Work in a Changing World, 1300–1600* (New York: Oxford University Press, 1996). Howell discusses brewsters as well, Howell, "Women, The Family Economy," 216. The loss of the control of a trade to men likewise happened to the London silkweavers in the sixteenth century. Kowaleski and Bennett, "Crafts, Gilds, and Women," 486.

[12] Maryanne Kowaleski, "Women's Work in a Market Town: Exeter in the Late Fourteenth Century," in *Women and Work in Preindustrial Europe,* 145–66. The exception to this general rule of a weak work identity was single women or relatively wealthy married women who had household help. As Martha Howell found for medieval Cologne, most working women were married and "had less uninterrupted time for market production than their male counterparts had." Howell, *Women, Production and Patriarchy*, 154.

[13] For a general discussion of the nature of women's work, see Mavis Mate's *Women in Medieval English Society* (Cambridge: Cambridge University Press, 1999), 45–56. See also Martha Howell, *Women, Production and Patriarchy in Late Medieval Cities* (Chicago: University of Chicago Press, 1986), chapter 1. Howell points out that while women's work may often have been relegated to the household, or it may have been lower paid, they could achieve high labor status depending on their situation, as well as to what degree they controlled production, distribution, and consumption. The complexities introduced by individual situation, the demand of labor, economic and demographic change, and other factors are important to keep in mind.

For Continental examples of premodern working women, see Merry Wiesner Wood, "Paltry Peddlers or Essential Merchants? Women in the Distributive Trades in Early Modern Nuremberg," *Sixteenth Century Journal* 12 (1981): 3–13; Judith C. Brown and Jordan Goodman, "Women and Industry in Florence," *The Journal of Economic History* 40, no.1 (1980): 73–80; Grethe Jacobsen, "Women's Work and Women's Role: Ideology and Reality in Danish Urban Society, 1300–1500," *The Scandinavian Economic History Review and Economy and History* 31 (1983): 1–20.

household economy becomes crucial as we reexamine women's lived experiences. The Husting wills suggest, through bequests of movable goods, daughters who operated in flexible spaces. The goods they inherited could help them in the supplementary occupations many of them were likely to pursue. Bequests of real estate to daughters also might have been used by many of these women in their marriages. Although sources can occlude their use of this property, because of coverture laws, a point I will return to, it was likely an essential contribution to the household economy.

The other cluster of scholarship on women and the economy has been on women's roles in the family, as discussed in detail in chapter 1. Although this scholarship has been wide ranging, from the connection between women's family roles, to the work they carried out within that economic unit, to the connection between family configuration and women's dowries, many scholars argue that women lost power due to changes in family structure and inheritance patterns. As medieval society shifted to a patrilineal family arrangement in the central Middle Ages and to placing emphasis on the first male heir, as the argument runs, daughters lost significant chances to inherit real estate. By extension, these women lost opportunities for influence in their worlds. This line of reasoning has extended to rural and urban studies alike.

Although scholars like Martha Howell allow for the instability of gender codes and for exceptional women who did not conform to new property regimes and inheritance structures,[14] the idea of economically impotent women by the late Middle Ages is a powerful one, and one that has resonated in numerous scholars' work. Yet, the Husting wills suggest that in late medieval London, women possessed significant opportunities to wield economic power. In the wills of Londoners at the Husting Court, 78 percent of all daughters represented received some amount of real estate, compared with 86 percent of all sons represented in the wills. In terms of movable wealth (money, goods, and so on), of all the instances in which movable property was bequeathed in these wills, an equal amount went to daughters as to sons. In short, the Husting wills do not reveal a strong bias for sons over daughters. The evidence from the London wills

---

[14] See Martha Howell, *The Marriage Exchange: Property, Social Place, and Gender in Cities of the Low Countries, 1300–1550* (Chicago: University of Chicago Press, 1998).

does not support the idea of daughters with diminishing economic strength. Although the heir may have remained privileged in rural and urban settings alike, due to an emphasis on patrilineage and primogeniture, town-dwellers sought alternative means to providing for all members of their families. By bequeathing property, movable and immovable, to daughters in their wills, parents gave their daughters opportunities to be financially stable and to actively participate in their economies.

Considering Women as Investors and Managers

The chasm between the two research avenues of working women and women in the household economy is filled by considering women's *use* of the property they acquired either with their dowries, in their widowhood, in addition to their dowries, outside of marriage, or in their occupations. Exploring the ways that women managed and invested their property and that of their family will help us bridge gaps between changing inheritance practices, testators' intentions, urban exceptionality, and women's economic influence. In part, the issue hinges on the question of whether women served merely as place holders for family property, or if they were active economic agents investing the property available to them, either from their marital or natal families. The handful of studies to date indicates that it was the latter: women were active in their economies through their participation in investment, credit methods, money lending, and real estate management. A brief review of these studies here will help us see how the daughters of London's elite may have pursued the opportunities presented to them in the wills, both as independent investors and proprietors and as acting in tandem with husbands for the interests of their families.

Women across medieval Europe participated in the worlds of property investment and management. These were worlds dominated by men, but women were by no means excluded. Women were active as investors and proprietors from the Mediterranean to the North Sea, investing their capital to earn the most return. As William Chester Jordan points out in his work on women and investment strategies in premodern societies, "the old orthodoxy that women, if they invested at all, always invested in risk-free enterprises or chose merely to spend down their capital on clothes and luxury goods seems untenable."[15] Instead, as Jordan points out, they diversified their investment portfolios to make the most of their property possessions.

There were regional economic differences that influenced these female financiers and their investment strategies. Jordan suggests a marked difference between women investors in Italy and England, for example, with higher-risk investments taking place in the former, usually in the form of long-distance maritime trade, and more conservative, lower-risk investments carried out by the latter, usually in real estate.[16] Indeed, in medieval Italy, women were actively investing their property as well as their husbands'. In his study of over four thousand *commenda* contracts from 1155–1216 in Genoa, Mark Angelos argues that as early as the twelfth century, women, particularly wives of traveling merchants, were savvy with credit, investing movable property and acting as competent business partners.[17] Georges Jehel argues that even though women in thirteenth-century Genoa had fewer opportunities than men to invest, due to status, law, and circumstance, they still were active in their economies.[18] In Siena, Eleanor Riemer has found middle and upper class women active in investment in the thirteenth century, although this activity waned as men sought to control women's use of capital.[19]

While urban versus rural economies can go a long way toward explaining differences in investment strategies by women and men alike (for example, proximity to maritime trade and the variety of urban opportunities), it will only take us so far. Time period is a crucial factor. As Angelos suggests in his study, in the twelfth cen-

---

[15] Jordan, *Women and Credit in Pre-Industrial and Developing Societies* (Philadelphia: University of Pennsylvania Press, 1993), 70.

[16] Jordan, *Women and Credit*, 67. However, Jordan's suggestion for England rests on work from rural early modern England, such as John Swain's *Industry before the Industrial Revolution: North-East Lancashire, c. 1500–1640* (Manchester: Manchester University Press, 1986). Jordan suggests London may have been a different case. Jordan, *Women and Credit*, 69, n. 82.

[17] Mark Angelos, "Urban Women, Investment, and the Commercial Revolution of the Middle Ages," in *Women in Medieval Western European Culture*, ed. Linda Elizabeth Mitchell (Taylor and Francis, 1999), 257–72.

[18] Jehel, "Le Rôle des Femmes et du Milieu Familial a Gênes dans les Activités Commerciales au cours de la première moitié du XIIIe siècle," *Revue d'histoire économique et sociale* 53, no. 2–3 (1975): 193–215, esp. 204.

[19] Riemer, "Women, Dowries, and Capital Investment in Thirteenth-Century Siena," in *The Marriage Bargain: Women and Dowries in European History*, ed. Marion A. Kaplan (Harrington Park Press, 1985), 59–80.

tury Genoa's economy was booming, which permitted greater opportunities for women to invest.[20] Toward the end of the Middle Ages, more opportunities were created for women in Northern Europe, as those cities became more heavily involved in long-distance trade. Regional cultures also played a role. I would suggest that in Italy, trade and investment opportunities for women also slowed toward the end of the Middle Ages due to Italy's increasing emphasis on dowry and the exclusion of women from inheritance in order to keep the patrimony in the agnate line. This specific dowry culture was absent in late medieval London.

Kathryn Reyerson has written about a situation different from that in Genoa.[21] Although Montpellier was a southern European town that also tapped into the lucrative long-distance Mediterranean trade, while women were active in all types of investment, their investments tended to remain in real estate and other low-risk endeavors. In early fourteenth-century Montpellier, women acted as sureties for others, were involved in payment and collection of debts for their children, loaned and borrowed money and land, engaged in contracts as did men, and were business partners in various types of trade. Reyerson found that these women tended to be more conservative than their male counterparts—they used credit less than men and were more involved in real estate investment, such as vineyards and house sales, rather than international trade.[22] Although low-risk, urban investments had advantages for women in Montpellier, Reyerson suggests the appeal for women of managing urban housing property: "Urban housing could be a profitable investment if rented out ... Housing management was less complex and less speculative than the administration of rural agricultural lands, whose yields might fluctuate enormously from year to year. Such facility may have been an attractive feature for urban women investors."[23]

Scholars have found evidence of women owning and managing property elsewhere in Europe as well. In her study of notarial and

---

[20] Angelos, "Urban Women, Investment."

[21] Kathryn Reyerson, "Women in Business in Medieval Montpellier," in *Women and Work in Pre-Industrial Europe*, 117–44. See also Reyerson's detailed study of the real estate economy of Montpellier in, "Land, Houses and Real Estate Investment in Montpellier: A Study of the Notarial Property Transactions, 1293–1348" in *Studies in Medieval and Renaissance History* 6 (Old Series, vol. 16) (1983), 37–112.

[22] Reyerson, "Women in Business," 134.

[23] Reyerson, "Women in Business," 134.

debt records from late medieval Avignon, Maryann Brink found evidence of women both owning and renting property. She notes one woman in 1307 who sold her *stare*, or place of business, of her own volition, and twenty-three women of 104 people who rented land and houses from the confraternity of the Petite Fusterie from 1326–1401. Brink concludes, "women in Avignon seem to have had enormous freedom in their property dealings. The only restrictions in practice seem to have been securing the husband's permission to alienate property and her family's permission, which a woman *and* her husband had to have to alienate dower property."[24]

Crossing the Channel in late medieval and early modern England through an examination of the royal equity court petitions, Marjorie McIntosh found women financially active in both the rural and urban spheres. McIntosh found that, like elsewhere in Europe, women's investment opportunities depended on outside factors. In England, their opportunities to participate in the economy fluctuated, due both to "gender-based handicaps" and the changing economy. McIntosh reiterates the argument emphasized by many scholars: working women were often at a disadvantage because of their gender. Women, unlike men, were often defined by their marital status rather than occupational status, often had fewer resources, and were often less mobile. These "handicaps" could discourage lenders from advancing loans to women.[25] Some opportunities for women were enhanced after the social and economic upheavals from the plague, while others were restricted in the sixteenth century as all production rose and credit devices formalized. Despite the restrictions, in late medieval England women were creditors and debtors, they operated as moneylenders and pawnbrokers, and they acted as sureties for others. Money lending for interest was a shrewd way to make a small profit on cash or goods and was used by unmarried, married, and widowed women alike; similarly, pawning could provide opportunities for women with few resources.[26] Not unlike their counterparts in

---

[24] Maryann E. Brink, "The Social Description of Property in Late Medieval Avignon," *Medieval Perspectives* 10 (1995): 67–76, quotation at 69.

[25] McIntosh, *Working Women in English Society, 1300–1620* (Cambridge, Cambridge University Press, 2005), 86. For another example of women managing property in northern Europe, see Shennan Hutton's work, "In Her Own Name: Property Management and Gender in Medieval Ghent" (paper, 2008 Berkshire Conference on the History of Women, Minneapolis, Minnesota, June 2008). My thanks to the author for permission to cite this work.

[26] McIntosh, *Working Women*, 98–109.

medieval Montpellier, women in late medieval England also leased their property to earn extra money. By the sixteenth century, the equity court petitions indicate urban women actively renting commercial and residential property for income.[27] These landladies sometimes lived in part of their rented property.[28]

Scholars' work on women proprietors in the rural landscape of late medieval England is suggestive. It reveals women using their resources to negotiate the best circumstances for their personal and family situations. Yet, urban-based women, like these London daughters, may have had even greater opportunities than rural-based women. The evidence in the Husting wills, I believe, shows a distinct urban aspect of inheritance, at least among the elite of London. The situation among daughters in London runs contrary to the situation in rural areas in which, in most cases, the patrimony was left to the first son. Daughters, if they received landed property, did so with their dowries. In the Husting wills, of all the real estate bequeathed in the fourteenth and fifteenth centuries, 20% of it descended to daughters and 27% to sons. In a rough comparison, in a study of English aristocratic women from 1450–1550, Barbara Harris found that of the estates of noblemen, only 12% descended to female heirs, and barely 7% among the estates of knights who sat in Parliament went to female heirs.[29] Just singling out tenements in London, the most frequently mentioned type of urban property in the Husting Wills, and looking at them from the standpoint of heirs rather than property, the percentage of daughters in the Husting wills who received tenements in the fourteenth and fifteenth centuries was 52%, while the percentage of sons was only slightly higher at 59%. Again, in comparison, a study of the landed aristocracy found rates of female inheritance to range from about 7% in the fourteenth century to 18% after the plague.[30]

Among peasants, the case of female inheritance was similar to that of the rural elite. On the manor of Brigstock before the plague, Judith Bennett found that, while daughters participated in the land market, sons were more likely to inherit land and daughters to receive gifts or participate in transactions while parents still lived. Bennett explains,

---

[27] McIntosh, *Working Women*, 114.

[28] McIntosh, *Working Women*, 115.

[29] Harris, *English Aristocratic Women*, 22.

[30] Simon Payling, "Social Mobility, Demographic Change, and Landed Society in Late Medieval England," *Economic History Review* 45 (1992): 51–62.

> women overall constituted only 21 percent of all participants in the Brigstock land market, so only one daughter conveyed or received land for every four sons who did so.... daughters were more likely than sons to bring partners to their land transfers and to rely on intrafamilial transactions.... sons were far more likely than daughters to receive future grants from parents, and daughters relied more heavily than sons on parental gifts of property.... The former reflects the preference of sons as heirs (since most future grants were designed to ensure proper inheritance), and the latter suggests that the weakened purchasing power of daughters forced them to lean more heavily on parental generosity than sons.[31]

Kim Phillips has noticed that peasant daughters' inheritance did change over time. When the plague hit, there was a brief period during which daughters on *some* manors had opportunities to hold land that they had not had before. However, these opportunities again diminished in the decades following the plague. For example, on the Essex manor of Havering, Majorie McIntosh noted that daughters appear in strong numbers in possession of land in the mid-fourteenth century, but by the mid-fifteenth century no women held tenancies alone. R. M. Smith has noted a similar development for daughters on the manor of Redgrave in Suffolk, stating that "fifteenth-century evidence 'shows little favour bestowed upon their daughters by men as they arranged for the dispersal of property after their death.'"[32]

This does not mean, of course, that women on rural manors did not inherit. In her study of manorial courts of Norwich, Elaine Clark found women, as well as men, negotiating continually with community and family members, as well as lords, in an effort to best control their lives. Clark has focused on these villagers negotiating choice of marriage partners and age at marriage, for example by paying fines to delay marriage. They also negotiated inheritance. Clark finds two sisters negotiating with their brother for a piece of his landed inheritance in exchange for an annual payment in crops.[33] While it is clear

---

[31] Bennett, *Brigstock*, 81–82.

[32] R. M. Smith, "Coping with Uncertainty: Women's Tenure of Customary Land in England c. 1370–1430," in *Enterprise and Individuals in Fifteenth-Century England*, ed. Jennifer Kermode (Stroud: Alan Sutton, 1991), 62; Marjorie McIntosh, *Autonomy and Community: The Royal Manor of Havering 1200–1500* (Cambridge: Cambridge University Press, 1986), 171–73. Both cited in Kim Phillips, *Medieval Maidens*, 125–26.

[33] Elaine Clark, "The Decision to Marry in Thirteenth- and Early Fourteenth-Century Norfolk," *Mediaeval Studies* 49 (1987): 507.

that London daughters had an advantage in comparison with their rural counterparts, in both locales women appear often as actors, negotiating with, or for, their property, rather than as more passive placeholders of that property.

Concentrating on Women in Urban England

Women in London benefited from burgage tenure, the freedom to devise property. Beginning at the start of the twelfth century, the freedom of devise developed at different times in England. The development of a uniform common law stopped the development in most rural areas, but in boroughs, because of their distinctive relationships with the king, it was allowed to continue. The freedom to devise property in boroughs, was applied both to hereditary and acquired land, and was aided by the development of the will of land (in the early Middle Ages, wills dealt almost entirely with movable goods).[34] London daughters also benefited from the lack of the custom of primogeniture followed in many other regions in the country. Primogeniture in the countryside did not dominate everywhere, but studies have shown a strong preference for the eldest male to inherit land and the younger siblings, including daughters, to inherit moveable goods.[35]

While population is impossible to estimate without parish records noting births and deaths, it is certain that London was the largest town in England. Estimates range from 60,000–100,000, with the likelihood of about 80,000 in the late Middle Ages.[36] In comparison, York likely had about 15,000, and Bristol, Lincoln, and Norwich about 8,000. About twelve other towns had over 5,000 inhabitants.[37] Does this exceptionality in size translate into exceptionality in inheritance by daughters? Is London an anomaly? I do not believe it was, or at least not entirely so. Burgage tenure did vary from town to

[34] Sheehan, *The Will in Medieval England*, 274–82.

[35] Erickson, *Women and Property in Early Modern England*, 77. There were exceptions to primogeniture. In Yorkshire, influenced by Norse tradition, daughters might have stood a better chance to inherit land along with their brothers.

[36] Barron, *London in the Later Middle Ages*, 238. For another population estimate of London, see P. Nightengale, "Growth of London in the Medieval English Economy," in *Progress and Problems in Medieval England*, ed. Richard Britnell and John Hatcher (Cambridge: Cambridge University Press, 2002), 89–109.

[37] Swanson, *Medieval Artisans*, 2–3.

town. In Ipswich, for example, male and female heirs inherited regardless of marital status. In Exeter, which had a population of about 3,100 in the fourteenth century,[38] there was an instance in the thirteenth century when a married daughter inherited property, along with a fourteenth-century case where a married daughter was excluded from inheritance because she already received her marriage portion.[39] By the late fourteenth century, it appears that Exeter allowed married daughters to inherit by right. Therefore, even within one borough, custom could change over time.[40]

Even allowing for the idiosyncrasies of custom in each borough, over thirty towns practiced burgage tenure, with some limitations, such as fees for alienation. Devise of property was completely free of any restrictions in twenty-five towns, including Oxford, York, Newcastle, Hereford, Lynn, Bristol, and Dublin, along with London.[41] Furthermore, research on a number of provincial towns suggests an economic situation for women similar to that of London. In Bristol, for example, as in London, daughters could and did inherit, could and did apprentice to crafts; when married, they could and did work with their husbands or alternatively trade as *femme sole* merchants; and as widows they could and did manage their property obtained through inheritance or jointure.[42] Similarly, in her work on merchants in York, Hull, and Beverley, Jennifer Kermode found evidence of women inheriting and managing real estate as well, along with daughters who received cash portions for marriage. For example, in York, Katherine Leversham was active in securing the inheritance for her children, and in Beverley two daughters of Stephen Coppendale inherited £100 each.[43] In addition to instances of daughters inheriting and women managing property in these towns, demographic evidence suggests that there were more single women, including young women, in towns and cities.[44] According to an early-sixteenth-centu-

---

[38] Maryanne Kowaleski, *Local Markets and Regional Trade in Medieval Exeter* (Cambridge: Cambridge University Press, 1995), 4.

[39] See Mary Bateson, *Borough Customs*, Selden Society (London: Bernard Quaritch, 1906), 2:132–133.

[40] See Maryanne Kowaleski, "The History of Urban Families in Medieval England," *Journal of Medieval History* 14, no. 1 (1988): 47–63, 60 n.7.

[41] Hemmeon, *Burgage Tenure*, 182–83

[42] Peter Fleming, *Women in Late Medieval Bristol* (Bristol: Bristol Branch of the Historical Association, 2001).

[43] Kermode, *Medieval Merchants*, 91, 100.

[44] Kowaleski, "Singlewomen," 49, 64. See also Kowaleski, "The History of Urban Families in Medieval England," 55.

ry census in Coventry, the percentage of single women in the adult population was perhaps as high as 43%, and 29.9% were represented in the 1377 poll tax (compared with around 20% in urban late medieval Tuscany and around 2% in rural Tuscany).[45] By extension, this might suggest that more women were present in towns to take advantage of increased inheritance opportunities, or opportunities to own, manage, rent, and sell properties more generally.

London was a giant compared to many provincial towns, yet it was similar to them legally and institutionally in many ways: most provincial towns, as did London, had civic regulation: many had ward courts, parishes, suburbs, craft guilds, powerful religious foundations, and, of course, immigration. With more case studies of daughters' inheritances, it might be shown that daughters across the towns of England faced similar opportunities in inheritance of real estate. With upwards of 15% of the entire population of England living in towns by 1300,[46] the possibilities gained through inheritance may have represented a substantial impact on women's lives. In light of this, we may need to adjust our views of women's opportunities in urban spaces.

Considering London Women

Returning to London and the possibilities for daughters in the capital, records outside of the Husting wills reveal women active in the real estate market. In her book *Wealth of Wives: Women, Law, and the Economy in Late Medieval London*, Barbara Hanawalt includes examples of London women renting properties along London Bridge. Her research reveals that on average, 7.4 percent of renters of the lucrative property along the bridge were women during a ten year-span for which rental records exist between 1460 and 1484. Hanawalt suggests that this number is small in part because the leases to women were probably for shorter time periods than to men, as single women may have married and then husbands' names would be listed.[47] Hanawalt also found women buying and selling real estate in

[45] Kowaleski, "Singlewomen," table A1 on pages 326–28. See also, See also Kowaleski, "The History of Urban Families in Medieval England," 55, 61 n.26.

[46] David M. Palliser, *Cambridge Urban History* (Cambridge: Cambridge University Press, 2000), 1:4.

[47] Hanawalt, *Wealth of Wives: Women, Law, and the Economy in Late Medieval London* (Oxford: Oxford University Press, 2007), 138–39.

land deeds: single women and widows were sellers in 6% of the deeds overall involving property from 1300–1474 and were buyers in 3%, while women acting with their husbands comprised one third of all of the selling transactions.[48] In addition, she also found women suing over their rights to property in the city's possessory assizes. In cases involving a range of properties, women comprised 20% of the litigants.[49] These numbers may be small and the evidence for London scattered, nevertheless taken together we are allowed a glimpse of busy London streets, where some daughters managed their inheritance.

Although women appear as actors in the records tracing real estate transactions, Barbara Hanawalt argues that London's burgage tenure and custom of inheritance meant that "real estate and liquid wealth passed through the hands of women,"[50] and that the "self-limiting patriarchy"[51] of late medieval London produced a horizontal social structure (rather than one that favored lineages as elsewhere in Europe) that built capital and reinforced the power of the town guilds. She argues that women were important to late medieval Londoners as "conduits of capital"[52] for the formation of the household economy.

It is clear that Londoners, by using the existing patriarchal structure, protected their daughters' rights to inherit. Yet, I would argue, alternatively, that these parents intended for their daughters to be active economic agents in the land market more than transmitters of wealth for the preservation of family or oligarchy. It is not clear in the wills whether the daughters were married or not—marital status is not consistently mentioned by the testators. As mentioned in chapter three, only 113 of 1,529 daughters are mentioned as married, or 7%, while only six sons are mentioned as married out of 1,854, less than 1%. In addition, the city's records do not require that real estate left to daughters in wills be used only for their dowries. Thus, it is plausible that married daughters could have received property in addition to the dowries they received from their parents *inter vivos* and that this inherited wealth could have been used by daughters for their own financial endeavors or for that of their future households. This

[48] Hanawalt, *Wealth of Wives*, 163–65.
[49] Hanawalt, *Wealth of Wives*, 165–66.
[50] Hanawalt, *Wealth of Wives*, 96.
[51] Hanawalt, *Wealth of Wives*, 12 passim.
[52] Hanawalt, *Wealth of Wives*, 208.

is in contrast to Hanawalt's statement that "almost all the wills and some of the court cases point to the female inheritance being directed toward an eventual marriage. If the father was alive, a daughter would receive her portion of inheritance when she married."[53] While the presumption of marriage may have indeed been great in medieval London, I found no hard evidence in the Husting wills that a daughter's inheritance would have been intended as dowry only or that if she was married she would be cut off from her father's inheritance.

Furthermore, it is also possible that daughters used their inheritances for other reasons than to lure a husband. In towns it was less common for women to marry than in the countryside, and it has been noted that there was a lower sex ratio in late medieval towns along with a surplus of single people, as compared with the countryside.[54] Thus, it is possible to entertain the idea that these daughters may have used their inheritance for reasons other than a marriage portion: to establish themselves in a trade, to purchase property, or to become proprietors. Therefore, I believe Hanawalt is right in the sense that many London women used their property for the benefit of the household economy. It was often in their best interest, as well as that of their families'. Yet, I do not believe this makes these women place holders or passive.

A key factor in the determination of women's involvement in investment and property management was their financial wherewithal as well as legal control. Since many women were most financially stable and free upon the death of their husbands, many of the works on women investors have focused on widows. In his work on women and credit in medieval and early modern Europe, Jordan heavily focused on widows, and with reason. Widows likely had greater capital to invest than single, unmarried women. Indeed, as Hanawalt notes, widows would have served to support the self-limiting patriarchy of London as channels of wealth, especially for the best interests of guilds. Single women, however, had the legal freedom to control what property they did have, and married women, with their husbands' support, could have considerable combined capital. As Marjorie McIntosh points out, a married woman who had the support of her husband "would potentially have had more capital to in-

[53] Hanawalt, *Wealth of Wives*, 8.

[54] See Kowaleski, "The History of Urban Families in Medieval England," 55.

vest in business or money-lending activity than a not-married woman."[55] Because husbands "covered" their wives *de jure* does not mean *de facto* that their wives were not involved in cases regarding real estate investment, or that it was not their wives' property they were leasing. We tend to see patriarchal structures, like England's coverture laws, and assume husbands made all decisions concerning real estate investment, even if their wives' inherited property was concerned. Yet, this might be an unfair assumption as we know from other studies that women in the past were adept at negotiating patriarchy to their advantage and many married women could be behind the investment decisions we see represented by their husbands' names in the records.

Unfortunately, it is not possible to see all of the financial actions of married women. If they appeared in court, many could have been in partnership with their husbands, or leading their husbands, but only their husbands would have needed to be named as the creditors or debtors. Married women could petition in England to trade on their own as *femmes soles* or they could have remained *femmes couvertes* and operated their own business with their husband's consent or collaboration. McIntosh argues that women in late medieval London more often did the latter, as it gave them more legal flexibility in various situations.[56] Barbara Hanawalt also supports this conclusion and explains that women acting as *femmes soles* are scanty in the London records, even though the law allows it.[57] All of the studies reviewed here suggest that the daughters of late medieval London, endowed with property, likely played important roles in the city's economy as autonomous traders or artisans who enhanced their family's income, as independent proprietors, or as business partners with their husbands.

The 3,081 wills enrolled with the Husting Court indicate that parents provided equally for their children. In particular, it is clear from the wills that these parents aimed to equip their daughters for economic success and to provide them with financial security, as they did for their brothers. Londoners, male and female alike, left an array

[55] McIntosh, *Working Women*, 97.

[56] See Marjorie McIntosh, "The Benefits and Drawbacks of *Femme Sole* Status," *Journal of British Studies* 44 (2005): 410–38.

[57] Hanawalt, *Wealth of Wives*, 138–39. For her discussion of *femme sole* status, see 171–73, 183 passim. *Femme sole* status was not unique to London; Bristol records also reveal *femme sole* registrations. Fleming, *Women in Late Medieval Bristol*, 7.

of movable goods to their daughters to use to set up a household, run a business, supplement a husband's income, or invest as capital: plate, cups, spoons, chests, pots, beds, cushions, brewing utensils, dresses, jewelry. These were tools that daughters could employ to conduct business and to pursue a livelihood, either as single women or independently within a marriage, or complimentary to the vocation of their husbands. Similarly, parents bequeathed a wide range of real estate to their daughters, even when they had brothers, which included tenements, shops, houses, and land. They also specified the type of inheritance, such as a joint fee tail, most likely to tailor to the daughters' personal situation as well as to best implement their own wishes. Daughters would have invested, rented, managed, or sold this property to their, or their families', best advantage. Even in the face of hardship, like the plague, parents were eager, when they could, to provide for their daughters who they viewed as viable heirs.

In addition, the secondary research on women and investment strategies uncovers women who operated, traded, and invested in a world dominated by men and influenced by ideas that women were inferior to men. These daughters in late medieval London, then, most likely explored diverse financial avenues with their inheritances—these were women who could invest their movable or immovable property in business and trading ventures; they could loan money; they could rent real estate, such as houses or tenements; they could mortgage land or buildings; they could use their capital to act as brokers or sureties for others. Further research into property management and investment by women in late medieval London should reveal that the daughters who appear in the Husting Wills harnessed the power made available to them by their parents in real and lasting ways.

Thinking Anew About Women's Experiences

Research into the investment strategies of medieval women is allowing a greater realization of the position of women in medieval society. Scholars' research has firmly established women's work as lower paid, less stable, relatively unskilled, and more diverse than men's. Yet, despite obstacles, we are becoming aware that they actively managed the resources at their disposal. Many different avenues of scholarship are converging in interesting ways. Research on the economic opportunities available to women suggests that the urban situation varied significantly from the rural one and that this situation may have also influenced family structure. In her study, Reyerson suggests that "one possible explanation for women's participation in business could lie, somewhat ironically, in the weaker and less traditional configuration of the family in the urban setting. Urban families were more fragile than rural families because of the difficult living conditions."[58] She posits that because of urban conditions, family configuration tended to fragment rather than follow patriarchal lines and thus forced women into greater roles of independence. This is a suggestive idea and one that brings together studies of women and family and women and the urban economy. It is clear that the daughters of the Husting wills were given economic opportunities different from their rural counterparts, or at least in different proportions. It seems probable that these women took advantage of these opportunities in a world that often deemphasized their influence.

Instead of primogeniture negatively influencing women's opportunities in the late Middle Ages, it is clear that some medieval cities cultivated positive environments for businesswomen or business-minded women. Women's identity in cities, as in the countryside, remained tied to the life cycle or family role (daughter, wife, widow), yet it is evident that in cities like late medieval London, these women were not mere placeholders. Instead, they were exercising power and influence through the property given to them by their parents. From a modern perspective, women defined by their familial roles, such as the daughters in the Husting wills, rather than identified as independent actors appears limiting, but it was not entirely so. These were women who were given access to power through inheritance rather than having their power reduced by inheritance. Changes in inheritance patterns did not appear to negatively affect the daughters in this late medieval city and may not have in other late medieval English cities either.

Most often, scholars studying women have considered their position (economic and otherwise) in comparison to their male counterparts. One central debate has been whether or not women experienced a "golden age" in the workplace in preindustrial societies, specifically

[58] Reyerson, "Women in Business," 137–38.

focusing on the period following the plague, as the epidemic influenced work opportunities and life-cycle changes for women.[59] Caroline Barron, the premier historian of late medieval London, has applied the classic question of women's history to London. She determined that women had a wider range of labor opportunities available to them in late medieval London than elsewhere, but due to the demographic rise, as occurred elsewhere, their economic prospects deteriorated by the sixteenth century.[60] The golden age argument has been redefined since the question was first posed, and scholars now deemphasize the near equality between men and women that early twentieth-century scholars saw before industrialization. Instead, they see a more nuanced picture of steady fluctuation with dips and peaks in the trajectory rather than highly emphasized golden, or oppositely, bleak, periods in history. Scholars also now agree that the dips and peaks affected women of varying social and economic statuses differently.

In her 1988 review article of scholars' research on working women, Judith Bennett argues that the history of working women from the twelfth to the nineteenth centuries is one of continuity rather than radical change. As she explains in her article, early twentieth-century scholars focused on medieval women active in work, as they themselves were some of the first to enter professional careers.[61] Since then, some modern scholars have continued this view wanting to see equality in a premodern era, while others, feeling the many oppressions of sexism today have painted a bleak picture of the opportunities for medieval women. Bennett argues that while the limitations women faced certainly changed over time, the overall picture remains one of women with weak work identities finding low-status work be-

---

[59] See Hanawalt, "Introduction," in *Women and Work in Pre-Industrial Europe*. See also, Hanawalt, "Golden Ages for the History of Medieval English Women," in *Women in Medieval History and Historiography*, ed. Susan Mosher Stuard (Philadelphia: Pennsylvania Press, 1987), 1–24. Two important works on the impact of the plague are: P. J. P. Goldberg, *Women, Work, and Life Cycle in a Medieval Economy: Women in York and Yorkshire c. 1300–1520* (Oxford: Clarendon Press, 1992); and Sandy Bardsley, "Women's Work Reconsidered: Gender and Wage Differentiation in Late Medieval England," *Past and Present: A Journal of Historical Studies* 165 (1999): 3–30. See also, Bennett, "'History that Stands Still': Women's Work in the European Past," *Feminist Studies* 14, no. 2 (1988): 269–283.

[60] Barron, "The 'Golden Age' of Women in Medieval London."

[61] Bennett, "History That Stands Still," 269–70.

cause of patriarchy. In her words, it is a story of "new designs embroidered on a cloth of oppression and deprivation."[62]

To some extent, searching for golden ages or particular turning points is fruitless because they either did not exist or, if they did, they did so only for a group of women circumscribed by factors like social class or personal circumstance. However, there are new avenues to be explored in women's history, which is made evident by the experiences of daughters in late medieval London. We should avoid becoming mired in describing the hopefulness or bleakness of medieval women's lives; it is neither glory nor guts. Instead, while most women were certainly barred from many aspects of life, especially political control, to carry on the textile metaphor, it is clear that they were integral fibers in the social and economic material of medieval life. The inheritances for London daughters, and perhaps those of daughters in other late medieval English cities, did not necessarily constitute a golden age for women, yet it was not a tarnished trough either.[63] Undeniably, as this scholarship converges, a new view of women in the medieval past is emerging. The past includes women who were living within the power structures that confined them or denied their engagement, and understanding their experiences and motives is important. They are experiences of negotiation, of working to improve their family and household finances, of utilizing social networks. These are not always women resisting medieval power structures or norms about women's place in society, and we should not award them more power than they actually possessed. Rather, these were women who were focusing on what would work best in their situations, in their day-to-day existence, and were pursuing economic options most viable for them.

It has been soundly established that women were not equal with men in the Middle Ages. We can recognize that medieval women lived in a male-privileged, male-dominated world where most everything was defined by a male model and still discuss the instances where women navigated this structure. For example, medieval people

---

[62] Bennett, "History that Stands Still," 280. See also her recent, excellent study in which she discusses the importance of continuity to feminist history. Bennett, *History Matters: Patriarchy and the Challenge of Feminism* (Philadelphia: University of Pennsylvania Press, 2006).

[63] Peter Fleming makes a similar argument in his review of women's status and work in Bristol. See *Women in Late Medieval Bristol* (Bristol: Bristol Branch of the Historical Association, 2001), 21.

derived a variety of dualistic ideas about gender roles from the fundamental construct of an ideal male model and a lesser female variant: superior, inferior; spirit, matter; power, submission. One of the most dominant dualistic gender constructs in medieval society was active, passive. Yet, the Husting wills, along with the research on women owning and managing property, reveal women with the resources to actively shape their financial interests and the real estate market in their towns. Certainly, female proprietors were in the minority, but this does not make their existence and actions less noteworthy. It is not useful to focus on women in the past solely as victims of patriarchy. Nor is it helpful to only seek out women in the past who were independent, powerful forces turning the system on its head out of self-awareness. These cases both exist, but, just as importantly and perhaps in the majority, the case of women who acted in their own interests, and in many cases as an extension of their families' interests, is a worthy pursuit.

Let us build upon the continuity that Bennett outlined over ten years ago, and reiterated in a recent work.[64] While recognizing the ways in which the power structures limited women's opportunities, we need to tell the story of women negotiating these structures in their lives: how they traversed restrictions, usurped powers usually denied to them, enhanced opportunities within their realm of influence, and even at times complied with patriarchy.[65] Scholars agree that women could not fully participate in their world and that they faced severe restrictions, even before industrialization, but now we can add to that by considering how they lived and worked within that world, how they negotiated those restrictions, and how they participated in their economies, societies, and governments.

Taken together, the results of this study on daughters' inheritance, the research into women's property ownership, and a consideration of daughters' inheritance in other English towns, reveals that while the late Middle Ages was not a golden age in terms of equal economic opportunities with men, these were women who chose various locations in which to work and pursue a means of livelihood: the hearth, the shop, the real estate market. In a patriarchal society that

---

[64] Judith Bennett, *History Matters*.

[65] Bennett emphasizes this idea and cites Deniz Kandiyoti's concept of "patriarchy bargains," in "Bargaining with Patriarchy," *Gender and Society* 2, no. 3 (1988): 274–90, which usefully describes the variety of actions taken by women, including supporting patriarchy to meet their own needs. Bennett, *History Matters*, 59.

stressed the patriliny and often tied women to family roles, daughters of late medieval London and their counterparts in other English towns and elsewhere in Europe were women who successfully navigated the patriarchal structures of their world. By considering daughterhood, we can see a broader swath of women, and these were women actively buying, selling, lending, borrowing, brokering, renting, and investing. Medieval daughters met up with many often-debilitating legal, social, and cultural restrictions that prevented them in almost all situations from competing with men. Yet, depending on their individual situations as well as the particular restrictions they encountered, these women were remarkable in how they navigated limitations to meet their needs and those of their families, and by extension how they were integral players in their society. The experiences of some of these London daughters temper the prevailing views at the time of women as subordinate, worth less, and inherently lustful and sinful.

Prescriptive sources are powerful in depicting strong notions of the gendered nature of property.[66] For example, in the Husting Wills more sons than daughters received commercial property in London. Yet, read carefully, prescriptive sources also reveal that these notions of gendered property were challenged, that they were more fluid than rigid. The design may indeed have been for women to be passive instruments in property matters, but the reality was not always so. Daughters of the London elite may have run up against the enduring patriarchal structures that women before and after them encountered, but they negotiated those limitations, as did many women before and after. Just as women today creatively work with the systems that they face, medieval women did the same. Let us exult in the continuity of women creatively managing circumstances as their world changed around them.

[66] My thanks to Martha Howell and Jean Howard for an excellent seminar, "Managing Property, Constructing Gender," at the 2008 Berkshire Conference that discussed ideas of gendered property.

APPENDIX ONE

TESTATORS

Year	Male Testators	Female Testators	Total Testators
1300	19	6	25
1301	11	2	13
1302	8	0	8
1303	14	4	18
1304	24	0	24
1305	24	8	32
1306	31	3	34
1307	43	11	54
1308	29	2	31
1309	28	4	32
1310	29	5	34
1311	37	5	42
1312	34	7	41
1313	29	5	34
1314	28	3	31
1315	24	4	28
1316	40	6	46
1317	15	4	19
1318	27	3	30
1319	15	1	16
1320	7	2	9
1321	25	1	26
1322	24	4	28
1323	24	4	28
1324	16	4	20
1325	18	3	21
1326	19	2	21

Year	Male Testators	Female Testators	Total Testators
1327	33	5	38
1328	48	3	51
1329	38	8	46
1330	20	1	21
1331	32	2	34
1332	31	4	35
1333	30	4	34
1334	16	4	20
1335	23	5	28
1336	21	3	24
1337	25	3	28
1338	12	4	16
1339	17	0	17
1340	19	2	21
1341	31	1	32
1342	26	5	31
1343	15	2	17
1344	11	1	12
1345	15	1	16
1346	21	1	22
1347	23	3	26
1348	94	22	116
1349	233	51	284
1350	27	7	34
1351	10	2	12
1352	14	3	17
1353	18	0	18
1354	15	0	15
1355	9	1	10
1356	14	1	15
1357	17	0	17
1358	14	1	15

Year	Male Testators	Female Testators	Total Testators
1359	11	1	12
1360	5	1	6
1361	116	17	133
1362	32	2	34
1363	19	1	20
1364	6	0	6
1365	13	1	14
1366	18	0	18
1367	10	0	10
1368	36	0	36
1369	15	1	16
1370	8	1	9
1371	11	0	11
1372	19	0	19
1373	7	2	9
1374	20	3	23
1375	34	1	35
1376	9	1	10
1377	9	0	9
1378	8	1	9
1379	15	1	16
1380	12	4	16
1381	9	1	10
1382	11	1	12
1383	11	2	13
1384	12	2	14
1385	10	0	10
1386	11	2	13
1387	8	3	11
1388	16	1	17
1389	7	1	8
1390	15	1	16

Year	Male Testators	Female Testators	Total Testators
1391	11	0	11
1392	9	0	9
1393	13	2	15
1394	12	2	14
1395	8	3	11
1396	12	0	12
1397	15	0	15
1398	6	1	7
1399	9	0	9
1400	12	3	15
1401	6	0	6
1402	3	1	4
1403	6	1	7
1404	9	2	11
1405	10	4	14
1406	10	2	12
1407	14	2	16
1408	12	2	14
1409	2	2	4
1410	13	1	14
1411	10	0	10
1412	8	0	8
1413	8	0	8
1414	7	0	7
1415	7	0	7
1416	9	0	9
1417	3	0	3
1418	4	0	4
1419	6	1	7
1420	11	0	11
1421	5	1	6
1422	6	0	6

Year	Male Testators	Female Testators	Total Testators
1423	6	0	6
1424	2	0	2
1425	7	0	7
1426	3	0	3
1427	9	2	11
1428	4	0	4
1429	5	1	6
1430	8	0	8
1431	3	2	5
1432	8	0	8
1433	15	0	15
1434	4	1	5
1435	6	0	6
1436	7	1	8
1437	3	1	4
1438	4	0	4
1439	9	0	9
1440	2	0	2
1441	11	0	11
1442	6	1	7
1443	5	4	9
1444	2	0	2
1445	4	0	4
1446	6	0	6
1447	2	0	2
1448	3	0	3
1449	4	0	4
1450	2	1	3
1451	2	1	3
1452	4	0	4
1453	2	0	2
1454	7	0	7

Year	Male Testators	Female Testators	Total Testators
1455	0	1	1
1456	5	0	5
1457	7	0	7
1458	2	1	3
1459	7	0	7
1460	5	0	5
1461	4	0	4
1462	1	0	1
1463	4	0	4
1464	2	0	2
1465	5	0	5
1466	3	0	3
1467	4	0	4
1468	7	2	9
1469	2	0	2
1470	2	0	2
1471	1	0	1
1472	4	0	4
1473	3	0	3
1474	2	0	2
1475	4	0	4
1476	1	0	1
1477	3	1	4
1478	3	0	3
1479	0	0	0
1480	6	1	7
1481	3	0	3
1482	4	0	4
1483	1	2	3
1484	1	1	2
1485	1	0	1
1486	1	0	1

Year	Male Testators	Female Testators	Total Testators
1487	0	0	0
1488	0	0	0
1489	2	1	3
1490	1	0	1
1491	2	0	2
1492	0	0	0
1493	0	0	0
1494	1	0	1
1495	2	0	2
1496	6	0	6
1497	2	1	3
1498	1	1	2
1499	3	0	3
1500	2	1	3
Totals	2718	363	3081

APPENDIX TWO

RECIPIENTS

Year	Male Recipients	Female Recipients	Unknown Sex	Total Recipients
1300	22	38	1	61
1301	20	11	1	32
1302	11	16	1	28
1303	19	21	1	41
1304	22	29	2	53
1305	44	54	1	99
1306	32	42	2	76
1307	64	70	3	137
1308	30	41	5	76
1309	38	35	1	74
1310	25	45	2	72
1311	49	61	3	113
1312	61	57	2	120
1313	48	46	2	96
1314	26	34	7	67
1315	32	35	2	69
1316	43	41	2	86
1317	22	15	0	37
1318	50	40	2	92
1319	11	18	1	30
1320	9	23	1	33
1321	23	39	1	63
1322	24	40	3	67
1323	31	20	0	51
1324	19	28	2	49
1325	22	19	3	44
1326	24	24	0	48

Year	Male Recipients	Female Recipients	Unknown Sex	Total Recipients
1327	45	52	1	98
1328	68	70	1	139
1329	43	57	3	103
1330	20	28	1	49
1331	50	54	1	105
1332	41	44	2	87
1333	37	44	1	82
1334	31	29	0	60
1335	37	31	1	69
1336	36	27	0	63
1337	28	32	1	61
1338	13	15	0	28
1339	23	24	0	47
1340	31	30	0	61
1341	39	57	2	98
1342	38	51	1	90
1343	21	30	1	52
1344	12	16	1	29
1345	29	25	0	54
1346	42	48	0	90
1347	30	54	1	85
1348	157	158	12	327
1349	334	291	12	637
1350	67	68	5	140
1351	38	27	0	65
1352	47	35	2	84
1353	32	28	1	61
1354	38	21	0	59
1355	17	27	0	44
1356	45	31	0	76
1357	34	33	1	68
1358	34	25	1	60

Year	Male Recipients	Female Recipients	Unknown Sex	Total Recipients
1359	17	17	0	34
1360	8	11	0	19
1361	210	201	13	424
1362	45	47	6	98
1363	24	25	2	51
1364	13	13	0	26
1365	44	28	0	72
1366	48	39	1	88
1367	23	20	0	43
1368	78	62	3	143
1369	18	24	2	44
1370	19	19	0	38
1371	20	15	0	35
1372	40	41	2	83
1373	21	15	0	36
1374	40	40	0	80
1375	64	55	1	120
1376	35	12	0	47
1377	25	18	0	43
1378	15	13	0	28
1379	39	25	1	65
1380	28	32	0	60
1381	17	21	1	39
1382	20	15	1	36
1383	24	18	1	43
1384	26	31	1	58
1385	11	16	1	28
1386	27	27	0	54
1387	13	12	0	25
1388	27	27	0	54
1389	14	15	1	30
1390	26	26	1	53

Year	Male Recipients	Female Recipients	Unknown Sex	Total Recipients
1391	24	22	1	47
1392	18	17	0	35
1393	40	37	0	77
1394	15	16	1	32
1395	19	22	0	41
1396	28	21	1	50
1397	36	27	0	63
1398	8	10	1	19
1399	15	10	0	25
1400	22	17	2	41
1401	4	8	1	13
1402	2	4	0	6
1403	5	6	1	12
1404	9	15	0	24
1405	13	10	1	24
1406	6	9	0	15
1407	26	14	0	40
1408	9	11	0	20
1409	8	1	0	9
1410	10	12	1	23
1411	8	16	3	27
1412	7	6	2	15
1413	7	11	0	18
1414	7	10	1	18
1415	16	12	1	29
1416	8	19	0	27
1417	2	5	0	7
1418	9	7	0	16
1419	7	7	1	15
1420	9	21	0	30
1421	10	10	0	20
1422	5	3	0	8

Year	Male Recipients	Female Recipients	Unknown Sex	Total Recipients
1423	6	11	0	17
1424	0	2	0	2
1425	4	6	0	10
1426	0	1	0	1
1427	3	7	0	10
1428	1	4	0	5
1429	0	4	1	5
1430	8	13	0	21
1431	0	6	0	6
1432	3	8	0	11
1433	9	9	0	18
1434	5	3	0	8
1435	10	13	1	24
1436	4	8	0	12
1437	5	3	0	8
1438	3	2	0	5
1439	5	7	2	14
1440	1	1	0	2
1441	2	5	0	7
1442	5	5	2	12
1443	4	5	0	9
1444	3	2	0	5
1445	4	5	0	9
1446	10	2	5	17
1447	0	3	0	3
1448	3	2	0	5
1449	0	3	2	5
1450	2	1	0	3
1451	5	4	0	9
1452	0	3	2	5
1453	2	1	0	3
1454	2	7	0	9

Year	Male Recipients	Female Recipients	Unknown Sex	Total Recipients
1455	3	1	0	4
1456	1	3	0	4
1457	8	12	0	20
1458	0	0	0	0
1459	3	6	1	10
1460	3	3	2	8
1461	6	5	0	11
1462	2	3	0	5
1463	2	1	0	3
1464	0	6	0	6
1465	3	7	0	10
1466	3	2	0	5
1467	1	7	1	9
1468	7	10	2	19
1469	3	5	0	8
1470	0	0	0	0
1471	0	0	0	0
1472	1	2	0	3
1473	0	1	0	1
1474	1	0	0	1
1475	1	1	0	2
1476	0	0	0	0
1477	6	6	0	12
1478	0	0	0	0
1479	0	2	0	2
1480	1	1	0	2
1481	4	4	0	8
1482	1	0	0	1
1483	4	0	0	4
1484	2	6	2	10
1485	0	0	0	0
1486	3	2	0	5

Year	Male Recipients	Female Recipients	Unknown Sex	Total Recipients
1487	0	0	0	0
1488	0	0	0	0
1489	0	4	0	4
1490	0	2	0	2
1491	0	0	0	0
1492	0	0	0	0
1493	0	0	0	0
1494	1	2	0	3
1495	3	3	2	8
1496	1	3	0	4
1497	3	1	1	5
1498	1	1	1	3
1499	0	1	0	1
Totals	4056	4169	185	8411

BIBLIOGRAPHY

Manuscript Sources

Corporation of London Records Office, London
Husting Rolls

The National Archives, Kew
Prerogative Court of Canterbury and Related Probate Jurisdictions: Will Registers, PROB 11

Printed Primary Sources

Bateson, Mary. *Borough Customs.* Vol. 2. London: Bernard Quaritch, 1906.

Bracton. *De Legibus Et Consuetudinibus Angliae.* Vol. 2. Edited by George Woodbine. New Haven: Yale University Press, 1915–1942. http://hlsl.law.harvard.edu/bracton/Unframed/English/v2/180.htm.

Sharpe, Reginald R., ed. *Calendar of Letter-Books Preserved among the Archives of the Corporation of the City of London at the Guildhall: Letter-Book K.* London: J. E. Francis, 1908.

Sharpe, Reginald R., ed. *Calendar of Wills Proved and Enrolled in the Court of Husting, London, A.D. 1258–1688.* 2 vols. London: John C. Francis, 1889–1890.

Calthrop, Henry. *Reports of Speciall Cases Touching Severall Customs and Liberties of the City of London.* London: Printed for Abel Roper, 1655.

Furnivall, Frederick J., ed. *The Fifty Earliest English Wills in the Court of Probate, London, 1387–1439.* London: Trubner and Co., 1882.

Glanvill. *A Treatise on the Laws and Customs of the Kingdom of England.* Edited by G. D. G. Hall. London: Thomas Nelson Ltd., 1965.

Secondary Sources

Abram, A. "Women Traders in Medieval London." *The Economic Journal* 26, no. 102 (1916): 276–85.

Agnelos, Mark. "Urban Women, Investment, and the Commercial Revolution of the Middle Ages." In *Women in Medieval Western European Culture,* edited by Linda Elizabeth Mitchell, 257–72. New York: Taylor and Francis, 1999.

Atkinson, Clarissa. *The Oldest Vocation: Christian Motherhood in the Middle Ages.* Ithaca: Cornell University Press, 1991.

Ågren, Maria, and Amy Louise Erickson, eds. *The Marital Economy in Scandinavia and Britain, 1400–1900.* Burlington, VT: Ashgate, 2005.

Baker, J. H. *An Introduction to English Legal History.* 2nd ed. London: Buttersworths, 1979.

Bardsley, Sandy. "Women's Work Reconsidered: Gender and Wage Differentiation in Late Medieval England." *Past and Present: A Journal of Historical Studies* 165 (1999): 3–30.

Barron, Caroline M. "The Education and Training of Girls in Fifteenth-Century London." In *Courts, Counties, and the Capital in the Later Middle Ages,* edited by Diana Dunn, 139-53. New York: St. Martin's Press, 1996.

______. "The 'Golden Age' of Women in Medieval London." In *Medieval Women in Southern England,* edited by Keith Bate and Malcolm Barber, 35-58. Reading, England: Graduate Centre for Medieval Studies, University of Reading, 1989.

______. "Introduction: The Widow's World." In *Medieval London Widows 1300–1500,* edited by Caroline M. Barron and Anne F. Sutton, xiii–xxxiv. London: Hambledon Press, 1994.

______. "London 1300–1540." In *Cambridge Urban History of Britain,* edited by D. M. Palliser, 395–440. Cambridge: Cambridge University Press, 2000.

______. *London in the Later Middle Ages: Government and People, 1200–1500.* Oxford: Oxford University Press, 2004.

Barron, Caroline, and Matthew Davies. "Ellen Langwith: Silkwoman of London (Died 1481)." *The Ricardian: Journal of the Richard III Society* 13 (2003): 39–47.

Barron, Caroline M., and Anne F. Sutton, eds. *Medieval London Widows 1300–1500.* London: Hambledon Press, 1994.

Beattie, Cordelia. "Governing Bodies: Law Courts, Male Householders, and Single Women in Late Medieval England." In *The Medieval Household in Christian Europe c. 850–c. 1550: Managing Power, Wealth, and the Body,* edited by Cordelia Beattie, Anna Maslakovic, and Sarah Rees Jones, 199–220. Turnhout: Brepols, 2003.

______. *Medieval Single Women: The Politics of Social Classification in Late Medieval England.* Oxford: Oxford University Press, 2007.

Beattie, Cordelia, Anna Maslakovic, and Sarah Rees Jones, eds. *The Medieval Household in Christian Europe, c. 850–1550.* Vol. 12, International Medieval Research. Turnhout: Brepols, 2003.

Bennet, Judith. *Ale, Beer, and Brewsters in England: Women's Work in a Changing World, 1300–1600.* New York: Oxford University Press, 1996.

______. *History Matters: Patriarchy and the Challenge of Feminism.* Philadelphia: University of Pennsylvania Press, 2006.

______. "'History that Stands Still': Women's Work in the European Past." *Feminist Studies* 14, no. 2 (1988): 269–83.

______. "Medieval Women, Modern Women: Across the Great Divide." In *Culture and History, 1350–1600: Essays on English Communities, Identities and Writing,* edited by David Aers, 147–75. New York: Harvester Wheatsheaf, 1992.

______. "Women and Men in the Brewers' Gild of London, ca. 1420." In *The Salt of Common Life: Individuality and Choice in the Medieval Town, Countryside and Church. Essays Presented to J. Ambrose Raftis,* edited by Edwin Brezette DeWindt, 181–232. Kalamazoo: Medieval Institute Publications, 1995.

______. *Women in the Medieval English Countryside: Gender and Household in Brigstock before the Plague.* New York: Oxford University Press, 1987.

Bennett, Judith, and Amy Froide, eds. *Singlewomen in the European Past, 1250–1800.* Philadelphia: University of Pennsylvania Press, 1999.

Bensch, Stephen P. *Barcelona and Its Rulers, 1096–1291.* Cambridge: Cambridge University Press, 1995.

Biancalana, Joseph. *The Fee Tail and the Common Recovery in Medieval England, 1176–1502.* Cambridge: Cambridge University Press, 2001.

Black, Henry Campbell. *Black's Law Dictionary: Definitions of the Terms and Phrases of American and English Jurisprudence, Ancient and Modern.* 6th ed. St. Paul: West Publishing Co., 1990.

Blackstone, William. *Commentaries on the Laws of England, 1765–1769, Book I, Chapter 15, Part III.* http://www.lonang.com/exlibris/blackstone/bla-115.htm.
Bloch, Marc. *Feudal Society.* Vol 1. Translated by L. A. Manyon. Chicago: University of Chicago Press, 1961.
Bowers, Richard H. "From Rolls to Riches: King's Clerks and Moneylending in Thirteenth-Century England." *Speculum* 58, no. 1 (1983): 60–71.
Brink, Maryann E. "The Social Description of Property in Late Medieval Avignon," *Medieval Perspectives* 10 (1995): 67–76.
Brown, Judith C., and Jordan Goodman. "Women and Industry in Florence." *The Journal of Economic History* 40, no.1 (1980): 73–80.
Burgess, Clive. "Late Medieval Wills and Pious Convention: Testamentary Evidence Reconsidered." In *Profit, Piety, and the Profession in Later Medieval England,* edited by Michael Hicks, 14–33. Gloucester: Alan Sutton, 1990.
Burkholder, Kristen. "Material Culture and Self-Presentation in Late Medieval England." PhD diss., University of Minnesota, 2001.
______. "Threads Bared: Dress and Textiles in English Wills." In *Medieval Clothing and Textiles.* Vol. 1, edited by Robin Netherton and Gale R. Owen-Crocker, 133–154. Boydell Press: 2005.
Butcher, A. F. "Rent and the Urban Economy: Oxford and Canterbury in the Later Middle Ages." *Southern History* 1 (1979): 11–43.
Carlier, Myriam, and Tim Soens, eds. *The Household in Late Medieval Cities, Italy and Northwestern Europe Compared.* Leuven: Garant, 2001.
Carlin, Martha. *Medieval Southwark.* London: Hambledon Press, 1996.
Carlson, Eric Josef. "The Historical Value of the Ely Consistory Probate Records." In *Index of the Probate Records of the Consistory Court of Ely 1449–1858 Part I: A–E,* edited by Elisabeth Leedham-Green and Rosemary Rodd, xvii–lix. London: British Record Society, 1994.
Cavallo, Sandra, and Lyndan Warner, eds. *Widowhood in Medieval and Early Modern Europe.* New York: Pearson Education Inc., 1999.
Chan, Mary, and Nancy Wright. "Marriage, Identity, and the Pursuit of Property in Seventeenth-Century England: The Cases of Anne Clifford and Elizabeth Wiseman." In *Women, Property, and the Letters of the Law in Early Modern England,* edited by Margaret W. Ferguson. Nancy E. Wright, and A. R. Buck, 162–82. Toronto: University of Toronto Press, 2004.
Cheney, C. R., and Michael Jones. *A Handbook of Dates.* Cambridge: Cambridge University Press, 2004.
Clark, Elaine. "The Decision to Marry in Thirteenth- and Early Fourteenth-Century Norfolk." *Mediaeval Studies* 49 (1987): 496–516.
Cohn, Samuel Kline. *The Cult of Remembrance and the Black Death: Six Renaissance Cities in Central Italy.* Baltimore: Johns Hopkins University Press, 1992.
______. *Death and Property in Siena, 1205–1800: Strategies for the Afterlife.* Baltimore: Johns Hopkins University Press, 1988.
Connolly, Margaret. "Another Medieval London Widow: The Story of Beatrice Cornburgh." *The Ricardian: Journal of the Richard III Society* 13 (2003): 148–58.
Coss, Peter. *The Origins of the English Gentry.* Cambridge: Cambridge University Press, 2003.
Crabb, Ann Morton. *The Strozzi of Florence: Widowhood and Family Solidarity in the Renaissance.* Ann Arbor: University of Michigan Press, 2000.
Daichman, Graciela S. *Wayward Nuns in Medieval Literature.* Syracuse, NY: Syracuse University Press, 1986.
Dale, Marian K. "The London Silkwomen of the Fifteenth Century." *The Economic History Review* 4, no. 3 (1933): 324–35.

Davis, Isabel, Miriam Müller, and Sarah Rees Jones, eds. *Love, Marriage, and Family Ties in the Later Middle Ages*. Vol. 11, International Medieval Research. Brepols: Turnhout, 2003.

Dean, Trevor, ed. *The Towns of Italy in the Later Middle Ages*. New York: Manchester University Press, 2000.

Dickens, Arthur Geoffrey. *Lollards and Protestants in the Diocese of York, 1509–1558*. London: Oxford University Press, 1959.

Didier, Noël. "Les Dispositions du Statut de Guillaume II de Foralquier sur les Filles Dotes (1162)." *Le Moyen Âge* 56, no. 1–2 (1950): 247–78.

Dockray-Miller, Mary. *Motherhood and Mothering in Anglo-Saxon England*. New York: St. Martin's Press, 2000.

Dronzek, Anna. "No Separate Spheres: The Household as Masculine and Feminine Space in Late Medieval England." Paper presented at the NACBS Annual Meeting, Baltimore, MD, November 2002.

Duby, George. *The Knight, the Lady, and the Priest: The Making of Modern Marriage in Medieval France*. Translated by Barbara Bray. New York: Pantheon Books, 1983.

______. *Medieval Marriage: Two Models from Twelfth-Century France*. Translated by Elbourg Forster. Baltimore: Johns Hopkins University Press 1978.

Dyer, Christopher. *An Age of Transition? Economy and Society in England in the Later Middle Ages*. Oxford: Oxford University Press, 2005.

______. *Standards of Living in the Later Middle Ages: Social Change in England c. 1200–1520*. New York: Cambridge University Press, 1989.

Epstein, Steven. *Wills and Wealth in Medieval Genoa, 1150–1250*. Cambridge: Harvard University Press, 1984.

Erickson, Amy Louise. "Common Law Versus Common Practice: The Use of Marriage Settlements in Early Modern England." *Economic History Review* 43, no. 1 (1990): 21–39.

______. "Coverture and Capitalism." *History Workshop Journal* 59 (2005): 1–16.

______. *Women and Property in Early Modern England*. New York: Routledge, 1993.

Evergates, Thomas, ed. *Aristocratic Women in Medieval France*. Philadelphia: University of Pennsylvania Press, 1999.

Farmer, Sharon. *Surviving Poverty in Medieval Paris: Gender, Ideology, and the Daily Lives of the Poor*. Ithaca: Cornell University Press, 2002.

Farr, James. *Artisans in Europe, 1300–1800*. Cambridge: Cambridge University Press, 2000.

Fisher, Anita Loy Beetham. "The Merchants of Medieval Bristol, 1350-1500." PhD diss., University of Oregon, 1987.

Fitch, Marc, ed. *Index to Testamentary Records in the Commissary Court of London*. Vol. 1, *1374–1488*. London: British Record Society, 1969.

______, ed. *Index to Testamentary Records in the Archdeaconry Court of London*. London: British Record Society, 1979.

Fleming, Peter. *Women in Late Medieval Bristol*. Bristol: Bristol Branch of the Historical Association, 2001.

Flower, C. T., ed. *Public Works in Medieval Law*. London: B. Quaritch, 1923.

Furnivall, Frederick J., ed. *The Fifty Earliest English Wills in the Court of Probate, London, 1387–1439*. London: Trubner and Co., 1882.

Gibson, Jeremy Sumner. *Probate Jurisdictions: Where to Look for Wills*. 4th ed. Baltimore: Genealogical Pub. Co., 1997.

Given-Wilson, Chris. *The English Nobility in the Late Middle Ages: The Fourteenth-Century Political Community*. London: Routledge, 1987.

Goldberg, P. J. P. "Household and the Organisation of Labour in Late Medieval Towns: Some English Evidence." In *The Household in Late Medieval Cities, Italy and Northwestern Europe Compared*, edited by Myriam Carlier and Tim Soens, 59–70. Leuven: Garant, 2001.

______. "The Public and The Private: Women in the Pre-Plague Economy." In *Thirteenth Century England III. Proceedings of the Newcastle-upon-Tyne Conference 1989*, edited by P.R. Coss and S.D. Lloyd, 75-89. Woodbridge, Suffolk: Boydell and Brewer, 1991.

______. "Women in Fifteenth-Century Town Life." In *Towns and Townspeople in the Fifteenth Century*, edited by John A. F. Thomson, 107–128. Gloucester: Alan Sutton, 1988.

______. *Women, Work, and Life Cycle in a Medieval Economy: Women in York and Yorkshire c. 1300–1520.* Oxford: Clarendon Press, 1992.

Goody, Jack. "Inheritance, Property and Women: Some Comparative Considerations." In *Family and Inheritance: Rural Society in Western Europe, 1200–1800*, edited by Jack Goody, Joan Thirsk, and E. P. Thompson, 10–36. New York: Cambridge University Press, 1976.

Goody, John R., and S. J. Tambiah. *Bridewealth and Dowry.* Cambridge: Cambridge University Press, 1985.

Goose, Nigel, and Nesta Evans. "Wills as an Historical Source." In *When Death Do Us Part: Understanding and Interpreting the Probate Records of Early Modern England*, edited by Tom Arkell, Nesta Evans, and Nigel Goose, 38–71. Oxford: Leopard's Head Press, 2000.

Grannum, Karen, and Nigel Taylor. *Wills and Other Probate Records.* Kew: The National Archives, 2004.

Grenville, Jane. *Medieval Housing.* London: Leicester University Press, 1997.

Guzzetti, Linda. "Women's Inheritance and Testamentary Practices in Late Fourteenth- and Early Fifteenth-Century Venice and Ghent." In *The Texture of Society: Medieval Women in the Southern Low Countries*, edited by Ellen E. Kittell and Mary A. Suydam, 79–108. New York: Palgrave Macmillan, 2004.

Hanawalt, Barbara. "At the Margins of Women's Space in Medieval Europe." In *"Of Good and Ill Repute": Gender and Social Control in Medieval England.* New York: Oxford University Press, 1998.

______. "Golden Ages for the History of Medieval English Women." In *Women in Medieval History and Historiography*, edited by Susan Mosher Stuard, 1–24. Philadelphia: Pennsylvania Press, 1987.

______. *Growing up in Medieval London: The Experience of Childhood in History.* New York: Oxford University Press, 1993.

______. *"Of Good and Ill Repute": Gender and Social Control in Medieval England.* New York: Oxford University Press, 1998.

______. "Reading the Lives of the Illiterate: London's Poor." *Speculum* 80, no. 4 (2005): 1067–86.

______. *The Ties That Bound: Peasant Families in Medieval England.* New York: Oxford University Press, 1986.

______. *Wealth of Wives: Women, Law, and the Economy in Late Medieval London.* Oxford: Oxford University Press, 2007.

______. "The Widow's Mite: Provisions for Medieval London Widows." In *Upon My Husband's Death: Widows in the Literature and Histories of Medieval Europe*, edited by Louise Mirrer, 21–45. Ann Arbor: The University of Michigan Press, 1992.

Harris, Barbara J. *English Aristocratic Women, 1450–1550: Marriage and Family, Property and Careers.* New York: Oxford University Press, 2002.

Heath, P. "Urban Piety in the Later Middle Ages: The Evidence of Hull Wills." In *Church, Politics, and Patronage in the Fifteenth Century*, edited by R. B. Dobson, 209–34. New York: St. Martin's Press, 1984.

Helmholz, Richard. "Married Women's Wills in Later Medieval England." In *Wife and Widow in Medieval England*, edited by Sue Sheridan Walker, 165–82. Ann Arbor: University of Michigan Press, 1993.

Hemmeon, Morley de Wolf. *Burgage Tenure in Mediaeval England*. Cambridge: Harvard University Press, 1914.

Herlihy, David. "The Making of the Medieval Family." In *Women, Family and Society in Medieval Europe: Historical Essays 1978–1991*. Providence: Berghahn Books, 1995.

Hinton, David A. *Gold and Gilt, Pots and Pins: Possessions and People in Medieval Britain*. Oxford: Oxford University Press, 2005.

Homans, George Caspar. *English Villagers of the Thirteenth Century*. Cambridge: Harvard University Press, 1941.

Horrox, Rosemary, ed. *The Black Death*. New York: Manchester University Press, 1994.

Hoskins, Janet. *Biographical Objects: How Things Tell the Stories of People's Lives*. New York: Routledge, 1998.

Howell, Martha. "Fixing Movables: Gifts by Testament in Late Medieval Douai." *Past and Present* 150 (1996): 3–45.

______. *The Marriage Exchange: Property, Social Place, and Gender in Cities of the Low Countries, 1300–1550*. Chicago: University of Chicago Press, 1998.

______. "The Properties of Marriage in Late Medieval Europe: Commercial Wealth and the Creation of Modern Marriage." In *Love, Marriage, and Family Ties in the Later Middle Ages*, edited by Isabel Davis, Miriam Müller, and Sarah Rees Jones, 17–61. Turnhout: Brepols, 2003.

______. "The Social Life of Pots, Beds and Dresses in Late Medieval Cities." Paper presented at the Center for Medieval Studies, University of Minnesota, Minneapolis, Minnesota, October 9, 2003.

______. *Women, Production, and Patriarchy in Late Medieval Cities*. Chicago: University of Chicago Press, 1986.

______. "Women, the Family Economy, and the Structures of Market Production in Cities of Northern Europe during the Late Middle Ages." In *Women and Work in Pre-Industrial Europe*, edited by Barbara Hanawalt, 198–222. Bloomington, IN: Indiana University Press, 1986.

Hughes, Diane Owen. "From Brideprice to Dowry in Mediterranean Europe." *Journal of Family History* 3 (1978): 262–96.

Hutton, Shennan. "In Her Own Name: Property Management and Gender in Medieval Ghent." Paper presented at the 2008 Berkshire Conference on the History of Women, June 2008.

Jehel, Georges. "Le Rôle des Femmes et du Milieu Familial a Gênes dans les Activités Commerciales au cours de la première moitié du XIIIe siècle." *Revue d'histoire économique et sociale* 53, no. 2–3 (1975): 193–215.

Jennings, John M. "The Distribution of Landed Wealth in the Wills of London Merchants 1400–1450." *Medieval Studies* 39 (1977): 261–80.

Jacobsen, Grethe. "Women's Work and Women's Role: Ideology and Reality in Danish Urban Society, 1300–1500." *The Scandinavian Economic History Review and Economy and History* 31 (1983): 1–20.

Jones, Sarah Rees. "Building Domesticity in the City: English Urban Housing after the Black Death." In *Medieval Domesticity: Home, Housing and Household in Medieval England*, edited by Maryanne Kowaleski and Jeremy Goldberg, 66-91. Cambridge: Cambridge University Press, 2008.

______."Property, Tenure and Rents: Some Aspects of the Topography and Economy of Medieval York." D. Phil. thesis, University of York, 1987.

______. "Women's Influence on the Design of Urban Homes." In *Gendering the Master Narrative: Women and Power in the Middle Ages*, edited by Mary Erler and Maryanne Kowaleski, 190–211. Ithaca: Cornell University Press, 2003.

Jordan, W. K. *The Charities of London, 1480–1660*. New York: Russel Sage Foundation, 1960.

______. *The Charities of Rural England, 1480–1660*. London: G. Allen & Unwin, 1961.

______. *Philanthropy in England, 1480–1660: A Study of the Changing Pattern of English Social Aspirations*. New York: Russel Sage Foundation, 1959.

Jordan, William C. *The Great Famine: Northern Europe in the Early Fourteenth Century*. Princeton: Princeton University Press, 1996.

______. *Women and Credit in Pre-Industrial and Developing Societies*. Philadelphia: University of Pennsylvania Press, 1993.

Jusserand, J. J. *English Wayfaring Life in the Middle Ages*. Translated by Lucy Toulmin Smith. Williamstown, MA: Corner House Publishers, 1974.

Kandiyoti, Deniz. "Bargaining with Patriarchy." *Gender and Society* 2, no.3 (1988): 274–90.

Karras, Ruth Mazo. *Common Women: Prostitution and Sexuality in Medieval England*. New York: Oxford University Press, 1996.

______. *Sexuality in Medieval Europe: Doing Unto Others*. New York: Routledge, 2005.

Keene, Derek. *Cheapside before the Great Fire*. London: Economic and Social Research Council, 1985.

______. *Historical Gazetteer of London before the Great Fire*. Cambridge, England: Chadwyck-Healey, 1987.

______. "Landlords, the Property Market and Urban Development in Medieval England." In *Power, Profit, and Urban Land: Landownership in Medieval and Early Modern Northern European Towns*, edited by Finn-Einar Eliassen and Geir Atle Ersland, 93–119. Brookfield, VT: Scolar Press, 1996.

______. *Survey of Medieval Winchester*. 2 vols. Oxford: Clarendon Press, 1985.

______. "Tanners' Widows, 1300–1350." In *Medieval London Widows 1300–1500*, edited by Caroline M. Barron and Anne F. Sutton, 1–28. London: Hambledon Press, 1994.

Keene, Derek, and Vanessa Harding. *A Survey of Documentary Sources for Property Holding in London before the Great Fire*. Vol. 22. London: London Record Society, 1985.

Keene, Derek, and Alan Vince. "Medieval Buildings and Property Development in the Area of Cheapside." *Transactions of the London and Middlesex Archaeological Society* 41 (1990): 89–105.

Kelly, Henry Ansgar. "Bishop, Prioress, and Bawd in the Stews of Southwark." *Speculum* 75, no. 2 (2000): 342–88.

Kermode, Jenny. *Medieval Merchants: York, Beverley and Hull in the Later Middle Ages*. Cambridge: Cambridge University Press, 1998.

Kettle, Ann J. "'My Wife Shall Have It': Marriage and Property in the Wills and Testaments of Later Mediaeval England." In *Marriage and Property*, edited by Elizabeth M. Craik, 89–103. Aberdeen: Aberdeen University Press, 1984.

King, C. E. *Renaissance Women Patrons: Wives and Widows in Italy c. 1300–1550.* Manchester: Manchester University Press, 1998.

Kiralfy, Albert. "Wills of Personality (Movables) in England from 1066–1500 A.D." In *Actes À Cause De Mort*, 35–45. Bruxelles: De Boeck Université, 1993.

Kittel, Margaret Ruth. "Married Women in Thirteenth-Century England: A Study in Common Law." PhD diss., University of California, Berkeley, 1973.

Kittell, Ellen. "Testaments of Two Cities: A Comparative Analysis of the Wills of Medieval Genoa and Douai." *European Review of History* 5 (1998): 47–83.

Kleineke, Hanes. "Alice Martyn, Widow of London: An Episode from Richard's Youth." *The Ricardian: Journal of the Richard III Society* 14 (2004): 32–36.

Kowaleski, Maryanne. "The History of Urban Families in Medieval England." *Journal of Medieval History* 14 (1988): 47–63.

______. *Local Markets and Regional Trade in Medieval Exeter.* Cambridge: Cambridge University Press, 1995.

______. "Singlewomen in Medieval and Early Modern Europe: The Demographic Perspective." In *Singlewomen in the European Past 1250–1800*, edited by Judith Bennett and Amy Froide, 38–81. Philadelphia: University of Pennsylvania Press, 1999.

______. ""Women's Work in a Market Town: Exeter in the Late Fourteenth Century." In *Women and Work in Preindustrial Europe*, edited by Barbara Hanawalt, 145–64. Bloomington, IN: Indiana University Press, 1986.

Kowaleski, Maryanne, and Judith Bennett. "Crafts, Gilds, and Women in the Middle Ages: Fifty Years after Marian K. Dale." *Signs* 14, no. 2 (1989): 474–501.

Kuehn, Thomas. "Law, Death, and Heirs in the Renaissance: Repudiation of Inheritance in Florence." *Renaissance Quarterly* 45 (1992): 484–516.

______. *Law, Family and Women: Toward a Legal Anthropology of Renaissance Italy.* Chicago: University of Chicago Press, 1991.

______. Review of *Death and Property in Siena*, by Samuel Cohn. *Journal of Modern History* 62 (1990): 624–26.

______. Review of *Wills and Wealth in Medieval Genoa*, by Steven Epstein. *Speculum* 61, no. 1 (1986): 143–45.

Lacey, Kay. "Production of 'Narrow Ware' by Silkwomen in Fourteenth and Fifteenth Century England." *Textile History* 18, no. 2 (1987): 187–204.

______."Women and Work in Fourteenth- and Fifteenth-Century London." In *Women and Work in Pre-Industrial England*, edited by Lindsey Charles and Lorna Duffin, 24–82. Dover, NH: Croom Helm, 1985.

Lavanchy, Lisane. *Écrire sa Mort, Decrier sa Vie: Testaments de Laïcs Lausannois (1400–1450).* Lausanne: Université de Lausanne, 2003.

Lewis, Katherine J., Noel Menuge, and Kim M. Phillips, eds. *Young Medieval Women.* New York: St. Martin's Press, 1999.

______. "Women, Testamentary Discourse and Life-Writing in Later Medieval England." In *Medieval Women and the Law*, edited by Noël James Menuge, 57–75. Woodbridge, Suffolk: Boydell Press, 2000.

Livingstone, Amy. "Noblewomen's control of property in early twelfth-century Blois-
Chartres" *Medieval Prosopography* 18 (1997): 55–72.

Loengard, Janet Senderowitz. "'Legal History and the Medieval Englishwoman' Revisited: Some New Directions." In *Medieval Women and the Sources of Medieval History*, edited by Joel T. Rosenthal, 210–36. London: The University of Georgia Press, 1990.

______. "'Which may be said to be her own': widows and goods in late-medieval England." In *Medieval Domesticity: Home, Housing and Household in Medieval England*, edited by Maryanne Kowaleski and Jeremy Goldberg, 162–176. Cambridge: Cambridge University Press, 2008.

Lorcin, Marie-Thérèse. *Vivre Et Mourir En Lyonnais: À La Fin Du Moyen Age*. Paris: Editions du CNRS, 1981.

Lynch, Joseph. *The Medieval Church: A Brief History*. London: Longman, 1992.

Maddern, Philippa. "Friends of the Dead: Executors, Wills and Family Strategy in Fifteenth-Century Norfolk." In *Rulers and Ruled in Late Medieval England: Essays Presented to Gerald Harriss*, edited by G.L. Harriss, Rowena E. Archer, and Simon Walker, 155–63. London: Hambledon Press, 1995.

Maillet, J. "De L'exclusion Coutumière des Filles Dotes à La Renunciation à Succession Future dans les Coutumes de Toulouse et Bordeaux." *Revue historique de droit français et étranger* 30 (1952): 514–45.

Martin, Claire A. "Dame Margery Astry." *The Ricardian: Journal of the Richard III Society* 14 (2004): 1–31.

Mate, Mavis. *Daughters, Wives and Widows after the Black Death: Women in Sussex 1350–1535*. Woodbridge, Sussex: Boydell Press, 1998.

______. "Property Investment by Canterbury Cathedral Priory 1250–1400." *The Journal of British Studies* 23, no. 2 (1984): 1–21.

______. *Women in Medieval English Society*. Cambridge: Cambridge University Press, 1999.

Maxeiner, Andrea Dianne Bessac. "Dower and Jointure: A Legal and Statistical Analysis of the Property Rights of Married Women in Late Medieval England." PhD diss., Catholic University of America, 1990.

Mayali, Laurent. *Droit Savant et Coutumes: L'exclusion des Filles Dotées XIIème Siècles*. Frankfurt: Klostermann, 1987.

McFarlane, K. B. *The Nobility of Later Medieval England*. Oxford: Clarendon Press, 1973.

McIntosh, Marjorie. *Autonomy and Community: The Royal Manor of Havering 1200–1500*. Cambridge: Cambridge University Press, 1986.

______. "The Benefits and Drawbacks of *Femme Sole* Status." *Journal of British Studies* 44 (2005): 410–38.

______. *Working Women in English Society, 1300–1620*. Cambridge: Cambridge University Press, 2005.

McKinley, R. A. *A History of British Surnames*. New York: Longman, 1990.

McNamara, JoAnn. *Sisters in Arms: Catholic Nuns through Two Millennia*. Cambridge: Harvard University Press, 1996.

______. "Women and Power through the Family Revisited." In *Gendering the Master*
Narrative, edited by Mary C. Erler and Maryanne Kowaleski, 17–30. Ithaca: Cornell University Press, 2003.

McNamara, Joann, and Suzanne Wemple. "The Power of Women through the Family in
Medieval Europe." Special double issue, *Feminist Studies* 3/4
(1973): 126–41.

McSheffrey, Shannon. "'I Will Never Have None Ayenst My Faders Will': Consent and the Making of Marriage in the Late Medieval Diocese of London." In *Women, Marriage, and Family in Medieval Christendom: Essays in Memory of Michael M. Sheehan, C.S.B.*, edited by Constance M. Rousseau and Joel T. Rosenthal, 153–74. Kalamazoo: Medieval Institute Publications, 1998.

______. "Place, Space, and Situation: Public and Private in the Making of Marriage in Late-Medieval London." *Speculum* 79, no. 4 (2004): 960–90.

Meek, Christine. "Women, Dowries, and the Family in Late Medieval Italian Cities." In *The Fragility of Her Sex?: Medieval Irish Women in Their European Context*, edited by Christine Meek and Katharine Simms, 136–52. Dublin: Four Courts Press, 1996.

Megson, Barbara E. "Mortality Among London Citizens in the Black Death." *Medieval Prosopography* 19 (1998): 125–133.

Milsom, S. F. C. "Inheritance by Women in the Twelfth and Early Thirteenth Centuries." In *On the Laws and Customs of England: Essays in Honor of Samuel E. Thorne*, edited by Samuel Edmund Thorne and Morris S. Arnold, 60–89. Chapel Hill: University of North Carolina Press, 1981.

Mirrer, Louise, ed. *Upon My Husband's Death: Widows in the Literature and Histories of Medieval Europe*. Ann Arbor: University of Michigan Press, 1992.

Miskimin, Harry A. "The Legacies of London: 1259–1330." In *The Medieval City*, edited by David Herlihy, Harry A. Miskimin, and A. L. Udovitch, 209–27. London: Yale University Press, 1977.

Mitchell, Linda E. *Portraits of Medieval Women: Family, Marriage and Social Relationships in Thirteenth Century England*. New York: Palgrave McMillan, 2003.

Moore, John S., ed. *The Goods and Chattels of Our Forefathers*. London: Phillimore, 1976.

Munro, John. "The Consumption of Spices and Their Costs in Late-Medieval and Early-Modern Europe: Luxuries or Necessities?" Lecture, University of Toronto, rev. Nov. 5, 2005. http://www.economics.utoronto.ca/munro5/SPICES1.pdf. Accessed Jan. 21, 2009.

Murray, Jacqueline. "Kinship and Friendship: The Perception of Family by Clergy and Laity in Late Medieval London." *Albion* 20, no. 3 (1988): 369–85.

Murray, Mary Charles. "Property and 'patriarchy' in English History." *Journal of Historical Sociology* 2 (1989): 303–27.

Nicholas, D. *The Domestic Life of a Medieval City: Women, Children and the Family in Fourteenth-Century Ghent*. Lincoln: University of Nebraska Press, 1985.

Nichols, John A., and Lillian Thomas Shank, eds. *Medieval Religious Women*. 3 vols. Kalamazoo, MI: Cistercian Publications, 1984–1995.

Nightengale, P. "Growth of London in the Medieval English Economy." In *Progress and Problems in Medieval England*, edited by Richard Britnell and John Hatcher, 89–109. Cambridge: Cambridge University Press, 2002.

Palliser, David M. *Cambridge Urban History*. Vol. 1. Cambridge: Cambridge University Press, 2000.

Parsons, John Carmi, ed. *Medieval Queenship*. New York: St. Martin's Press, 1993.

______."Mothers, Daughters, Marriage, Power: Some Plantagenet Evidence, 1150–1500." In *Medieval Queenship*, edited by John Carmi Parsons, 63–78. New York: St. Martin's Press, 1993.

Payling, Simon. "Social Mobility, Demographic Change, and Landed Society in Late Medieval England." *Economic History Review*, 45 (1992): 51–73.

Pederson, Frederik. *Marriage Disputes in Medieval England*. London: Hambledon Press, 2000.

Pegues, Frank. "The *Clericus* in the Legal Administration of Thirteenth-Century England." *The English Historical Review* 71 (1956): 529–59.

Phillips, Kim M. *Medieval Maidens: Young Women and Gender in England, 1270–1540*. Manchester: Manchester University Press, 2003.

Piponnier, Françoise, and Perrine Mane. *Dress in the Middle Ages*. Translated by Caroline Beamish. New Haven, CT: Yale University Press, 1997.

Platt, Colin. *King Death: The Black Death and Its Aftermath in Late-Medieval England*. Toronto: Toronto University Press, 1997.
Pollock, Frederick, and Frederic Maitland, eds. *The History of English Law before the Time of Edward I*. Cambridge: Cambridge University Press, 1924.
Poos, L.R. "Population Turnover in Medieval Essex: The Evidence of Some Early Fourteenth-Century Tithing Lists." In *The World We Have Gained*, edited by L. Bonfield, 1–22. New York: Blackwell, 1986.
Postles, David A. "Record-Keeping in the Medieval Borough: Proof of Wills." *Archives: The Journal of the British Records Association* 16 (1983): 12–15.
______. *Talking Ballocs: Nicknames and English Medieval Sociolinguistics*. Leicester: University of Leicester, 2003.
Pounds, N. J. G. *The Culture of the English People: Iron Age to the Industrial Revolution*. Cambridge: Cambridge University Press, 1994.
Power, Eileen. *Medieval English Nunneries c. 1275 to 1535*. Cambridge: Cambridge University Press, 1922.
______. *Medieval Women*. New York: Cambridge University Press, 1975.
Queller, Donald E., and Thomas F. Madden. "Father of the Bride: Fathers, Daughters, and Dowries in Late Medieval and Early Renaissance Venice." *Renaissance Quarterly* 46, no. 4 (1993): 685–711.
Razi, Zvi. *Life, Marriage and Death in a Medieval Parish: Economy, Society and Demography in Halesowen 1270–1400*. Cambridge: Cambridge University Press, 1980.
Reaney, P. H. *A Dictionary of English Surnames*. 3rd ed. Oxford: Oxford University Press, 1997.
Reyerson, Kathryn. "Land, Houses and Real Estate Investment in Montpellier: A Study of the Notarial Property Transactions, 1293–1348." *Studies in Medieval and Renaissance History* 6 (Old Series, vol. 16) (1983): 37–112.
______. "Women in Business in Medieval Montpellier." In *Women and Work in Pre-Industrial Europe*, edited by Barbara Hanawalt, 117–144. Bloomington, IN: Indiana University Press, 1986.
Richardson, Catherine. "Household Objects and Domestic Ties." In *The Medieval Household in Christian Europe, c. 850–1550: Managing Power, Wealth, and the Body*, edited by Cordelia Beattie, Anna Maslakovic, and Sarah Rees Jones, 433–48. Turnhout: Brepols, 2003.
Riddy, Felicity. "Mother Knows Best: Reading Social Change in a Courtesy Text." *Speculum* 71, no. 1 (1996): 66–86.
Riemer, Eleanor S. "Women, Dowries, and Capital Investment in Thirteenth-Century Siena." In *The Marriage Bargain: Women and Dowries in European History*, edited by Marion A. Kaplan, 59–80. Harrington Park Press, 1985.
______. "Women in the Medieval City: Sources and Use of Wealth by Sienese Women in the Thirteenth Century." PhD diss., New York University,1975.
Rosenthal, Joel T. *The Purchase of Paradise: Gift Giving and the Aristocracy, 1307–1485*. London: Routledge, 1972.
Ruiz, Teofilo F. *From Heaven to Earth: The Reordering of Castilian Society, 1150–1350*. Princeton: Princeton University Press, 2004.
Salter, Elisabeth Ellen. "Some Differences in the Cultural Production of Household Consumption in Three North Kent Communities, c. 1450–1500." In *The Medieval Household in Christian Europe, c. 850–1550*, edited by Cordelia Beattie, Anna Maslakovic, and Sarah Rees Jones, 391–408. Turnhout: Brepols, 2003.
Schofield, John. *Medieval London Houses, 1200–1600*. New Haven: Yale University Press, 1995.

______. "Urban Housing in England, 1400–1600." In *The Age of Transition: The Archaeology of English Culture, 1400–1600*, edited by David Gaimster and Paul Stamper, 127–44. Oxford: Oxbow Books, 1997.

Schofield, John, Patrick Allen, and Colin Taylor, with contributions by Derek Keene and Alan Vince. "Medieval Buildings and Property Development in the Area of Cheapside." *Transactions of the London and Middlesex Archaeological Society* 41 (1990): 39–237.

Scott, Joan Wallach. *Gender and the Politics of History.* New York: Columbia University Press, 1999.

Sheehan, Michael. "The Bequest of Land in England in the High Middle Ages: Testaments and the Law." In *Marriage, Property, and Succession*, edited by Lloyd Bonfield, 326–38. Berlin: Duncker and Humblot, 1992.

______. "English Wills and the Records of the Ecclesiastical and Civil Jurisdictions." *Journal of Medieval History* 14 (1988): 3–12.

______. "A List of Thirteenth-Century English Wills." *Genealogists' Magazine* 13 (1961): 259–65.

______. *The Will in Medieval England: From the Conversion of the Anglo-Saxons to the End of the Thirteenth Century*. Vol. 6. Toronto: Pontifical Institution of Mediaeval Studies, 1963.

______. "Wills and Testaments." In *Medieval England: An Encyclopedia*, edited by Paul E. Szarmach, M. Teresa Tavormina, and Joel T. Rosenthal, 792-3. New York: Garland, 1998.

Skinner, Patricia. "Women, Wills and Wealth in Medieval Southern Italy." *Early Medieval Europe* 2 (1993): 133–52.

Smail, Daniel Lord. "Démanteler le Patrimoine. Les Femmes et les Biens dans la Marseille Médiévale." *Annales - Histoire, Sciences Sociales* 52, no. 2 (1997): 343–68.

______. "Mapping Networks and Knowledge in Medieval Marseille, 1337–1362: Variations on a Theme of Mobility." PhD diss., University of Michigan, 1994.

Smith, Richard M. "Coping with Uncertainty: Women's Tenure of Customary Land in England c. 1370–1430." In *Enterprise and Individuals in Fifteenth-Century England*, edited by Jennifer Kermode, 43–67. Stroud: Alan Sutton, 1991.

______. "Demographic Developments in Rural England, 1300–48: A Survey." In *Before the Black Death: Studies in the "Crisis" of the Early Fourteenth Century*, edited by B. Campbell, 25–77. New York: Manchester University Press, 1991.

______. "Families and Their Land in an Area of Partible Inheritance: Redgrave Suffolk 1260–1320." In *Land, Kinship and Life-Cycle*, edited by Richard M. Smith, 135–95. New York: Cambridge University Press, 1984.

______, ed. *Land, Kinship and Life-Cycle*. New York: Cambridge University Press, 1984.

______. "Some Issues Concerning Families and Their Property in Rural England 1250–1800." In *Land, Kinship and Life-Cycle*, edited by R. M. Smith, 1–86. Cambridge: Cambridge University Press, 2002.

______. "Women's Property Rights under Customary Law: Some Developments in the Thirteenth and Fourteenth Centuries." *Transactions of the Royal Historical Society* 36, no. 5 (1986): 165–94.

Spufford, Margaret. *Contrasting Communities: English Villagers in the Sixteenth and Seventeenth Centuries*. Cambridge: Cambridge University Press, 1974.

______. "The Limitations of the Probate Inventory." In *English Rural Society, 1500–1800: Essays in Honour of Joan Thirsk*, edited by J. Chartres and D. Hey, 139–74. Cambridge: Cambridge University Press, 1990.

Stafford, Pauline. *Queens, Concubines and Dowagers: The King's Wife in the Early Middle Ages*. Athens: University of Georgia Press, 1998.

Stahl, Alan M. "Coins and Coinage." In *Medieval England: An Encyclopedia*, edited by Paul E. Szarmach, M. Teresa Tavormina, Joel T. Rosenthal, 201-3. New York: Garland, 1998.

Stave, Susan. *Married Women's Separate Property in England, 1660–1833*. Cambridge: Harvard University Press, 1990.

Stevens, Henry John. *New Commentaries on the Laws of England*. London: Butterworths, 1874.

Stuard, Susan Mosher. *Gilding the Market: Luxury and Fashion in Fourteenth-Century Italy*. Philadelphia: University of Pennsylvania Press, 2006.

______. "Recycling Luxuries in the First Age of Fashion." Paper presented at Medieval Domesticity: Home, Housing and Household Conference, Fordham University, New York, March 12–13, 2005.

Swain, John. *Industry before the Industrial Revolution: North-East Lancashire, c. 1500–1640*. Manchester: Manchester University Press, 1986.

Swanson, Heather. *Medieval Artisans: An Urban Class in Late Medieval England*. Oxford: Basil Blackwell, 1989.

Tanner, Norman P. *The Church in Late Medieval Norwich, 1370–1532, Studies and Texts*. Toronto: Pontifical Institute of Mediaeval Studies, 1984.

Thrupp, Sylvia. *The Merchant Class of Medieval London*. Ann Arbor: University of Michigan Press, 1962.

Trafford, Claire de. "Share and Share Alike? The Marriage Portion, Inheritance and Family Politics." In *Studies on Medieval and Early Modern Women: Pawns or Players?*, edited by Christine Meek and Catherine Lawless, 36–48. Dublin: Four Courts Press, 2003.

Trigg, Stephanie. "'Ye Louely Ladyes with Youre Longe Fyngres': The Silkwomen of Medieval London." *Studia Anglica Posnaniensia* 38 (2002): 469–84.

Vernarde, Bruce. *Women's Monasticism and Medieval Society: Nunneries in France and England, 800–1215*. Ithaca: Cornell University Press, 1997.

Walker, Sue Sheridan, ed. *Wife and Widow in Medieval England*. Ann Arbor: University of Michigan Press, 1993.

Walne, Peter. *English Wills: Probate Records in England and Wales with a Brief Note on Scottish and Irish Wills*. Richmond: Virginia State Library, 1964.

Ward, Jennifer C. "Elizabeth De Burgh, Lady of Clare (D. 1360)." In *Medieval London Widows 1300–1500*, edited by Caroline M. Barron and Anne F. Sutton, 29–46. London: Hambledon Press, 1994.

______. *English Noblewomen in the Later Middle Ages*. New York: Longman, 1992.

Wedgwood, Josiah, ed. *History of Parliament, Biographies of the Members of the Commons House 1439–1509*. London: His Majesty's Stationery Office, 1936.

Weetman, Jamieson Floyd. "London Wills and the Black Death: The Pursuit of Stability in Religious Practise in the Husting Rolls Wills, 1315–1359." Master's thesis, University of Calgary, 1999.

Wemple, Suzanne. *Women in Frankish Society: Marriage and the Cloister, 500–900*. Philadelphia: University of Pennsylvania Press, 1987.

Wensky, Margret. "Women's Guilds in Cologne in the Later Middle Ages." *Journal of European Economic History* 11, no. 3 (1982): 631–50.

Westlake, H. F. *The Parish Gilds of Mediaeval England*. New York: The MacMillan Company, 1919.

Whittle, Jane. "Inheritance, Marriage, Widowhood and Remarriage: A Comparative Perspective on Women and Landholding in North-East Norfolk, 1440–1580." *Continuity and Change* 13, no. 1 (1998): 33–72.

______. "Servants in Rural England c. 1450–1650: Hired Work as a Means of Accumulating Wealth and Skills before Marriage." In *The Marital Economy in Scandinavia and Britain, 1400–1900*, edited by Maria Ågren and Amy Louise Erickson, 89–107. Burlington, VT: Ashgate, 2005.

Williams, Gwyn A. *Medieval London: From Commune to Capital.* London: Athlone Press, 1962.

Woolf, Virginia. *A Room of One's Own.* New York: Harcourt, Brace and Company, 1929.

Wood, Merry Wiesner. "Paltry Peddlers or Essential Merchants? Women in the Distributive Trades in Early Modern Nuremberg." *Sixteenth Century Journal* 12 (1981): 3–13.

Wray, Shona Kelly. *Communities and Crisis: Bologna during the Black Death.* Leiden: Brill Academic Publishers, 2009.

______. "Last Wills in Bologna During the Black Death." PhD diss., University of Colorado, 1998.

______. "Women, Family, and Inheritance in Bologna During the Black Death." In *Love, Marriage, and Family Ties in the Later Middle Ages*, edited by Isabel Davis, Miriam Müller, and Sarah Rees Jones, 205–16. Turnhout: Brepols, 2001.

Wright, Nancy E., and Margaret W. Ferguson. "Introduction." In *Women, Property, and the Letters of the Law in Early Modern England*, edited by Nancy E. Wright, Margaret W. Ferguson, and A. R. Buck. Toronto: University of Toronto Press, 2004.

Zell, Michael L. "Fifteenth- and Sixteenth-Century Wills as Historical Sources." *Archives: The Journal of the British Records Association* 14 (1979): 67–74.

______. "The Use of Religious Preambles as a Measure of Religious Belief in the Sixteenth Century." *Bulletin of the Institute of Historical Research* 50, no. 122 (1977): 246–49.

Ziegler, Philip. *The Black Death.* New York: Harper Torchbooks, 1969.

INDEX

Page numbers in *italics* indicate figures, tables, and other illustrative material. Names of medieval people are alphabetized by the first major element of the surname; thus Spicer, Johanne le, will be found under S.

Later Medieval Europe

Managing Editor
Douglas Biggs

ISSN: 1872-7875

Brill's *Later Medieval Europe* series deals with all aspects of European history and culture from ca. 1100 to ca. 1600 (with the majority covering the Late Medieval time period of 1100-1500). All areas of Europe will be included; however, there will be a focus on the territories of modern-day France, Germany and Great Britain, as well as on the Low Countries. Economic, social, political history and the history of culture and mentality will also be given special emphasis.

1. Armstrong, L., Elbl, I. & M. M. Elbl (eds.). *Money, Markets and Trade in Late Medieval Europe*. Essays in Honour of John H.A. Munro. 2007. ISBN-13: 978 90 04 15633 3, ISBN-10: 90 04 15633 X
2. Butler, S.M. *The Language of Abuse*. Marital Violence in Later Medieval England. 2007. ISBN-13: 978 90 04 15634 0, ISBN-10: 90 04 15634 8
3. Thiery, D.E. *Polluting the Sacred*. Violence, Faith and the 'Civilizing' of Parishioners in Late Medieval England. 2009. ISBN 978 90 0417387 3
4. Doležalová, L. (ed.). *The Making of Memory in the Middle Ages*. 2010. ISBN 978 90 04 17925 7
5. Mazour-Matusevich, Y. & A.S. Korros (eds.). *Saluting Aron Gurevich*. Essays in History, Literature and Other Related Subjects. 2010. ISBN 978 90 04 18650 7
6. Turner, W.J. (ed.). *Madness in Medieval Law and Custom*. 2010. ISBN 978 90 04 18749 8
7. Ward, A. *History and Chronicles in Late Medieval Iberia*. Representations of Wamba in Late Medieval Narrative Histories. 2011. ISBN 978 90 04 20272 6
8. Staples, K.K. *Daughters of London*. Inheriting Opportunity in the Late Middle Ages. 2011. ISBN 978 90 04 20311 2

brill.nl/lme

